Palgrave Practical Guides in Communication

Palgrave Practical Guides in Communication provides accessible introductions to all key topics in the field, with an emphasis on interpersonal, intercultural, and organizational communication, as well as public speaking and rhetoric. The series includes both textbooks geared towards specific courses taught in communication studies programs across the globe, and practical guides geared toward both advanced students and practitioners. Volumes in the series emphasize not just the what, but the how: they help readers improve specific communication skills and practices. In order to do that, volumes in the series include a variety of exercises, activities, and other pedagogical features, some of which can be multimodal (e.g., video and/or audio). Informed by cutting-edge research by leading scholars, volumes in the series help readers become more effective communicators in today's rapidly changing world.

Ronald Yaros

# The Digital Engagement Model

## How to Capture and Keep Audience Attention

palgrave
macmillan

Ronald Yaros
University of Maryland, College Park
College Park, MD, USA

ISSN 3004-9032 ISSN 3004-9040 (electronic)
Palgrave Practical Guides in Communication
ISBN 978-3-032-03821-0 ISBN 978-3-032-03822-7 (eBook)
https://doi.org/10.1007/978-3-032-03822-7



This Palgrave Macmillan imprint is published by the registered company Springer Nature Switzerland AG
The registered company address is: Gewerbestrasse 11, 6330 Cham, Switzerland

*To my loving wife, Carey, whose kindness, brilliance, and unwavering presence embody the extraordinary person that you are. Through the years of research and teaching, and the countless hours of writing that brought me to this point, you offered grace, patience, and quiet strength to every step of the journey. This book bears the imprint of your support on every page, and I am forever grateful.*

# Preface

This book is based on a simple realization: It doesn't matter how important your message is if no one pays attention to it.

Content creators, engagement teams, journalists, educators, and researchers must confront the simple reality: Users can't learn something, trust something, or be influenced in any way by content without meaningful engagement.

Infinite scrolling, push notifications, and algorithms have changed everything. A "like" isn't understanding. A "share" isn't a reflection. These are signals from users who chose to interact, but what about the majority who didn't? Clicks and likes do not measure whether content was processed deeply enough to influence one's knowledge, trust, behavior, or beliefs. We cannot assume content communicated important information about the economy, public health, climate change, or democracy unless we know the content was consumed, not just accessed. To learn, be persuaded, or build community, a user's attention must be sustained. Sustaining that attention is impossible without first capturing it.

What's surprising is that new models for producing content haven't emerged, even though supporting research in fields such as neuroscience and human-computer interaction has. Since completing my doctoral research that synthesized journalism with information processing, audience analytics have shown that traditional practices might briefly capture the attention and "likes" of some users, but are often not sufficient to sustain the engagement of most. Rather than teasing all users to explore "how" something happens, "why" something is important, or "x number of ways" to learn something, content should *immediately* inform diverse populations who encounter it with varying amounts of time and distraction. Every user decides if they have the time and interest to continue, and some scanners might even be "converted" to readers.

This book explains how and why different users consume different types of content. Without those insights, we risk producing text that continues to vanish into the scroll.

College Park, MD Ronald Yaros

# List of Terms

| *Concepts* | *Definition* |
| --- | --- |
| Digital | Internet-connected technologies (i.e., devices, apps, delivery systems, etc.). |
| Engagement | A user's active attention, behavioral, and/or emotional interaction with digital content leading to comprehension and knowledge gain. |
| Digital "DIET" | An acronym representing four key variables all users bring to any content. |
| Individual interest | A longer-term preference for, or personal connection to, a topic or source developed over time by previous exposure, experiences, and education. |
| Situational interest | Short-term interest sparked only by how content is presented—often incidentally in social media. |
| User environment | Includes a physical environment (e.g., distractions) and a technological environment (devices and connectivity). |
| Attention momentum | The ability for content to build users' attention following the initial exposure to content. The more time invested, the more likely engagement is to continue. |
| SPICE content | An acronym representing five variables in content that is scannable, personalized, interactive, curates curiosity, and, which appropriate, emotional as defined below. |
| Scannable content | Easy-to-consume content (headlines, bullet points, visuals, etc.), facilitating a user's consumption of useful information independent of subsequent content. Does not include short titles or teasing "clickbait" requiring time to be informed. |
| Personalized content | Content that is tailor-made to a user through explicit preferences, identity, relevance, or algorithmic targeting. |

(*continued*)

(continued)

| *Concepts* | *Definition* |
|---|---|
| Interactive content | User actions include wiping, scrolling, liking, sharing, commenting, or responding to links, polls, and visuals. |
| Curated curiosity | The intentional design of content that continues to provoke curiosity and interest following an initial click or content. |
| Emotional content | Content that taps into core human feelings—joy, outrage, empathy, fear, or awe—to strengthen connection, memory, and shareability. Emotion is a powerful driver of attention and retention. |
| Dwell time | The amount of time a user pauses or lingers on content while scrolling, even without clicking or interacting. It reflects attention capture and is used as a behavioral signal of relevance or resonance even in microseconds. Longer dwell time can indicate cognitive or emotional engagement and is increasingly tracked by platforms to optimize content delivery. |
| Compound headline | A title or headline that includes one informative, explanatory declarative sentence followed by a related "teasing" sentence, such as posing a question or offering a consequence. This headline informs all users and teases those with the time to continue engagement. |
| Smart scrolling | A strategic content design tactic where one topic for a short video is distributed across multiple short, scroll-optimized videos to maintain user interest and extend exposure to the topic over time. It leverages the scroll behavior typical of social feeds, turning one unit of content into a series of "micro-engagements" that cumulatively increase time spent, recall, and retention. |
| Progressive disclosure | A strategy in a user interface that reveals only a portion of the total amount of content after initial content is consumed. Includes the automatic appearance of content, or a user's interactivity (e.g., clicks, scrolls, etc.) that reveals additional information in replacement of content presented in its entirety. |
| Smart Story Suite | A user interface providing a coordinated collection of textual and visual content elements including, but limited to, explanatory headlines, titles, subheadings, and visual, scannable content, and labeled links to additional sections of content that align with either a linear or nonlinear consumption of selectable content. The suite supports reduced cognitive load enabling short- and/or longer-term consumption of content with multiple user options that reinforce interest and attention momentum through layered reveals of selected content. |

# Acknowledgments

This book is the product of several years and four careers in communication, shaped by the new and evolving ways people seek, process, and engage with digital information and includes:

- Five years as a radio news reporter during my high school and undergraduate days
- Seven years as a broadcast meteorologist in Madison, Wisconsin, and St. Louis, Missouri, while I pursued a master's in education to explore how people learn about complex topics such as science and health
- Thirteen years directing a successful corporation that distributed innovative educational software to millions of classrooms through a nationwide community program adopted by local television stations
- Five years as a doctoral student and teaching assistant at the University of Wisconsin–Madison
- And the past 20 years of teaching and researching, at the University of Utah and continuing at the University of Maryland

The list of people to thank on this long journey could be its own chapter. So, to all the friends, coworkers, collaborators, scholars, and the thousands of undergraduate and graduate students I have had the privilege to teach and learn from, I offer a heartfelt "thank you" for your interest, support, and yes, your *engagement*, a term that is often used, but rarely defined. Here, *engagement* means more than moments of attention, comments and compliments, or a fleeting professional connection. It represents thoughtful conversations, lasting friendships, respected collaborations, and sincere curiosity about my enduring passion. That passion is understanding how and why diverse populations of users seek, select, share, and consume digital information.

That passion for communicating information was forged early—from broadcasting weather informaton from a Michigan farm in high school to producing Emmy Award-winning broadcasts following college, including the nation's first multi-part series on the EPA's climate change predictions in 1981. The passion also included partnerships with respected meteorologists from major newsrooms including those in Chicago, Dallas, and Washington, D.C., to smaller newsrooms in Rockford, Lansing, and Fort Wayne.

Across all of these settings and the work completed, one question lingered: *Of all the people this reached, how many engaged with it in a meaningful way?*

Reporting news, broadcasting science, creating lesson plans, and publishing research—none of it matters without meaningful engagement. In an age when the number of followers, likes, and shares can be mistaken for impact, we must remember that the *reach* of any content is not the same as *engagement with it.* Simply distributing content—whether it is to classrooms, households, or on social media—does not ensure attention, understanding, or lasting value.

Despite dramatic advances in technology, much of the important digital content still fails to earn the attention it deserves. Key information is often buried within pages of long-fom text or poorly designed presentations, which assume that if a user is interested, they will spend the time to consume it. Videos longer than a few seconds are often skipped or fast-forwarded. Clickbait can seduce clicks to pages that often fail to sustain a user's interest. In an age when users are bombarded with digital content, it's no longer enough to just produce quality content. That content must be presented in ways that address the wide variations in users' time, needs, and environments, as well as the hardwired limits of the human brain to process information effectively.

This book is the culmination of decades spent observing, experimenting, teaching, and listening to audiences, students, scholars, and skeptics. It reflects a lifelong belief that engagement is not a byproduct of content but a function of how well that content meets the needs of those who consume it. If my work contributes in some small way to advancing that understanding—to helping create digital content that not only reaches people, but connects with them, the years of effort, classroom discussions, and research will have been worth it.

For every moment along that journey, I am thankful.

As one might imagine, the list of people to thank on this long journey could match the length of this book. So, to all the friends, coworkers, collaborators, scholars, and the thousands of undergraduate and graduate students I have had the privilege to teach and learn from, I offer a heartfelt "thank you" for your interest, support, and—yes—your engagement, a term that is often used, but rarely defined. **Along the way, I benefited from thoughtful editorial stewardship, and I thank Jasmin Naim for her care, patience, and guidance in bringing this manuscript to fruition**.

*Competing Interests* The author has no competing interests to declare that are relevant to the content of this manuscript.

# Contents

# List of Figures

# List of Tables

CHAPTER 1

# Introduction: Rethinking Engagement in a Distracted Digital World

- Digital engagement drives the impact of information, entertainment, education, and even democracy. Why isn't more done to update it for today's digital world?
- The *Digital Engagement Model* draws on cognitive science and human-computer interaction to design new ways for content to attract and sustain user attention.
- This book details theoretical frameworks, practical strategies, and evidence-based approaches to help scholars and practitioners understand how content can attract more users to consume more content for longer periods of time.



R. Yaros, *The Digital Engagement Model*, Palgrave Practical Guides in Communication,
https://doi.org/10.1007/978-3-032-03822-7_1

Substantial resources are invested in creating digital content, including research, expert interviews, award-winning writing, and engaging visuals. Unfortunately, in a global media landscape where all content competes with one another, the clarity, accuracy, and credibility of that content alone are no longer sufficient for many users. For them, unless content is presented in ways that reflect their needs, behaviors, and cognitive abilities, much of what they encounter will be ignored. The question is no longer solely how to write better, shoot video better, or report news better—but how to package engaging content so that it informs more people, even if it's just a portion of the larger message.

We live in a media ecosystem overflowing with content but starving for attention. Traditional models of engagement, designed for print and broadcast, often fail in a world where users quickly skim text, scroll through short videos, scan visuals, and listen to only part of a podcast, easily distracted at any moment. The time many users have is not always sufficient to read lengthy storytelling or view entire videos and complex visualizations before they can decide if that content is relevant to them. That means *all* content must immediately present the virtual argument that, if consumed, will offer value, which is what many social media users seek as they continuously scroll through short videos. In an environment of endless choices and shrinking time to focus, the real challenge isn't how to get more clicks on specific content. It's about facilitating consistent and meaningful engagement with any content for *all* users.

That's the goal this book tackles head-on.

The *Digital Engagement Model* (DEM) represents the culmination of years of researching, observing, and instructing the next generation of information consumers that grew up in a digital world. Since many readers of this book did not experience that new technology in their formative years, the model and its concepts introduced provides a new framework of variables for creating and presenting any type of digital content, grounded not only in interdisciplinary research in communication, cognitive psychology, neuroscience, and design, but also in the needs and behaviors of today's consumers.

This book does not claim that applying the model will engage every with every message. Its objective is to enhance the chances of engagement, particularly for users who are incidentally exposed to content they did not seek but might explore if it were presented differently. All users, regardless of interest, are compelled to make an immediate decision: Is this content worth my time? Too often, the structure of that content responds with a "no." If the only option for a user is to read lengthy paragraphs or watch extended minutes of video before deciding to engage, many will not even begin, regardless of the significance of that content.

Consider commonly used labels such as "A 7-minute read." This isn't a value proposition; it may actually deter users who are unwilling to spend that amount of time to engage with the content. For any user, a page filled with text, even with a few bolded words, still appears as a block of reading. What if the content were organized in a way that allows scanning users to grasp key points in just seconds? This approach doesn't discourage the creation and consumption of long-form content; it simply makes it easier for users looking for short-form information to also digest what they need.

Some producers have been trained to believe that enticing users with titles and headlines that pose questions, promise numbered lists, or feature vague titles is the most effective way to engage the largest number of users. While these may work for users who have the time to delve into the details, what about those users who don't? Why does some content use titles such as "Why this matters"? Give users the info so they can decide *if* it matters (to them). Why does some content use short titles that are typically found in term papers to merely introduce a topic? A more informative subhead offers valuable information for all users, including those users in a rush to get to work, start a class, or board a plane.

Throughout my years of sharing this work with educators, students, scholars, and practitioners, some have suggested that a cognitive approach to content is irrelevant to those working outside the field of psychology. The response is it is relevant to all users consuming any type of digital content. Ignoring the first critical moments a user decides to engage with a website, mobile app, or social network risks losing many users and subscribers before they even grasp the main message.

Admittedly, shifting how content is structured and presented isn't easy. Many producers are understandably more comfortable presenting pages of scrolling text, even when analytics and revenue streams show that users quickly "bounce" from them to other content. For producers of topics with broad appeal, the transition from a focusing on a narrow "target audience" to the larger group of users also exposed to the same content can be challenging. For example, when Facebook changed its layout and features in 2008, many users revolted not because the changes were ineffective, but because they disrupted familiarity and habits. This book isn't about the comfort of producing or consuming predictable and comfortable formats. These chapters do not suggest reinventing the message itself but rethinking how it is delivered.

Unfortunately, a printed book can only go so far in replicating the live, interactive digital experiences that this model is designed to support. Digital engagement occurs not in reading chapters filled with text, but during the scrolls, swipes, scanning, skimming, viewing, and clicking that users make in real time. The following chapters do not cover every aspect of cognition or engagement, but offer empirical, theoretical, and practical insights into how content structures, interface designs, and multimedia features can be arranged to create more dynamic, user-centered content.

Chapter 2: Digital Engagement Shifts to a New Era

Technology has transformed how we consume information, more rapidly than most content can adjust. Users interact with content in highly fragmented ways—glancing at a post while waiting in line at the store, scanning headlines between tasks, or skipping through a video during their commute. Despite these common scenarios, much of today's content is still presented as if users will read a full article uninterrupted, as they did when newspapers were the primary sources of information. Pages filled with dense, "one-size-fits-all" text are still common despite the significant changes in users' needs and behaviors. Chapter introduces a framework grounded in cognitive science, communication theory, and neuroscience that directly addresses these shifts.

The *Digital Engagement Model* (DEM) does not discard the need for quality writing, strong reporting, or compelling multimedia. Instead, it emphasizes structuring this content in ways that account for how users process information, particularly in the first few seconds of encountering it. We will analyze how demographic traits, attention span, environment, interest, time, and device usage affect content consumption. These variables can vary for the same user at different times, which is why a rigid linear format for content can be ineffective. This model suggests an adaptive presentation: Content that can cater to users with diverse needs.

One challenge in writing this type of book was defining its target audience. Scholars need rigorous theory, while practitioners require practical results. However, both groups—and their audiences—confront the same reality: Engagement is fragile. This book serves as a bridge, grounded in empirical research but intended for application in news, education, marketing, and engagement teams.

Chapter 3: A New Model Fills Some Theoretical Gaps

A book chapter outlining a theoretical foundation for engagement must refer to foundational theories such as Uses and Gratifications [1–3], and theoretical concepts, such as selective exposure [4–6]. This chapter critiques how some traditional theories fall short when addressing today's mobile users accessing, processing, and interacting with fragmented digital content, particularly on social media [7–9]. The DEM aligns with and expands Uses and Gratifications theory but frames individual differences with new shared similarities that all users bring to any digital content [10]. This chapter discusses how traditional media effects theories may not always capture the nuanced ways users respond to specific content, such as political news, because those theories do not consider the relationships between new user traits, such as interest, environments, time and content characteristics [11–13].

Educational psychologists have categorized interest into two categories [14]. One relates to Self-Determination Theory (SDT) [9, 15]. This chapter elaborates on how Self-Determination Theory (SDT) posits that a user's autonomy, competence, and relatedness can significantly influence their motivation for engagement. For autonomy, users seek content that allows them to feel a sense of freedom and control. The vast array of digital media choices—from personalized news feeds to curated entertainment—satisfies autonomy by aligning content with individual preferences, even when such content has not been specifically sought by a user.

Competence is addressed when users engage with content that helps them to develop skills or knowledge, fulfilling their desire to feel effective. Finally, social media, discussions, and other interactive platforms can satisfy a user's need for relatedness by creating a sense of connection. Users tend to gravitate toward content that fosters a sense of belonging, such as content centered on shared concerns. Situational interest—which is generated only by how content is presented—can build "attention momentum" that sustains a user's attention. The process of attention momentum in content can transform a user's fleeting curiosity into meaningful interactions with information. Understanding these dynamics can help content creators to engage their audiences with information more effectively.

Chapter 4: Your Mind on Media

What if newsrooms could tap into a deeper, more sustained form of engagement—one that holds users' meaningful attention over time? This suggests that attention can be built and sustained by aligning the placement of multimedia with the way the human brain processes information. This is because the brain responds better to information presented in ways that minimize cognitive overload. Several studies demonstrate that the brain can handle only a limited amount of information at any one time before becoming overwhelmed [16–18]. When content is segmented and scannable with visuals and interactive features, that content can align with how the brain processes information in working memory. The *Digital Engagement Model* leverages these insights by suggesting producing content in ways that the brain can process more effectively.

This chapter explores the cognitive neuroscience of attention and information processing. Too many interactive elements, such as long videos or complex graphics, can overwhelm users and detract from their engagement. The chapter also explores how headlines, text styles, and visual cues can affect attention. Producers of less popular but arguably more important content (e.g., health, science, etc.) face the challenges of not only attracting users' attention but retaining it. Those who produce content that fails to keep users engaged for more than a few seconds should ask if they may be bombarding users with too much information.

In sum, the research from cognitive psychology, educational psychology, human-computer interaction, and neuroscience—traditionally siloed fields—converges in the proposed model to address the complex challenges of engaging modern audiences with more digital content.

Chapter 5: Social Media Uniquely Builds Attention

One of the most significant impacts of social media for journalism and education is the ability of social media to foster audience engagement [19]. This chapter examines how social media continues to revolutionize communication and journalism by transforming the way content is produced, distributed, and consumed, particularly by younger users. Popular platforms, including TikTok [8, 20], X [21], Facebook [22, 23], and Instagram [24], enable instant sharing and creating direct user connections. Interactive features such as likes, shares, and comments can now contribute to the news cycle. This two-way communication can also strengthen the relationships between news organizations and the public, enhancing transparency and accountability [25–27]. Social media platforms also facilitate the analysis of public interest, sentiment [28], and trending topics, making it easier to gauge audience reactions in real time. Emphasizing multimedia storytelling by incorporating photos, videos, and infographics enhances engagement, making content more accessible and impactful. The ability to craft interactive narratives makes social media an essential tool for modern journalism, supporting immersive and engaging reporting. However, this increased engagement also brings challenges. The need to capture attention can lead some media organizations to prioritize sensational or highly shareable stories on social media, sometimes at the cost of in-depth journalism. Nonetheless, content producers who effectively harness social media can stay relevant in the evolving digital landscape.

Younger social media users are particularly adept at recognizing the dominant behaviors that drive their interactions with content. The DEM is designed to meet the needs of a wide range of users, not just traditional target audiences, and helps content producers better understand how to attract and retain users in the fast-paced, fragmented digital environment. This chapter also critiques current practices, focusing on improving social media analytics or using artificial intelligence to increase reach. While social media may increase audience reach, it does not necessarily result in sustained engagement. For organizations that rely on larger audiences for additional advertising or subscription revenue, this poses a significant challenge.

Chapter 6: All Users Have a “Digital DIET”

This chapter focuses on four key user variables of demographics, individual interests, environment, and time. All are essential when creating content that resonates with a wide audience.

1. Demographics: Users' age, gender, education, and cultural background shape how they engage with content. However, the DEM moves beyond focusing solely on demographics and instead incorporates these factors into a broader understanding of shared user behaviors.
2. Individual Interests: A user's personal interests influence their content choices. Content creators must strike a balance between long-term user interests of a target audience and momentary curiosity by those outside the target audience to reach a broader audience. The model suggests that individual interests are correlated with the motivations users have when seeking and selecting content. Curiosity, however, is one of five key variables to be addressed by the content.
3. Environment: The physical, social, and technological environments in which users consume content—whether on a mobile device in a crowded environment or a desktop in their room at home—can affect how they will interact with the material. The DEM emphasizes adapting content to fit these varied technological and environmental contexts.
4. Time: One of the most overlooked factors when producing digital content is the amount of time users have to engage with it. The DEM encourages content that caters to both quick scanners and deep readers, recognizing that time constraints influence how much of the material can and will be consumed. It is not impossible to produce content for both short form and long form consumption, which can negate the need to limit for the number of words presented.

By addressing the user-centered "DIET" variables, the DEM helps content to meet users where they are, whether they are scanning briefly or engaging deeply. This approach also highlights the limitations of traditional engagement metrics, such as quantifying the number of clicks and time spent on the page. By focusing on shared user "DIET" traits before assembling the final content to be presented, content producers can enhance both engagement in an increasingly fragmented and fast-paced media landscape.

Chapter 7: SPICE Content Generates Situational Interest

This chapter builds on the foundation laid by the digital DIETS framework by focusing on the content itself. This chapter introduces the five key "SPICE" content variables, which multiple studies have demonstrated to enhance information processing in different ways. Content that is scannable, personalized, interactive, and curates curiosity after the initial click, while also evoking emotion, generates situational interest in content that some users would otherwise ignore. In other words, situational interest originates only with the content, not the user. This chapter stresses that the more of these five content variables are incorporated into digital material, the greater the likelihood of engaging more users.

The chapter emphasizes that users often avoid content they consider "boring," even if it that content is important, which presents a challenge for producers presented information that some users typically ignore. Incidental exposure to content outside a user's personal interests can still tap the power of strategically designed content. The DEM explains that when specific cognitive triggers are activated by content, more users can be attracted to the content. This expands the scope of what types of content can attract more users by tapping into the psychological factors that influence how users engage with content. By combining the five SPICE content variables, the DEM enables content creators to craft more material that resonates on a cognitive level, ultimately enhancing engagement across user groups. The strategies introduced in this chapter offer practical ways to enhance all content.

Chapter 8: Photos and Charts Must Explain Quickly

This chapter applies the DEM variables to enhance the effectiveness of how photos and data charts can communicate more information quickly to non-expert audiences. In an age where we are inundated with information, making visuals and data accessible and instantly understandable is crucial for broad audiences. Data visualizations transform complex, data-heavy content into digestible and visually appealing graphics. These charts can quickly convey specific messages to users without requiring prior knowledge by simplifying intricate data. Rethinking the role of explanatory features allows even basic bar and line charts to help non-expert audiences quickly grasp key measures, trends, or relationships in the data. The chapter also examines the concept of explanatory photos versus "point-and-shoot" photos. Standard "point-and-shoot" photos focus only on a primary subject (e.g. a building). Unlike point-and-shoot photos, which often depend on captions or accompanying text to explain the scene, this chapter describes how an explanatory photo can instantly communicate more information with little to no text. They achieve this by featuring a primary subject a secondary element, which provides the user with more context. Explanatory visuals reduce cognitive load by guiding viewers toward an immediate understanding of the content.

Chapter 9: The Smart Story Suite Offers a New Approach: Not a Single Template

This chapter introduces and tests a new *Smart Story Suite* based on all of the concepts and variables discussed in the book's first eight chapters. Instead of pages of scrollable linear text, this user interface presents users with a single page featuring selectable buttons that direct them to specific sections of the content. These buttons apply SPICE variables to provide the user with the freedom to select what they are most interested in. This chapter explains why engagement varies depending on how certain content is arranged and presented. Engagement is facilitated by the ***progressive disclosure*** of content that addresses a user's digital DIET with SPICE content variables to generate ***attention momentum***.

The user-selective clusters of content in the *Smart Story Suite* challenge the assumption that all users consume large blocks of digital text. Storytelling often assumes users read digital text linearly, as many do with printed text. Given the complexity of digital environments, however, users can navigate vast amounts of continuous information. In this case, their shifting interests and varied time constraints are addressed through a more dynamic approach to content presentation. The solution lies in presenting content in an interface that can effectively serve both scanners and readers simultaneously by focusing on the ten DIET and SPICE variables.

A key takeaway from Chap. 9 is the recognition that the various ways users interact with content should be considered when creating that content. The DEM posits that while some users may engage deeply with long-form articles, others may have only a brief time for consumption. A strategic arrangement of content variables enables engagement on multiple levels, thereby increasing the likelihood of capturing the attention of a broader audience. The introduction of the *Smart Story Suite* marks a significant development in content production. By focusing on the intersection of user needs and a powerful combination of content variables, the structure offers a more flexible approach to increasing engagement in a fragmented and fast-paced digital landscape.

## References

1. Blumler, J. G., and E. Katz. 1974. The uses of mass communications: Current perspectives on gratifications research. In *Sage annual reviews of communication research*, vol. 3, 318. Beverly Hills: Sage Publications.
2. Sundar, S. S., and A. Limperos. 2013. Uses and Grats 2.0: New gratifications for new media. *Journal of Broadcasting & Electronic Media* 57 (4): 504–525.

3. Ruggiero, T. 2000. Uses and gratifications theory in the 21st century. *Mass Communication and Society* **3** (1): 3–37.
4. Knobloch-Westerwick, S. 2012. Selective exposure and reinforcement of attitudes and partisanship before a presidential election. *Journal of Communication* **62** (4): 628–642.
5. Knobloch-Westerwick, S. 2015. The selective exposure self-and affect-management (SESAM) model: Applications in the realms of race, politics, and health. *Communication Research* **42** (7): 959–985.
6. Zillmann, D., et al. 2004. Effects of lead framing on selective exposure to Internet news reports. *Communication Research* **31** (1): 58–81.
7. de Zúñiga, H. G., and Z. Cheng. 2021. Origin and evolution of the news finds me perception: Review of theory and effects. *Profesional de la Información* **30** (3): 1–17.
8. Falgoust, G., et al. 2022. Applying the uses and gratifications theory to identify motivational factors behind young adult's participation in viral social media challenges on TikTok. *Human Factors in Healthcare* **2**:100014.
9. Martela, F. 2020. Self-determination theory. In *The Wiley-Blackwell encyclopedia of personality and individual differences*, ed. B. J. Carducci and C. S. Nave. Wiley-Blackwell.
10. Sidnam, M. E., and P. Monge. 2024. Individual differences and technology affordances combine to predict mobile social media distraction behaviors and consequences. In *Proceedings of the CHI conference on human factors in computing systems*.
11. Vraga, E., L. Bode, and S. Troller-Renfree. 2016. Beyond self-reports: Using eye tracking to measure topic and style differences in attention to social media content. *Communication Methods and Measures* **10** (2–3): 149–164.
12. Xu, Q., and S. S. Sundar. 2016. Interactivity and memory: Information processing of interactive versus non-interactive content. *Computers in Human Behavior* **63**:620–629.
13. Yaros, R. A., and A. E. Cook. 2011. Attention versus learning of online content: Preliminary findings from an eye-tracking study. *International Journal of Cyber Behavior, Psychology and Learning* **1** (4): 49–69.
14. Renninger, K. A., and S. E. Hidi. 2022. Interest development, self-related information processing, and practice. *Theory Into Practice* **61** (1): 23–34.
15. Ryan, R. M., and E. L. Deci. 2000. Self-determination theory and the facilitation of intrinsic motivation, social development, and well-being. *American Psychologist* **55** (1): 68–78.
16. Paas, F., A. Renkl, and J. Sweller. 2003. Cognitive load theory and instructional design: Recent developments. *Educational Psychologist* **38** (1): 1–4.
17. Plass, J., R. Moreno, and R. Brunken. 2010. *Cognitive load theory*. New York: Cambridge University Press.
18. Beauvais, C., T. Olive, and J.-M. Passerault. 2011. Why are some texts good and others not? Relationship between text quality and management of the writing processes. *Journal of Educational Psychology* **103**:415–428.

19. Hermida, A. 2016. *Tell everyone: Why we share and why it matters.* Anchor Canada.
20. Miller, E. 2020. As TikTok grapples with weightier topics, journalists are tuning in to deliver the news. https://www.poynter.org/reporting-editing/2020/as-tiktok-grapples-with-weightier-topics-journalists-are-tuning-in-to-deliver-the-news/.
21. Huberman, B. A., D. M. Romero, and F. Wu. 2009 Social networks that matter: Twitter under the microscope. *First Monday* 14(1) [April 1, 2010]. http://firstmonday.org/htbin/cgiwrap/bin/ojs/index.php/fm/article/view/2317/2063.
22. Thorson, K., et al. 2021. Algorithmic inference, political interest, and exposure to news and politics on Facebook. *Information, Communication & Society* **24** (2): 183–200.
23. Oeldorf-Hirsch, A., and S. S. Sundar. 2015. Posting, commenting, and tagging: Effects of sharing news stories on Facebook. *Computers in Human Behavior* **44**:240–249.
24. Swart, J., and M. Broersma. 2023. What feels like news? Young people's perceptions of news on Instagram. *Journalism* **25** (8): 1620–1637.
25. Vraga, E. K., et al. 2019. Accidentally attentive: Comparing visual, close-ended, and open-ended measures of attention on social media. *Computers in Human Behavior* **99**:235–244.
26. Ortiz-Ospina, E. 2019. The rise of social media. OurWorldInData.org.
27. Fletcher, R., and R. K. Nielsen. 2018. Are people incidentally exposed to news on social media? A comparative analysis. *New Media & Society* **20** (7): 2,450–2,468.
28. Choi, J., S. Y. Lee, and S. W. Ji. 2021. Engagement in emotional news on social media: Intensity and type of emotions. *Journalism and Mass Communication Quarterly* **98** (4): 1017–1040.

CHAPTER 2

# Digital Engagement Shifts to a New Era

- Consumer behaviors are outpacing content presentations.
- Overwhelming content outpaces the brain's limited processing.
- Content can reach beyond a limited target audience.
- A new digital engagement model targets diverse populations.
- Human creativity and emotions are still unmatched by AI.



R. Yaros, *The Digital Engagement Model*, Palgrave Practical Guides in Communication,
https://doi.org/10.1007/978-3-032-03822-7_2

Pages of text are failing to recruit sufficient readers amid distracting environments or time constraints as they navigate vast amounts of information from countless sources. Our *Digital Engagement Model* (DEM) extends content beyond a target audience and applies years of multidisciplinary research in cognitive psychology, human-computer interaction, and neuroscience.

New user variables—and innovative ways to present content—can significantly boost engagement. The goal is to provide users with multimedia content in both short and long forms, tailored to their specific needs. Importantly, this chapter also acknowledges the challenges of adapting the well-established skills and practices of newsrooms and classrooms to a fundamentally new mindset for communication in an increasingly mobile world.

The impact of any content, whether text, photos, or videos, on any topic, from news and sports to social media, depends on its ability to capture and retain attention. Our research demonstrates that the way content is presented, whether as bullet points, a clickbait headline, a news story, a social media post, or a video, book, or movie, is influenced by a complex interplay of user and content variables. Applying a "one-size-fits-all" content strategy—even if it's one new model or checklist of strategies for content—is not the answer in an age of ubiquitous digital media.

Relying on single content strategies, such as loading up social media, writing sensational headlines, prioritizing brevity, or increasing the use of video, may help to attract users, but those strategies alone will not always maximize the potential number of users to engage. A more comprehensive approach to presenting digital content is essential if it is to meet the needs of diverse populations. This requires a unique blend of multidisciplinary research, years of experimentation, and a new user interface that scholars, practitioners, teachers, and students have yet to see.

This book offers such an interface, which no longer relies solely on excellent writing, compelling photography, or engaging video. Nor does it address the broader, conceptual notions of engagement, which are commonly discussed in other books and journals. Instead, the chapters in this book synthesize a combination of multidisciplinary cognitive, behavioral, and content variables that facilitate user attention in the critical first seconds of exposure. These variables, long studied across various scientific disciplines, are presented together in these chapters for the first time.

Ironically, the first challenge in writing a book about digital audiences was to define its audience. Producing content that benefits both communicators and scholars feels impossible, as each group views digital content through their unique lenses of needs, expectations, and goals. Communicators prioritize practical and innovative strategies for audience engagement, while scholars seek theoretical depth to support those strategies. Scholars expect empirical evidence based on literature and meta-level theories. Practitioners seek an ideal model that can be applied in a fast-paced digital environment, yielding measurable outcomes in terms of user engagement, retention rates, and opportunities to monetize content. Addressing these expectations requires a production model for engagement that offers theoretical depth, pedagogical value, and practical application. Ultimately, an empirical model must serve as a useful framework for understanding and addressing real-world challenges, capturing the attention of a broader audience, and sustaining it.

This book aims to bridge the gaps between producing content and consuming it with a model that honors each perspective. It attempts to strike a balance between rigorous research that addresses scholarly expectations and actionable industry-focused strategies. Our new model makes this book ambitious but essential. That's because it helps to explore and understand the variables, behaviors, and neurologically processing that digital users share. The model seeks a middle ground between addressing a specific "target audience" while accounting for "individual differences." The result is an innovative and comprehensive guide that advances theoretical understanding and fosters practical innovation to enhance attention to content in a complex digital landscape.

Through this book's tripartite structure, which emphasizes empirical depth, innovative appeal, and commercial relevance, each chapter challenges the predictable and scrollable structures of mainly text. What is the downside of attracting more users to more content, especially when it is important information that many users ignore or avoid? The same question applies to organizations wishing to increase subscriptions to their content. The answer to both questions is a more engaging interface that can attract, retain, and inform more users.

To address the core challenges in sustaining users' attention, this book examines how content consumption and interaction with that content, whether it is selectively sought [1] or encountered incidentally [2, 3], vary widely. While research has described how curiosity-driven information seeking initiates user engagement [4], and another has examined how selective exposure shapes attention, these behaviors reflect different entry points into digital consumption [5]. Users who share [6], consume [7], or avoid content [5, 8] determine their levels of attention and engagement. Dismissing innovative approaches that can engage more users beyond a narrow target audience may be missing opportunities to maximize the reach and impact of your content.

The strategies, models, and interfaces proposed in this book offer innovation for eight categories of readers. The two primary groups are:

- **Communicators** seeking new concepts from the other disciplines of cognitive psychology, human-computer interaction, and neuroscience. In addition to producing the good content they've been producing, communicators will explore new ways to present that content to address what we know about users' behavior, attention, and content selection.
- **Scholars** who can reflect on why content distributed on online, mobile devices, and social media does not guarantee that the content was consumed or made an impact. Shorter periods of engagement with content suggest that the generalizability of some media effects may be more limited than they were in the pre-digital era. Emerging theories that address users' incidental and selective exposure to

content, avoidance, and information overload warrant discussion and experimentation.

Other groups can also benefit from these chapters.

- **Writers** can cast a wider net beyond their target audience to reach more users who are exposed to their content, even unintentionally, on social media. Good writing means aligning with users' varying expectations and interests, as well as the time a user has to appreciate it.
- **Reporters** in newsrooms that apply the model would no longer be confined to a word limit for only short-form or long-form stories. The new interface offers both. Unlike scrollable pages that force users to read text if they want to be informed, users can now determine how much they wish to read, view, or scan, to be informed based on the amount of time they have. Some will consume short-form summaries, while others can still learn the long-form details.
- **Editors** will understand why different media sustain attention in different ways. They'll learn how content that continues to generate curiosity *after* a headline or title can build "attention momentum."
- **Audience development teams** can look beyond the interactivity of social media likes and shares as a primary measure of engagement and understand how more users could interact with more content, or why more time spent on the content can signal less comprehension.
- **Web managers** who apply some or all of the components of a new user interface will offer every user more choices for personalized content that serves their needs.
- **Professors** wishing to enlighten the next generation of producers and consumers with concepts not discussed in other classes can address real-world challenges of communicating more effectively in a complex world.

## 2.1 Consumer Behaviors Outpace Content Presentation

Attention to digital content among user groups is the product of an interrelated mix of key content and user variables. To explore user variables, we investigate the needs of different demographics [9, 10], individual interests [11–14], physical and technological environments [15–17], and available time [18, 19]. Producing content that incorporates as many of the five key variables to be discussed could generate interest and engagement, thereby maximizing the content's reach across diverse populations. This approach supports the need for adaptive content presentation that aligns with the evolving behaviors of digital consumers.

> ***Are we consuming digital content or is it consuming us?***

Sundar and Limperos [20] noted that Internet users are so actively engaged that the term "audience" may no longer be adequate, as dividing users in this way may be artificial. Regardless of some user-specific needs, the ways attention is captured and the ways different media are processed remain fundamental to the engagement process. Whether a page displays text, a photo, or a video, cognitive processes dictate the extent to which users engage, disengage, or ignore the content [21], ultimately shaping their perceptions, responses, and interactions with it [22, 23].

While we know that users with established interests often seek specific information [24, 25], most users also consume incidental content, guided in part by the structure of the content. Short social media videos can divert and mesmerize users [26]. Even content curated by algorithms [27] and social media [15, 28, 29] depends on structures that direct users with fragmented attention patterns.

For years, we have known that different content drives varying engagement levels across different media on different platforms [30]. For instance, while some interested users may dedicate time to reading text-heavy pages, others might only have the time or interest to scan text quickly, missing key information that is buried in the content [31, 32].

Research confirms that users with shorter attention spans often skim content rather than read in-depth [31, 33–35]. This challenges any assumption that all users consume text in a linear manner. Eye-tracking has revealed multiple scanning patterns that differ from linear reading [31, 36]. In the context of news, the traditional inverted pyramid structure can efficiently deliver key facts to users who have the time to read them, but it falls short of effectively catering to the fragmented consumption patterns of readers [14, 37]. These behaviors evolved from technology that was prevalent in the 1980s [38].

Specifically, changes began with the 1981 *San Francisco Examiner's* venture into digital territory that offered an electronic version of its newspaper that users could download to their home computers over a phone line in about two hours [39]. Despite that extended download time, the innovation marked the beginning of digital news distribution. Smartphones were still decades away, and most news was still printed in more than 1700 newspapers in the United States alone. Stories typically followed the inverted pyramid structure that places the most important details first and the least important last [40].

In 1994, 13 years after its initial electronic experiment, the *San Francisco Examiner* and *San Francisco Chronicle* published their print editions online. In the UK, *The Daily Telegraph* took a similar step, launching its web version as the *Electronic Telegraph*. This marked another pivotal moment in the evolution of digital journalism. These early efforts foreshadowed the tectonic shifts that would forever reshape news consumption. Those who were 18 and older in 1994 stood on the cusp of a dramatic transformation in how most content would be accessed and experienced.

Between 1987 and 2003, more than 300 US newspapers ceased publication [41] as the media industry began to shift. The launch of the first social network, *Six Degrees*, in 1997 introduced social connectivity, but it would be another 13 years before smartphones enabled users to access content on the go. By 2005, more than 6000 news websites were still relying on the traditional story structure of a headline and a photo embedded in paragraphs of text. This reflected only limited adaptation to evolving user behaviors.

Few could have envisioned in 2005 that smartphones would provide instant access to virtually any information one could want. Technological advances have since enabled greater convenience for interacting with mobile content, social media, and streaming platforms at any time and from anywhere [42]. Today, most users can't imagine a day without their devices.

In response, some scholars have focused on researching customizable experiences that attract users [43]. This shift emphasized the importance of relevance, interactivity, and personalization in effectively engaging users. However, these broad concepts, including user motivations and interactivity, are often overlooked in the second-by-second cognitive decisions that users make to read, scan, like, share, or avoid content.

By 2024, more than seven billion mobile devices worldwide provided users with on-demand access to unlimited information, while more than 500 US newspapers ceased operations for various reasons. Those that survived depended on the traditional format of headlines, photos, and pages of scrollable text, along with ads. A few papers added AI-generated reading of the text and video, but without a systematic structure for multimedia.

Some sites adopted the strategy of pop-up windows for subscribers, employing clickbait headlines to capture clicks or more detailed headlines to inform scanners. But clicking on headlines most often exposed users to pages dominated by scrollable text, as the attention span of many users quickly dwindled. The inverted pyramid structure originated in the 1860s and, some 160 years later, remains the dominant structure for news. If you access a digital news site, the predictable headline-photo-text format will likely dominate most pages.

To reassure readers, some publishers provide the estimated read-time for consuming their content, but a five-minute read, for example, could arguably deter users with, say, just one minute to read even well-crafted text. Audience analytics suggest [44], while roughly half of all users may engage with at least part of an article, the other half disengages with the content within 15 seconds [45]. Even when factoring in dedicated news consumers, the average visit to news sites such as CNN or *The Washington Post* in December 2024 totaled just under three minutes [46]. For audience development teams, achieving an average visit duration of at least 15 minutes would likely spark newsroom celebrations.

These statistics raise a critical question that newsrooms and journalism textbooks have yet to fully address: Why does digital content disengage at least half of those who encounter it? And why do 80% of users leave a site after viewing just a single page [47]? This book explores potential answers and solutions, focusing on whether new structures could better serve those who seek in-depth information *and* those with limited time to scan content quickly for key information. Could innovative formats help foster more loyal users with an interface that caters to varying attention spans and preferences? We explore these possibilities in each chapter, examining how rethinking traditional structures may be the key to retaining more users.

The evidence suggests that shifts in user behaviors, driven by technology providing overwhelming, on-demand content, have outpaced the innovation in how content is delivered.

## 2.2 Attention Shifts to Multiple Sources

Before the internet, news consumers typically relied on a single, scheduled news source, including the daily printed newspaper or evening network news broadcast. However, digital technology and 24/7 access to information have disrupted these fixed routines.

Abandoning structured times for reading the daily paper, more random mobile news consumption grew from 76% in 2019 to 87% by 2024, confirming the role of mobile devices as the preferred source for on-the-go news access. Laptop use for news also grew significantly, rising from 58% to 71% over the same period. In contrast, traditional media continued its downward trend. TV news, once dominant, slid from 68% in 2019 to 62% in 2024, while print news overall saw the steepest drop, with usage falling from 40% to just 25%. These shifts underscore a growing reliance on content with 24/7 access [47].

Instead of devoting time to reading a paper or watching a newscast, in 2023, users in the United States spent an average of 144 micro sessions on their phones per day [48, 49]. Time spent texting, viewing apps, watching videos, and scrolling social media on a single device can total up to seven hours per day [50]. Based on cumulative screen time across multiple devices, an 18-year-old could spend nearly 16 years of their life viewing screens by the time they reach 65.

The sheer volume of devices and media sources fuels the widely acknowledged fact that we are inundated with information [51]. Attention is fragmented across a variety of websites, social media platforms, mobile apps, text alerts, email newsletters, and podcasts on multiple devices, including phones, smartwatches, tablets, laptops, and desktop computers. Each is vying for attention.

At the same time, social media has equipped a growing user base with the tools to quickly produce, edit, and distribute content that used to take hours. Users who allocate limited time to content typically divide their attention across multiple platforms [52, 53]. The question is how journalism and education fit into this complexity. To what extent will any content, including video, be viewed in its entirety by the largest possible population of diverse users?

Video-based platforms have experienced significant global growth, becoming the primary news source for an increasing number of users [54]. To engage the next generation effectively with information, many publishers are focusing on short-form video production. This format resonates with younger audiences because it aligns with their consumption habits

[55]. This also reflects yet another shift toward quick, easily digestible media. Will today's social media users maintain their loyalty to their favorite social platforms as they grow older, or will they eventually shift to more mainstream news sources?

Meeting the needs of diverse audiences may necessitate revising some frameworks, including the well-established Uses and Gratifications Theory. The theory initially focused on how audiences actively seek content to fulfill their specific needs. Scholars have since modified the theory to account for the fragmented, fast-paced environment where users constantly shift between brief interactions and deeper engagement. Updating and testing new models can eventually help content creators design experiences that align more closely with today's user behaviors [56, 57], including selective exposure [1].

At the same time, research claiming any impact of digital content hinges on whether that content was actually consumed, not just whether its distribution could have reached a large number of followers, some of whom may not have even seen it. The potential reach of content does not equate to genuine engagement. Consumption of content is not synonymous with the number of likes or clicks. Meaningful engagement means going beyond surface-level metrics to understand how users process and interact with information in ways that will drive retention and influence.

## 2.3 We Must Extend Beyond a Target Audience

Topic-specific websites—such as those focused on cooking or gardening, for example—have and should continue to cater to niche groups, but existing users of these sites are not those who will benefit most from new ways to present content. A target audience also often represents only a portion of a much larger user base. Research into human-computer interaction supports this claim, suggesting that users often share traits that go beyond traditional audience categorizations. Analytics also indicate that to engage a wider range of users, the presentation of content must be versatile enough to appeal to multiple population segments simultaneously.

The DEM variables and the companion user interface we introduce in subsequent chapters will focus on users who either scan or avoid content, especially when exposed to it incidentally on social media. Some scholars suggest that incidental exposure might even offset earlier worries about declining news consumption among younger users [58], while others argue that clicking on a link does not equate to meaningful engagement with the following content [59].

The mobile environment has led to increased incidental exposure to content [2, 27, 60]. Social media's role in news distribution has led to what some researchers refer to as the perception that "news finds me," a phenomenon whereby younger users believe they don't need to seek out news to stay informed [61]. For these users, news surfaces organically within their social feeds. This incidental exposure represents one way that varied sources continue to reshape content consumption and highlights the limitations of a one-size-fits-all approach.

Regardless of how users are exposed to information, our model posits that producing more engaging content, whether organically discovered or curated by algorithms, means understanding how, when, and where text and multimedia can be presented to align with the cognitive sequences in which it will be consumed.

Meanwhile, much of today's digital content is shaped by efficient yet formulaic content management systems (CMS), which quickly populate text and media into standardized templates. These templates operate under the outdated assumption that all users process content in the same way. While some organizations have attempted to make content more user-friendly by incorporating shorter paragraphs and bullet-point summaries, to any casual scanner, a page of text remains just that—a page of text. Declining news audiences and revenues, and increasing machine learning algorithms have increased the need and desire to reach beyond a narrowly defined target audience.

Experimental research has demonstrated that restructuring original news stories on health topics such as breast cancer or complex topics such as nanotechnology can significantly boost user interest and comprehension among participants with little to no prior knowledge [37]. Another study found that incorporating explanatory links to specific terms alongside the main text of complex stories can significantly boost interest and understanding of the content by users who would not typically seek or select it [11]. Modifying the traditional inverted pyramid can therefore reach a broader audience. Story details were more accurately recalled when presented in a narrative style rather than the traditional inverted pyramid format [62].

When deciding to explore ways to engage more users outside a target audience, the challenge lies in defining what engagement is.

## 2.4 Defining Engagement Can Be Complex

Engagement is complicated because definitions vary, the digital landscape is fragmented, and users switch between sources and platforms. Moreover, the term "engagement" describes various conditions and extends beyond citizen involvement in local communities or student engagement in classes [23, 34, 63–67]. This complexity necessitates a nuanced understanding of engagement, especially as it applies to users' varied interactions across multiple digital platforms.

Audience analytics define engagement through micro-level measures, such as the number of clicks, likes, or shares of content received. However, as stated above, clicking on a headline does not necessarily indicate true engagement with the following content. Metrics focused solely on quantifiable interactions may overlook a substantial population of passive users who scan or read the content without any overt interaction.

Other approaches measure engagement by time spent on content; however, this can also be misleading, as other simultaneous activities and distractions may inflate time-based metrics, obscuring the accurate measurement of meaningful engagement. Rather than relying on surface-level metrics from a single user population on one website, our new model suggests that the different needs of various user types—scanners, readers, and passive consumers—require content structures that cater to all users. Only by addressing diverse user preferences can metrics begin to accurately reflect the complex engagement process, moving beyond surface-level measures to understand how different user groups engage with content on a deeper level.

The model introduced in this book defines engagement as a multidimensional concept that explains how certain content attracts attention after initial exposure. Figure 2.1 outlines a basic set of components that represent a more complex cognitive process, illustrating how different motivations can be shaped by variables commonly shared across users. Goal-directed information seeking guides attention, but what about the significant portion of users who encounter content, such as news stories or social media posts, incidentally rather than intentionally? The model contends that conventional content structures, such as headlines or titles, paired with photos or videos and scrollable text, are not equally effective in serving different motivations. Even before the rise of digital media, some scholars argued that not all gratifications associated with information seeking should be classified as need-based or problem-solving. Allen [68] noted that some gratifications may fulfill broader desires such as entertainment or socialization, which fall outside the narrow scope of traditional information needs.

Specifically, we define engagement through three core dimensions—cognitive, interactive, and emotional, which shape how users attend to and process information.

- *Cognitive engagement* describes the mental processes users employ to absorb and understand content, even when they are not actively interacting with it. Skimming news headlines or deeply engaging with news stories both require cognitive engagement, albeit at different levels. While essential for knowledge acquisition and critical

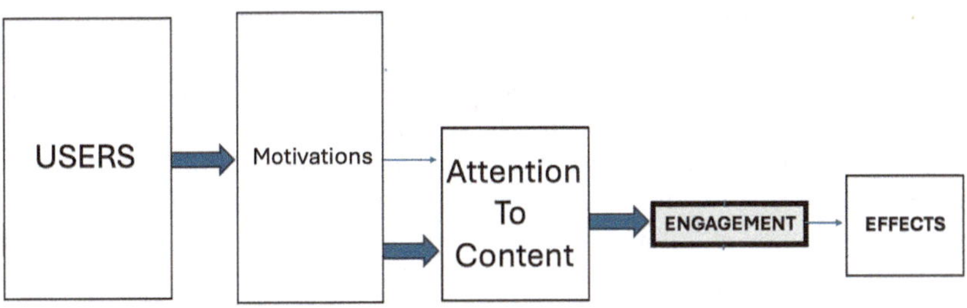


**Fig. 2.1** Basic components for variables in the digital engagement model

thinking, cognitive engagement alone may not always lead to interactive behaviors.

- *Interactive engagement*, on the other hand, requires direct user participation—liking, sharing, or commenting on content. While interactivity is easier to measure than cognitive engagement, it doesn't always indicate deeper understanding. Users can quickly interact with content without needing to consume or process it all.
- *Emotional engagement* is the extent to which content resonates with users to enhance cognitive and interactive behaviors [69]. Compelling stories, images, or videos that evoke emotional responses can drive greater interaction and also make content more memorable [23].

Understanding the cognitive, interactive, and emotional dimensions of engagement can inform a model designed to sustain attention and foster engagement beyond brief interactions. However, it must also account for the barriers that naturally limit engagement. One such barrier lies within the brain's hard-wired tendencies, which affect how users process and respond to content.

## 2.5 The Brain Is Fast but Still Limited

As detailed in the next chapter, our brains have about 100 billion neurons, and each one has between 1000 and 10,000 connections with other neurons [70]. Each neuron acts as a messenger, sending and receiving information through rapid electrical impulses and chemical signals, enabling us to think, move, and feel. The complexity and speed of these interactions are staggering, and they form the foundation of our cognitive and emotional experiences.

However, the brain also faces a notable limitation in terms of attention. Daniel Kahneman's seminal book, *Attention and Effort*, conceptualized attention as a limited resource [71]. His *Capacity Model of Attention* explained that, as the brain processes stimuli and completes tasks, it allocates cognitive resources accordingly. In other words, the brain has a finite capacity for processing information, which must be carefully distributed based on the relative demands of each task and motivational factors. This underscores why maintaining engagement is challenging, especially when content must compete for the brain's limited resources.

In media contexts, Kahneman's model was further developed through the *Limited Capacity Model of Motivated Mediated Message Processing* [72,

73]. Lang's adaptation integrates insights from cognitive psychology, information processing, and motivated cognition to explain how media messages are processed. The model posits that media messages compete for a finite pool of cognitive resources, with both the structure of a message and the user's motivations playing critical roles in how effectively content is processed and addressed. Lang's model has been particularly influential in helping to understand user engagement within complex media environments, where attention is constantly divided, and motivations are key to sustaining engagement [74, 75].

## 2.6 Content Presentations Now Need to Outpace Users

The concepts, strategies, and designs presented in this book are grounded in two words: ***radical change***. Some have questioned the future viability of the news industry, highlighting the urgent need for transformative change. In response, this book not only identifies abstract concepts of engagement but also focuses on the importance of the first five seconds during which users encounter digital information.

To keep pace—or even catch up—with shifts in users' needs and preferences, digital content producers can't afford to ignore new ways to package and present information. Referral traffic from social media has already declined significantly. Specifically, in 2023, referrals from Facebook news sites decreased by 48%, and referrals to news sites from X/Twitter decreased by 27% [76]. By 2024, nearly 30% of users cited social media as their primary news source [50], with TikTok becoming a key platform for 28% of that group. Meanwhile, Facebook's role as a news source continued to wane, falling from 36% in 2014 to 26% by 2024, a trend some attribute to changes in Facebook's algorithm that deprioritized news content.

Where will users be in five or ten years? The future role of social media and news remains uncertain, especially as today's students grow into tomorrow's employees with family responsibilities. If producers do not adopt new methods of multimedia storytelling, text-based content could be produced more quickly by artificial intelligence.

The goals for transformation align with those set out in the 2020 Group Report by *The New York Times*. "We have not yet created a news report that takes full advantage of all the storytelling tools at our disposal and, in the process, does the best possible job of speaking to our potential audience." This call for change emphasizes the urgency of rethinking traditional content strategies and adopting innovative approaches that can genuinely engage and resonate with today's audiences [77].

Change was similarly the objective for *The Washington Post* in July 2024, when CEO William Lewis announced the creation of a third newsroom designed to build the skills necessary to meet untapped audiences "where they are" [78, 79]. The initiative aims to adapt to the evolving news ecosystem by engaging users who are "less likely to subscribe to traditional offerings," addressing the need for news organizations to reach beyond conventional subscriber bases and connect with new audiences.

Numerous initiatives have emerged to preserve and adapt journalism, such as Solutions Journalism [80] and Constructive Journalism, which launched its series of *Psychology for Journalists* articles in 2023 [81]. While it's essential to understand what topics interest users the most, prior interests alone do not reveal all users' needs or explain the varying behaviors users exhibit when consuming digital content.

The 2024 *Reuters Digital News Report* suggests that journalists can enhance engagement by focusing on relatable local stories, actively listening to communities, and providing solutions-based coverage [21]. While these are valuable recommendations, they remain broad and do not address the crucial seconds when a user encounters specific content and structures. Effectively capturing attention in these brief moments requires a more granular understanding of how users engage with content at first glance.

Our book does not rely only on theories, user motivations, and social media likes to introduce a unique cognitive model. Instead, we emphasize the importance of delivering high-quality content that fosters deeper engagement in a matter of seconds for many users and encourages the consumption of more content that users would typically ignore. This is not to suggest that all users will consume all content, but any incremental increase in the consumption of content that some users would typically overlook if it were presented as a page of text could lead to a more informed society, while increasing revenues for struggling marketers and news organizations.

We introduce a unique micro-level cognitive model that incorporates user and content variables and strategies that are not widely taught or addressed. This emphasizes the delivery of high-quality content that facilitates deeper engagement, enabling more users to consume more content for more extended periods of time. Our innovative methods capture and sustain user attention in a fragmented digital landscape.

By catering to user behaviors and preferences, this model aligns content presentation with cognitive processes, creating more personalized experiences that maximize engagement. It is designed to adapt to how users consume media, especially as incidental exposure is increasingly common. The framework anticipates and accommodates common media behaviors, including scanning, sporadic engagement, and multitasking, which are prevalent in mobile environments. By addressing the barriers to engagement, our model introduces new content features to appeal to a broader audience.

We promote the need for an alternative model and a definition of engagement beyond simply the number of page views or social media shares. The definition of engagement is then unpacked further, examining its key dimensions and introducing strategies to foster deeper, more enduring connections between content and users.

## 2.7 The Digital Engagement Model Targets Diverse Users

Attention to content can't be ensured solely with clickbait [82], text brevity [83], or interactivity [84]. Facilitating sustained attention requires foundational concepts from cognitive psychology and neuroscience, which describe how users process and retain information. We can examine attention as it naturally occurs by studying attention within users' technological environments [85].

Our cognitive *Digital Engagement Model* is represented in Fig. 2.2 and detailed in the following chapters. Through theoretical foundations, empirical evidence, and practical strategies, it reconfigures traditional content presentation practices to enhance engagement.

Rooted in multidisciplinary research, the DEM maps the cognitive processes and decision-making paths that users follow, aiming to offer tailored presentation strategies for today's digital landscape.

Since users' needs vary, a multifaceted approach is essential to reimagine content delivery in ways that sustain attention. The DEM focuses on synthesizing three key components of engagement (Fig. 2.2). This approach acknowledges the fragile relationships that all users bring to all content, and the goal for producers to engage more users with important

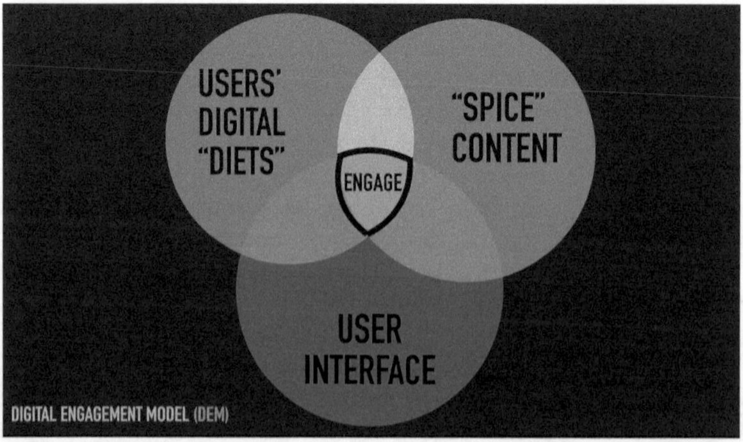


**Fig. 2.2** The three core components of the digital engagement model

information that busy users may not consume if presented as pages of scrollable text.

The proposed model and its strategies cannot guarantee universal engagement with all content, but they do increase the likelihood of capturing and sustaining attention. As illustrated in Fig. 2.1, the model synthesizes user variables, content variables, and a unique interface to create a tailored approach to engagement. By aligning these components, the DEM offers a more adaptable and user-centered framework for presenting content that addresses users' varying needs.

Some of the DEM's strategies may not be essential for attracting users with a strong interest in a topic and ample time to engage with it. The model is designed to extend beyond this core audience by engaging a broader group of users with limited time. Even mobile users with strong interest may have only limited time to pursue details. For marketers, nonprofit organizations, government agencies, and news organizations competing with often entertaining social media video and animation, the model argues that even brief engagement with more important content is better than no engagement. Accommodating the needs and behaviors of today's digital audiences will only enhance the likelihood of capturing the attention of an aging generation that grew up with social media.

To be clear, well-written text remains essential, but the model specifies specific cues in text for users with different needs and then combines them with multimedia in ways that align with how the brain allocates attention. Long-form storytelling that some users avoid is prompting publishers to adopt more video and audio content [79]. As users increasingly turn away from less engaging content, even when it provides important information [8, 16, 86, 87], it becomes essential to explore new formats that will draw more users in.

The DEM goes beyond single-solution approaches, such as specific link types or shorter paragraphs. Instead, it integrates a variety of strategies that work together to address how users select content. This multifaceted approach considers varying attention spans and engagement styles, providing a more adaptable framework for a tailored user experience. Clickbait-style headlines and titles emerged in the 1990s and were initially believed to be the most effective way to attract users. The empirical evidence suggests otherwise.

Research indicates that users' clicks and average dwell time on content are closely tied to the perceived relevance of the information. Factors such as specificity, length, and readability also play critical roles in shaping user satisfaction. The optimal content strikes a balance between attention-grabbing headlines and scannable information, catering to users with different time constraints. By providing both appeal and accessibility, content can attract and sustain scanners and readers alike.

An early study found that humans are hardwired to select danger-related content [88], while later research revealed that subheads emphasizing conflict and agony encourage more selective exposure [89]. These findings suggest that content highlighting threats or distressing events naturally captures attention, indicating an innate tendency to prioritize information that suggests potential harm.

Interdisciplinary research indicates that users process content in varied ways [90–93]. Considering factors such as a user's interests, environment, available time, and preferred engagement style—and whether they are scanning, skimming, or reading—the DEM introduces our *Smart Story Suite*. This interface enables users to quickly select and structure information that meets their needs, departing radically from traditional headline/photo/text formats. The SSS empowers users to personalize their content experience without requiring them to focus solely on long-form text.

The user-centered interface presents a single screen featuring bullet-point highlights, an introductory paragraph of text, a photo or video, and a series of buttons for accessing additional content at the bottom of the screen. Users determine which information they are interested in based on their available time. This means each user can consume content as either short form or long form. One of the selectable buttons is a fact-check button, providing instant access to the sources of the information to minimize perceptions of misinformation. News, for example, typically repeats previously known information related to the story for users who are encountering the story for the first time. Users who engaged previously with the story before new details were known could skip details they already knew. This explains how and why more users could engage with more content [94]. The model can also be used for testing new theories and building knowledge [95]. We refrain from theorizing about the effects of content, such as trust or bias, without first confirming that meaningful engagement has occurred.

Research on content production, which we cover in the initial chapters of this book, underpins the practical strategies for content delivery presented later. Emphasizing the first critical seconds of user exposure, this book examines the variables that influence the attention given to content. In this way, we show how understanding cognitive and neurological processes offers fresh insights into the needs and behaviors of digital consumers.

Importantly, this book does not equate the potential reach of social media content with meaningful engagement. Instead, it acknowledges that reach alone is an inadequate measure of genuine engagement without considering the variety of user behaviors shaped by digital technology. This nuanced approach highlights the importance of depth over mere visibility, focusing on the quality of user interaction. A blend of concepts from cognitive psychology, educational psychology, and neuroscience provides a roadmap for enhancing the communication of virtually any digital content, not just news.

Shrinking news audiences and revenues, the rise of algorithms, and the flood of information combine to make capturing and sustaining user attention increasingly challenging. Text-heavy pages are often perceived as less engaging than short social media videos [26]. At the same time, more serious content related to health, science, the economy, or the environment cannot and should not be reduced to entertainment, strategically combining and presenting multimedia alongside text that can quickly inform scanners and guide readers to more details, can capture more attention, and inform more users. Well-structured content like this can effectively reach a broad range of users, extending beyond those with the time for and interest in lengthy articles. This approach enables news organizations to accommodate diverse consumption habits without sacrificing the depth or integrity of the content.

Instead of depending solely on algorithms or grabbing attention, the DEM promotes building deeper connections with users by aligning content presentation with natural cognitive processing. This approach emphasizes delivering information effectively rather than merely chasing clicks to cultivate a more profound and lasting interaction with digital content.

## 2.8 Human Creativity Is Unmatched by AI

Artificial intelligence tools can generate headlines, text, and visuals more quickly than human creators. Still, the complexity of the Digital Engagement Model necessitates human judgment, skills, emotional sensitivity, and decision-making to effectively apply the appropriate strategies, placements, and combinations of multimedia. AI's ability to create cognitively and emotionally engaging multimedia, organize specific information into a new multimedia structure, and present it in a way that supports human processing of the content does not yet convincingly exist. AI may always lack the sensitivity to produce content that communicates or generates empathy, nuanced interpretations, and deep contextual understanding. Even ChatGPT acknowledges its own limitations in replicating the following human skills:

1. **Contextual Understanding**: AI can detect and generate emotional content but lacks the deeper contextual insight and cultural awareness that humans contribute to content creation.
2. **Ethical Considerations**: AI's ability to manipulate emotions raises ethical concerns. Human oversight is essential to ensure responsible use of emotional content, preventing exploitation or harm.
3. **Creativity and Subtlety**: While AI can automate certain tasks, human creators bring empathy, creativity, and subtlety that AI often struggles to replicate. Additionally, humans can adapt content in real-time based on feedback and changing contexts.
4. **Complex Emotional Layering**: AI can regenerate basic emotional content, but the nuanced emotional layering present in human storytelling continues to be a challenge for AI.

Producing digital content with multiple DEM variables and strategies requires creativity, skill, and ethical judgment that only human producers can provide. While AI may be able to regenerate previously produced emotional content, it lacks the intuitive ability to create original reporting, creativity, and cultural nuances that human producers offer. Human intuition and experience are essential in crafting emotionally impactful narratives that resonate more deeply with users.

Whether you're a communications professional, teacher, scholar, or student, this book aims to inspire you to rethink some traditional practices that AI can replicate, such as writing or creating visuals. When attention becomes the new measure of success, your evaluation of the variables in the DEM ultimately depends on how quickly you want to test new approaches and the opportunities they present. That said, not every content producer may wish to adopt our model despite the positive effects it could offer in terms of enhanced user attention.

## 2.9 For Some, a New Model Can Be Challenging

Several communication sectors are seeking solutions to address the dominance of mobile devices, the rising popularity of social media, increased use of algorithms, threats from artificial intelligence, and decreasing revenues due to shrinking audiences spending less time on more sources. In his 1962 book *The Structure of Scientific Revolutions*, Thomas Kuhn focused on the challenges that motivated a major paradigm shift in science. Kuhn argued that significant transformations do not emerge gradually from routine practices. Instead, he contended that when existing models fail to meet new challenges, a crisis prompts a revolutionary shift, not merely an incremental change. Kuhn's call for bold, structural changes is more urgent than ever in a digital environment that hasn't endured if legacy media, which established many production strategies still practiced today.

Rethinking traditional practices that have not kept pace with user behaviors can our understanding of how the brain responds to various media, and adopting new strategies that align with how users consume content despite having different amounts of time to process it. This shift may involve several incremental changes, ranging from addressing more user variables when producing content to incorporating new content variables in its presentation.

Some producers will recognize that addressing the urgent need to test new strategies for serving the diverse digital consumers of tomorrow has no downside. The research to design this model was motivated years ago by the rapid increase in technologies and the growing number of users who rely on them, regardless of time and location. While established practices and approaches may feel more comfortable for some, they are often not equipped to address the fragmented nature of digital consumption experienced by distracted users who are bombarded with continuous information on demand.

It can be disheartening for those who spend countless hours writing award-winning stories that ultimately reach a limited number of interested users. Keeping users engaged requires more than just capturing their attention. Attracting and maintaining interest in content a user may not have sought is no different from a social media user engaging with incidental content they did not expect. Clearly, important or serious information will never possess the entertaining appeal of short social media videos, but more skills and strategies could draw that attention.

The DEM refutes those who believe that artificial intelligence can or will replicate the creativity and emotional sensitivity of human producers. If current content structures persist, AI poses a threat. In the context of Kuhn's paradigm shifts, the DEM challenges the assumption that well-written and well-sourced texts are the sole criteria for presenting content. Well-written text enhanced by new approaches that align with how the brain processes information—regardless of a user's level of interest and time—represents a transformation. By addressing the paradigm shift directly, the DEM aims to add depth, focus, and coherence to digital content, particularly news, where the stakes for attracting and engaging citizens in news stories are higher than ever.

The reality is that text-heavy content cannot, nor should it, compete with the endless multimedia available at the fingertips of most users. Envisioning a larger audience to attract and inform, strategies based on the individual similarities all users bring to content, and addressing the needs of more users could spark greater interest in important issues—issues that would otherwise be overlooked.

Content producers of traditional formats who need to shorten their texts to fit prescribed templates will find relief, as the DEM presents all content as both short and long-form information. This means that all text can be as lengthy as needed, but scanner users are never obligated to engage for as long as readers must. In other words, producers can leverage the web's innovative features without sacrificing quality or quantity. Furthermore, the content might even convert some scanners into readers when they encounter an innovative and user-friendly interface.

A model that guarantees that all content will engage every user will never exist. A model can only increase the likelihood that more users will consume more content for longer periods of time. The transformation proposed in this book involves re-evaluating, developing, and applying new skills and strategies. It also requires replacing predictable structures with those that facilitate consumption for users with varying motivations. Such efforts respond to evolving user behaviors and the cognitive processing of multimedia.

## References


1. Knobloch-Westerwick, S. 2015. *Choice and preference in media use: Advances in selective exposure theory and research.* Routledge.
2. Takano, M., et al. 2021. Effects of incidental brief exposure to news on news knowledge while scrolling through videos. *IEEE Access* **9**:37,772–37,783.
3. Kim, Y., H. T. Chen, and H. Gil de Zuniga. 2013. Stumbling upon news on the internet: Effects of incidental news exposure and relative entertainment use on political engagement. *Computers in Human Behavior* **29**:2707–2614.
4. Wilson, T. D. 2024. Approaches to information-seeking behavior in psychology; a comparison of early and contemporary studies. *Information Research an International Electronic Journal* **29** (1): 34–53.
5. Volk, S. C., A. Schulz, S. Blassnig, S. Marschlich, M. H. Nguyen, and N. Strauß. 2025. Selecting, avoiding, disconnecting: A focus group study of people's strategies for dealing with information abundance in the contexts of news, entertainment, and personal communication. *Information, Communication & Society* **28** (1): 21–40.
6. Oeldorf-Hirsch, A., and S. S. Sundar. 2015. Posting, commenting, and tagging: Effects of sharing news stories on Facebook. *Computers in Human Behavior* **44**:240–249.
7. Kim, Y. H., D. J. Kim, and K. Wachter. 2013. A study of mobile user engagement (MoEN): Engagement motivations, perceived value, satisfaction, and continued engagement intention. *Decision Support Systems* **56**:361–370.
8. Carbone, M., S. Soroka, and J. Dunaway. 2024. The psychophysiology of news avoidance: Does negative affect drive both attention and inattention to news? *Journalism Studies* **25** (12): 1460–1475.
9. American Press Institute. 2014. *Social and demographic differences in news habits and attitudes* [cited 2015 February 6]. http://www.americanpressinstitute.org/publications/reports/survey-research/social-demographic-differences-news-habits-attitudes/.
10. Yaros, R., et al. 2015. Serving the needs of the Latina community for health information. *Health, Culture and Society* **8** (1): 20–33.

11. Crone, W. C., et al. 2011. Informal science education: A practicum for graduate students. *Innovative Higher Education* **36** (5): 291–304.
12. Yaros, R. 2005. Effects of explanatory structure building on interest in and understanding of hypertext news about science and technology. In *School of Journalism and Mass Communication*, 168. Madison, WI: University of Wisconsin-Madison.
13. Flowerday, T., G. Schraw, and J. Stevens. 2004. The role of choice and interest in reader engagement. *The Journal of Experimental Education* **72** (2): 93–114.
14. Yaros, R. 2011. Effects of text and hypertext structures on user interest and understanding of science and technology. *Science Communication* **33** (3): 275–308.
15. Kümpel, A. S. 2022. Social media information environments and their implications for the uses and effects of news: The PINGS framework. *Communication Theory* **32** (2): 223–242.
16. Toff, B., and A. Kalogeropoulos. 2020. All the news that's fit to ignore. *Public Opinion Quarterly* **84** (S1): 366–390.
17. Yaros, R., and J. Misak. 2020. Completing college writing assignments on mobile phones: Comparing students' attitudes and engagement across disciplines and age. *Journalism & Mass Communication Educator* **76** (2): 216–227.
18. Zheng, J., and G. Gao. 2024. Fragmented moments, balanced choices: How do people make use of their waiting time? In *Proceedings of the CHI Conference on Human Factors in Computing Systems*. Honolulu, HI, USA: Association for Computing Machinery.
19. Lioudis, N. 2019. Using the Engaged Time metric to grow audiences, unlock loyal readership. https://blog.chartbeat.com/2019/08/16/using-engaged-time-data-grow-loyal-audience/.
20. Sundar, S. S., and A. Limperos. 2013. Uses and Grats 2.0: New gratifications for new media. *Journal of Broadcasting & Electronic Media* **57** (4): 504–525.
21. Newman, N., and E. Heinrichs. 2024. Seven things journalists can do to counter news avoidance.
22. Wahl-Korgensen, K. 2020. An emotional turn in journalism studies? *Digital Journalism* **8**:175–194. https://doi.org/10.1080/21670811.2019.1697626.
23. Choi, J., S. Y. Lee, and S. W. Ji. 2021. Engagement in emotional news on social media: Intensity and type of emotions. *Journalism and Mass Communication Quarterly* **98** (4): 1,017–1,040.
24. Falgoust, G., et al. 2022. Applying the uses and gratifications theory to identify motivational factors behind young adult's participation in viral social media challenges on TikTok. *Human Factors in Healthcare* **2**:100014.
25. Petri, H. L., and J. M. Govern. 2012. *Motivation: Theory, research, and application*. 6th ed. Independence, KY: Cengage Learning.
26. Chen, Y., et al. 2023. The effect of short-form video addiction on users' attention. *Behaviour & Information Technology* **42** (16): 2893–2910.

27. Thorson, K. 2020. Attracting the news: Algorithms, platforms, and reframing incidental exposure. *Journalism* **21** (8): 1067–1082.
28. Wei, Z., et al. 2024. Social media distractions alter behavioral and neural patterns to global-local attention: The moderation effect of fear of missing out. *Computers in Human Behavior* **157**:108258.
29. Trielli, D., and N. Diakopoulos. 2019. Search as news curator: The role of Google in shaping attention to news information. In *Proceedings of the 2019 CHI Conference on Human Factors in Computing Systems*. Glasgow, Scotland, UK: Association for Computing Machinery.
30. Eveland, W. P., M. Krisztina, and M. Seo. 2004. Moving beyond "just the facts": The influence of online news on the content and structure of public affairs knowledge. *Communication Research* **31** (1): 82–107.
31. Pernice, K. 2019. Text scanning patterns: Eyetracking evidence. https://www.nngroup.com/articles/text-scanning-patterns-eyetracking/.
32. White, S. J., et al. 2015. Eye movements during reading and topic scanning: Effects of word frequency. *Journal of Experimental Psychology: Human Perception and Performance* **41** (1): 233–248.
33. Fatmawan, A. R., N. P. A. Dewi, and I. P. A. D. Hita. 2023. Skimming and scanning technique: Is it effective for improving Indonesian students' reading and comprehension. *Edusaintek: Jurnal Pendidikan, Sains dan Teknologi* **10** (3): 1,181–1,198.
34. Freiling, I., and L. Weidmuller. 2017. Scan method tracks reader attention, engagement. *Newspaper Research Journal* **38** (4): 449–461.
35. Eveland, W. P., et al. 2002. *How Web site organization influences free recall, factual knowledge, and knowledge structure*. New Orleans: National Communication Association.
36. Yaros, R., and A. Cook. 2013. Attention versus learning of online content: Preliminary findings from an eye-tracking study. In *Evolving Psychological and Educational Perspectives on Cyber Behavior*, ed. R. Z. Zheng, 132–154. Hershey, PA: IGI Global.
37. Yaros, R. 2006. Is it the medium or the message? Structuring complex news to enhance engagement and situational understanding by non-experts. *Communication Research* **33** (4): 285–309.
38. Yaros, R. 2009. Digital natives: Following their lead on a path to a new journalism. In *Nieman Reports*. Nieman Foundation for Journalism at Harvard University.
39. KRON-TV. 1981. *1981 primitive Internet report on KRON* [video]. https://youtu.be/5WCTn4FljUQ?feature=shared.
40. BBC. 2024. *A history of mobile phones and smartphones*. Bitesize Topical.
41. Cho, H., H. J. Martin, and S. Lacy. 2006. An industry in transition: Entry and exit in daily newspaper markets, 1987–2003. *Journalism and Mass Communication Quarterly* **83** (2): 381–396.

42. Sundar, S. S. 2009. Social psychology of interactivity in human-website interaction. In *Oxford handbook of internet psychology*, ed. A. Joinson et al. Oxford, UK: Oxford University Press.
43. Huang, E. 2009. The causes of youths' low news consumption and strategies for making youths happy news consumers. *Convergence* **15** (1): 105–122.
44. Newman, N., R. Fletcher, C. T. Robertson, A. Ross Arguedas, and R. K. Nielsen. 2024. *Reuters institute digital news report 2024.* Reuters Institute for the Study of Journalism.
45. Haile, T. 2014. What you think you know about the web is wrong. *Time.*
46. SimilarWeb. 2024. *Visit duration metrics.* SimilarWeb.
47. Behre, J., S. Hölig, and J. Möller. 2024. *Reuters institute digital news report 2024.* Reuters Institute for the Study of Journalism.
48. Bazen, A. 2025. *Journal of Consumer Research.* Consumer affairs.
49. Pew Research Center. 2024. *Mobile fact sheet* [November 13, 2024]. https://www.pewresearch.org/internet/fact-sheet/mobile/.
50. Guttmann, A. 2024. Average daily media use in the U.S., 2023 by medium. In *Statista.* Statista, June 20, 2024.
51. Eppler, M. J., and J. Mengis. 2004. The concept of information overload: A review of literature from organization, science, accounting, marketing, MIS, and related disciplines. *The Information Society* **20**:325–344.
52. Lee, P. S., and L. Leung. 2008. Assessing the displacement effects of the Internet. *Telematics and Informatics* **25** (3): 145–155.
53. De Waal, E., and K. Schoenbach. 2010. News sites' position in the mediascape: Uses, evaluations and media displacement effects over time. *New Media & Society* **12** (3): 477–496.
54. Newman, N., et al. 2023. Digital news report 2023. Available from: https://reutersinstitute.politics.ox.ac.uk/digital-news-report/2023.
55. Newman, N. 2024. *Technology trends and predictions 2024.* Available from: https://reutersinstitute.politics.ox.ac.uk/journalism-media-and-technology-trends-and-predictions.
56. Blumler, J. G. 1979. The role of theory in uses and gratifications studies. *Communication Research* **6**:9–36.
57. Katz, E., J. G. Blumler, and M. Gurevitch. 1973. Uses and gratifications research. *The Public Opinion Quarterly* **37** (4): 509–523.
58. Lenhart, A., et al. 2010. *Social media & mobile internet use among teens and young adults.* Millennials.
59. Barnidge, M. 2015. The role of news in promoting political disagreement on social media. *Computers in Human Behavior* **52**:211–218.
60. Fletcher, R., and R. K. Nielsen. 2018. Are people incidentally exposed to news on social media? A comparative analysis. *New Media & Society* **20** (7): 2,450–2,468.

61. de Zúñiga, H. G., and Z. Cheng. 2021. Origin and evolution of the news finds me perception: Review of theory and effects. *Profesional de la Información* **30** (3): 1–17.
62. Wise, K., et al. 2009. When words collide online: How writing style and video intensity affect cognitive processing of online news. *Journal of Broadcasting & Electronic Media* **53** (4): 532–546.
63. Omar, B., et al. 2024. Unlocking young people's engagement with online news: affective or cognitive? *Online Information Review* 48 (5): 944–958.
64. Ikwunne, T., L. Hederman, and P. J. Wall. 2020. Understanding user engagement in information and communications technology for development: An exploratory study. In *HCI international conference on human computer interaction*, 710–721. Cham: Springer International Publishing.
65. Kaakinen, J. K., et al. 2018. Fluctuation in cognitive engagement during reading: Evidence from concurrent recordings of postural and eye movements. *Journal of Experimental Psychology: Learning, Memory, and Cognition* **44**:1671–1677.
66. Cohen, S. S., et al. 2018. Neural engagement with online educational videos predicts learning performance for individual students. *Neurobiology of Learning and Memory* **155**:60–64.
67. Yardley, L., et al. 2016. Understanding and promoting effective engagement with digital behavior change interventions. *American Journal of Preventive Medicine* **51** (5): 833–842.
68. Allen, B. 1996. *Information tasks: Toward a user-centered approach to information systems*, 308. Academic Press, Inc.
69. Knobloch, S., et al. 2004. Affective news: Effects of discourse structure in narratives on suspense, curiosity, and enjoyment while reading news and novels. *Communication Research* **31** (3): 259–287.
70. Kandel, E., and L. Squire. 2000. Neuroscience: Breaking down scientific barriers to the study of brain and mind. *Science* **290** (5494): 1113–1120.
71. Kahneman, D. 1973. *Attention and effort*, 246. Englewood Cliffs, N.J.: Prentice-Hall.
72. Lang, A. 2000. The limited capacity model of mediated message processing. *Journal of Communication* **50**:46–70.
73. Lang, A. 1989. Effects of chronological presentation of information on processing and memory for broadcast news. *Journal of Broadcasting & Electronic Media* **33**:441–452.
74. Lang, A., et al. 2002. Captured by the World Wide Web: Orienting to structural and content features of computer-presented information. *Communication Research* **29** (3): 215–245.
75. Lang, A., J. E. Newhagen, and B. Reeves. 1996. Negative video as structure: Emotion, attention, capacity, and memory. *Journal of Broadcasting & Electronic Media* **40**:460–477.

76. Neary, J. 2023. Tracking the reader journey: A year of subscriber trends. https://blog.chartbeat.com/2024/02/29/tracking-the-reader-journey-a-year-of-subscription-trends/.
77. New York Times. 2017. The New York Times' 2020 group report.
78. Maher, B. 2024. Washington Post "third newsroom" creation gets underway. https://pressgazette.co.uk/north-america/washington-post-third-newsroom-krissah-thompson-will-lewis/.
79. Bruell, A. 2024. Washington post CEO plans a mysterious 'Third Newsroom.' His past offers a clue.
80. Solutions Journalism. 2024. *Solutions Journalism Network* [cited 2024]. https://www.solutionsjournalism.org/who-we-are.
81. Alpuim, M., and K. Ehrenberg. 2023. How insights from psychology can improve journalism. *Psychology for Journalists* [cited 2024 April 2, 2023]. https://www.bonn-institute.org/en/news/psychology-in-journalism.
82. Lefebvre, R. C. 2007. The new technology: The consumer as participant rather than target audience. *Social Marketing Quarterly* **13** (3): 31–42.
83. Van Dijk, T. A. 1983. Discourse analysis: Its development and application to the structure of news. *Journal of Communication* **33** (2): 20–43.
84. Kiousis, S. 2002. Interactivity: A concept explication. *New Media & Society* **4** (3): 355–383.
85. Hamilton, K. A., J. K. Yamashiro, and B. C. Storm. 2023. Special issue of applied cognitive psychology: Rethinking cognition in a digital environment. *Applied Cognitive Psychology* **37** (4): 683–685.
86. Betakova, D., H. Boomgaarden, S. Lecheler, and S. Schäfer. 2025. I do not (want to) know! The relationship between intentional news avoidance and low news consumption. *Mass Communication and Society* **28** (3): 413–440.
87. Palmer, R., B. Toff, and R. K. Nielsen. 2023. Examining assumptions around how news avoidance gets defined: The importance of overall news consumption, intention, and structural inequalities. *Journalism Studies* **24** (6): 697–714.
88. Shoemaker, P. J. 1996. Hardwired for news: Using biological and cultural evolution to explain the surveillance function. *Journal of Communication* **46** (3): 32–47.
89. Zillmann, D., et al. 2004. Effects of lead framing on selective exposure to Internet news reports. *Communication Research* **31** (1): 58–81.
90. Sternadori, M. M., and K. Wise. 2010. Men and women read news differently. *Journal of Media Psychology* **22** (1): 1–11.
91. Jenkins, J. R., et al. 2003. Sources of individual differences in reading comprehension and reading fluency. *Journal of Educational Psychology* **95** (4): 719.
92. Owen, L. H. 2018. People read news differently (i.e., worse) on phones than they do on desktop, new research suggests. https://www.niemanlab.org/2018/04/people-read-news-differently-i-e-worse-on-phones-than-they-do-on-desktop-new-research-suggests/.

93. Mulupi, D., F. H. C. Wong, and R. A. Yaros. 2025. Investigating the effect of a physician's race and gender on user engagement with and perceived credibility of COVID-19 vaccine news. *Newspaper Research Journal* **46** (1): 96–117.
94. Järvelin, K., and T.D. 2003. Wilson On conceptual models for information seeking and retrieval research. *Information Research* **9**:9–1.
95. Mershon, C., and O. Shvetsova. 2019. *Formal modeling in social science*, 256. University of Michigan Press.

CHAPTER 3

# A New Model Fills Some Theoretical Gaps

- We begin with Uses and Gratifications Theory.
- Uses and Gratifications is expanded.
- Other communication theories emerged.
- Newer theory defines the concepts of interest.
- A lack of user interest can also lead to avoidance of content.
- Six new propositions are presented to expand the concept of engagement.



R. Yaros, *The Digital Engagement Model*, Palgrave Practical Guides in Communication,
https://doi.org/10.1007/978-3-032-03822-7_3

This chapter explores theories of media consumption with a focus on Uses and Gratifications theory (U&G) and the Elaboration Likelihood Model (ELM). U&G posits that individuals actively select media to fulfill their need for information, entertainment, and social interaction. We build on both by differentiating the dimensions of interest, as users either seek specific content or pay attention to content that generates interest, but content they would not typically seek or select. The chapter discusses why we should consider users who only scan or avoid content equally important as users who engage with content.

Uses and Gratifications Theory [1] posits that audiences are active participants, seeking media to satisfy their psychological and social needs. Agenda-setting theory [2] provided insights into how the media influence the public's perception of issues. Spiral of Silence theory [3, 4] highlighted the role of perceived majority opinions in shaping one's willingness to express dissenting views. These theories continue to inform important research about influence, perception, and media power. At the same time, there is a gap in the frameworks that address the time users spend engaging or not engaging with digital content. Arguably, those moments are equally important as the broader theoretical concepts to engagement, since the application of any theory or claims of media effects ultimately depends on whether users consumed and understood the content.

In the context of digital media, where attention is fragmented, interfaces constantly shift, and interactions occur in milliseconds, conceptual models often lack the precision to explain moment-to-moment user needs, attention, and psychological processes, which occur before users derive gratification from the media. There is no downside to theorizing how, when, and why users cognitively process digital information. What triggers or interrupts a user's attention, and what ultimately drives user behavior at the micro-level?

This is where other disciplines can help fill the theoretical gap. Fields such as cognitive psychology, human-computer interaction, and neuroscience have already developed concepts that are empirically grounded and highly relevant to digital engagement with different forms of content, not just news. Although some of the peer-reviewed models were published well before the first iPhone, their core ideas remain applicable. Their original contexts may relate to early web navigation, interface design, or decision-making environments, but with adaptation, they can enrich and extend the field of communication theory to the digital world. Here are just three examples of theories that may not be known to some:

**Information Foraging Theory** [5–7] conceptualizes users as rational agents trying to maximize the value of information per unit of effort, much like animals foraging for food. The theory has been used to explain the navigation, attention allocation, and search behaviors that continue today.

**Dual-Process Models of Cognition** [8, 9] distinguish between fast, automatic thinking and slow, deliberate thinking, offering a framework for understanding how users process headlines, information, and social media videos in real-time.

**Nudge Theory** [10, 11] explains how subtle design elements in digital environments can influence user behavior without limiting freedom of choice. This concept is relevant for everything from the design of notifications to the placement of content.

These theories and others are often overlooked in communication and journalism research, not due to a lack of relevance, but rather because of disciplinary boundaries. Many scholars have made the case for greater interdisciplinarity in the field, especially as digital environments evolve in complexity and speed [12, 13]. At the same time, there is understandable hesitation among some producers to adopt or even test unfamiliar frameworks outside their education, research, or training.

This chapter seeks to bridge that gap. It begins by reviewing traditional communication and journalism theories that remain foundational to understanding engagement. Then, it introduces additional theoretical models from adjacent fields that have been rigorously tested. By integrating these perspectives, the chapter provides a comprehensive framework for understanding digital engagement—one that seamlessly transitions between macro-level motivations and micro-level cognition.

If we want to create new media products that fulfill their purpose and convey well-crafted messages to their audiences, the first step is to appreciate the underlying theory. Given the need to bridge the gap between theory and practice, this chapter reviews the essential concepts from Uses and Gratifications (U&G) theory to the Elaboration Likelihood Model (ELM) to show how they jointly form the cornerstone of understanding digital attention. We then build upon these concepts for enhanced user engagement.

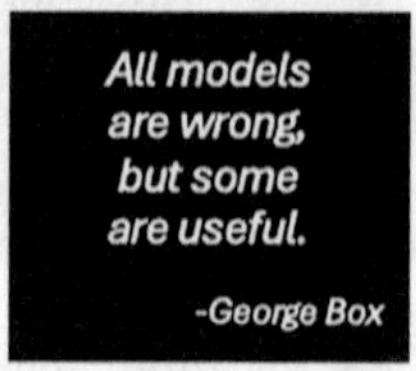


At one end of the scale, many textbooks focus primarily on the latest developments in media production, such as digital storytelling, audience analytics, or algorithm-driven content strategies. These prioritize practical application over theoretical concepts, often treating theory as an academic tool rather than essential guidance for shaping media practice [14].

At the other extreme, scholarly publications provide a conceptual basis for research, underpinned by theory [15]. Peer-reviewed publications typically apply theory and pay less attention to its practical applications [16]. Some have argued that this forms "psychological blinders," narrowing researchers' perceptions to expectations that either confirm or refute their theories [17]. If this is true, scientists' observations can be influenced by prevailing paradigms that constrain their openness to alternative explanations. In other words, existing theories shape, but can sometimes restrict, scientific inquiry.

In the media context, theory can serve as a lens for understanding user preferences, anticipating technological innovation, and shifts in audience behavior [18]. Any perceived divide between theory and practice may therefore hinder meaningful contributions, both to research and industry. While theory may seem abstract to some practitioners, and some might hesitate to apply theory when producing daily digital content, both camps stand to benefit from the more integrated approach introduced by the Digital Engagement Model.

Theory also provides a framework for generalization, allowing the findings from individual studies to contribute to a broader understanding of media dynamics [19]. Without theory, media research risks becoming a collection of disconnected case studies, lacking coherence and predictive power [20]. For this reason, we argue that theory can also guide practitioners in navigating changing engagement patterns and the reasons for those changes, whether in the evolution of content presentation, social media algorithms, or ethical concerns in content creation [21].

In our view, multidisciplinary theory should not be an exclusively abstract academic requirement, but a powerful bridge between research and practice [22]. We address concerns about the validity of a solid foundation in theoretical research when predicting future engagement, demonstrating how a new model can surpass the often-temporary trends uncovered by historical audience analytics. Analytics can provide a limited view into meaningful audience engagement because they attempt to quantify the attention users pay to information, rather than the degree of attention and level of comprehension.

By integrating theoretical perspectives into media production, we can address relevant real-world applications. This is because a systematic understanding of communication processes can then inform the content structure [23]. Instead of existing in separate spheres, theory and practice can be complementary, each enhancing the other's value. By grounding both research and practice in theoretical insights, when possible, a more informed, adaptive, and innovative approach can cultivate an understanding of media while addressing user cognition in the digital age [24].

The cognitive revolution of the 1950s introduced the concept of the mind as an information processor, analogous to a computer. In so doing, it laid the groundwork for the algorithms that mimic human problem-solving and decision-making processes today.

In particular, Chomsky's theory of transformational-generative grammar emphasized the human mind as the engine of language processing, thus impacting the way that artificial intelligence (AI) models understand and generate human language [25]. The *Logic Theorist* program was designed in 1956 to simulate human problem-solving and is often regarded as one of the first AI systems, demonstrating how cognitive psychology principles can be applied to machine learning [26]. These early theories provided insights into human cognition, memory, problem-solving, and information retention—processes that are to some extent hardwired into the brain and have influenced our approach to data processing and decision-making today.

Atkinson and Shiffrin's Multi-Store Model of Memory [27] conceptualized memory as a sequential process consisting of three distinct stages:

1. **Sensory Memory** is the brief storage of sensory input, allowing individuals to perceive their environment momentarily before transferring relevant information to the next stage.
2. **Short-Term Memory** is a temporary storage system with limited capacity, influenced by Miller's earlier work on chunking and information retention [28].
3. **Long-Term Memory** is a more permanent storage system where information is encoded and retrieved when necessary.

Their model represents memory as a structured process, whereby information moves through these stages in a linear progression. This thinking went on to influence later AI models whose machine-learning algorithms mimic human memory structures. Newell and Simon's Information-Processing Theory introduced a computational perspective, treating the mind as an information-processing system similar to a computer [29]. The same team also developed the *General Problem Solver* (GPS), one of the first computer-based models designed to simulate human thought. This ground-breaking research laid the groundwork for the way that modern-day AI systems use heuristics (mental shortcuts) and decision trees to simulate human reasoning.

While these early theories provided a foundation for understanding cognition, they primarily addressed linear, text-based information processing. Because these models were developed in an era focused on reading and verbal learning, they did not fully account for the increasing complexity of mediated messages in digital and multimedia environments.

## 3.1 It Began with Uses and Gratifications Theory

Well before the advent of the internet and smartphones, Uses and Gratifications Theory (U&G) proposed that audiences actively select media based on their individual needs and motivations, rather than passively consuming content [1]. The theory defined gratifications as:

1. Social (interacting with others)
2. Diversion (escaping from current environments)
3. Status and credibility (seeking recognition or validation)
4. Emotions (enjoying entertainment or mood regulation)
5. Cognitive (acquiring new information)

Building on the U&G concepts, McQuail [30] broadly categorized users' motivations for media use into the four primary functions of:

1. Information
2. Personal identity
3. Integration and social interaction
4. Entertainment [15, 30]

With each edition of the model, McQuail emphasized that media consumption is shaped by individual needs, context, and media availability, reinforcing the idea that audiences actively choose content based on personal and social gratifications.

Since its publication in 1973, the paper that first proposed U&G theory has been cited more than 6000 times, even though it was introduced 34 years before the first iPhone. Concepts from the original framework have been applied to analyze the effects of social media, including Instagram [31], Facebook [32, 33], and Pinterest [34]. Other studies have focused on photo sharing [35] or users' motivations for using YouTube, finding that information-seeking and social interaction are the key drivers for viewing and sharing videos [36]. Many scholars conclude that uses and gratifications from media occur when selected content satisfies users' expectations and needs.

The theory continues to be cited as a basis for researching the effects of cell phones and social media [37–39]. For example, Falgoust and associates report six motivations for using *TikTok* predicted by U&G theory, including:

1. Entertainment
2. Convenience and utility for widespread communication
3. Increasing social interaction
4. Finding social support
5. Seeking and sharing information
6. Escaping from everyday life

Other scholars argue that since U&G theory focuses on broad motivational categories and the subsequent gratifications for digital consumers from media use, it falls short of addressing the predictable behaviors that relate to cognitive processing. Although the ways users select and engage with information partially direct media use, some scholars believe U&G theory does not thoroughly address the roles of self-directed selectivity and attention to different content. In other words, U&G theory can explain media selection behaviors, but not predict how exposure to media messages leads to attitude formation or change [40].

U&G assumes that once an audience has consumed content, subsequent media effects depend on individual motivations. In this way, the theory addresses user behavior but does not distinguish between different degrees of cognitive engagement with the content. Others propose that the affordances of technology can influence why users engage with, disengage from, or avoid certain sources and content based on preconceptions [41–43]. For example, even when misinformation is consumed by a user because they believe it is a trusted source, misperception can result.

## 3.2 Uses and Gratifications Theory Is Expanded

Traditional media targeted broad audiences in a unified way, but new technologies offer users more personalized experiences, allowing them to select, filter, and customize specific content in their preferred media environments. Indeed, platforms such as Netflix, YouTube, and personalized news feeds exemplify how media consumption is tailored to individual preferences. Unlike traditionally scheduled TV programs or printed newspapers, digital media enables users to access content anytime, from anywhere. On-demand consumption has reduced the constraints of real-time broadcasting, giving users more control over when and how they engage with content.

While U&G provided a valuable perspective on audience agency, it does not account for all of the rapidly changing features, availability and uses of digital technology.

These limitations explain why the Elaboration Likelihood Model (ELM) expanded U&G by shifting the focus from media selection to message processing and persuasion. Developed in 1986, the ELM explains how individuals use different levels of cognitive effort to engage with persuasive messages, ultimately determining whether a message leads to a temporary or lasting attitude change [9]. By doing so, the ELM moved beyond U&G's emphasis on why media is used to consider how media messages can influence thinking.

The ELM extends U&G in other ways. U&G described an active audience but did not differentiate between levels of cognitive processing. To illustrate how the depth of message engagement can affect outcomes, the ELM introduced both "central" and "peripheral" processing routes. In this way, the ELM explains when and why persuasion can be either long-lasting or temporary. U&G assumes audience members are generally active, but the ELM specifies the conditions under which individuals engage. In particular, if a user's motivation and cognitive ability are high, it can encourage "central processing," reinforcing and stabilizing the effects of the content. Conversely, low motivation or cognitive constraints result in "peripheral processing," where effects such as persuasion depend on the perceived credibility or emotional appeal of the message.

The ELM provides an explanation for why individuals process social media and political messages differently, depending on their level of engagement with those messages. To illustrate, clickbait content relies on peripheral cues to tease, while more detailed long-form news articles promote central processing when users are highly motivated to understand an issue.

Although U&G theory originated in the era of mass communication, many believe it remains a valuable framework for understanding media use in the Internet age [40]. However, digital media alters users' interactions with content, meaning we must reconsider some of U&G's core assumptions. Unlike one-way communication in traditional media (e.g., television, radio), digital platforms offer two-way engagement, allowing users to respond, modify, and create content. Social media, discussion forums, and online gaming platforms enable real-time feedback loops, making gratifications more dynamic. This shift means that users are not only consumers but also active participants, allowing them to influence content creation and distribution.

Ruggiero [40] also identifies three characteristics that differentiate newer media from traditional media, thereby expanding the U&G framework. These markers of modern consumption behaviors include interactivity, demassification, and synchronicity. Ruggiero critiques earlier U&G research that relies too heavily on users' self-reported motivations, which can often be subjective and inconsistent. Ruggiero calls for more empirical studies using newer methods, such as tracking online behavior, to enhance the understanding of user engagement in digital contexts. Other research found that depending on technology for gratification is linked to users' needs, motivations, and satisfaction [40], but these do not predict the resulting level of engagement.

Subsequent research has examined concepts such as interactivity from the perspective of U&G, while also integrating the ELM [43, 44]. Sundar's MAIN model introduced a heuristic approach to understanding the effects of technology on engagement. Furthermore, Sundar and Limperos [45] revisited and expanded the U&G framework to account for the affordances of digital and interactive media. They observe that the traditional U&G framework did not fully account for these technological affordances or the unique interactive features of digital platforms that help to shape user motivations and gratifications. Recognizing this gap, the researchers proposed Uses and Gratifications 2.0 to integrate how digital media affordances can influence engagement with the gratifications users derive from media use.

These researchers also argue that the structure and capabilities of digital media can generate new gratifications. Unlike earlier, mostly static media formats, digital platforms have introduced elements of interactivity, customization, and user agency, which redefine how users engage with content. Like Ruggiero, they propose that the affordances of digital media contribute to a more dynamic relationship between technology and user behavior, where gratifications are no longer simply sought by users but shaped by a platform's design. Four types of affordances of new media that extend U&G theory include:

1. **Modality** refers to the way information is presented, which can significantly impact user engagement and satisfaction. For example, immersive experiences in virtual reality (VR) or interactive storytelling enhance the modality-based gratifications of realism and sensory immersion.

2. **Agency**. Users' ability to create, modify, and distribute content directly has an impact on the gratifications of self-expression and control. Social media platforms, such as YouTube, TikTok, and Instagram, enable users to engage as both consumers and producers, fulfilling user needs that traditional mass media cannot address.
3. **Interactivity** is the extent to which users can engage with and modify content. It has the potential to increase their involvement and perception of control. Interactive elements such as polls, comment sections, and visualizations can fulfill users' needs for engagement and responsiveness.
4. **Navigability** is the ease with which users can move through and filter content influences how efficiently they can retrieve and consume information. Personalized recommendations on platforms such as Netflix or Spotify provide gratifications by reducing search efforts and increasing content relevance.

By integrating these affordances, Sundar and Limperos showed that media engagement in the digital age does not just fulfill pre-existing needs but also responds to the opportunities that new technologies provide. Their work predicts that emerging technologies can create entirely new motivations for media use, such as those related to algorithm-driven personalization of content, immersive experiences, and participatory engagement. For example, algorithm-driven content feeds on social media, such as Instagram, don't just satisfy users' desire for entertainment; they shape new habits around passive discovery and personalization, encouraging longer engagement times and repeat visits. These are particularly relevant for social media, digital marketing, and online journalism, where platform design has a direct influence on user behavior and satisfaction.

While modality, agency, interactivity, and navigability still describe general technological affordances, they do not address the nuanced interplay between digital content structures and individual user variables. Two users engaging with the same interactive platform may experience vastly different gratifications, based on a combination of a user's:

- Cognitive effort required to comprehend the content
- Relative interest
- Environment in which they are exposed to the content
- Time constraints to engage, even for information that is of interest to the user

This complexity calls for a new cognitive model that shifts from macro-level affordances to the meso- and micro-level interplay as users interact with dynamic content structures across various devices and environments.

## 3.3 Other Communication Theories Have Emerged

As digital media ecosystems have continued to evolve since 2013, engagement cannot solely be defined by broad user preferences or technological features. This is because user interactions with content also occur at micro-levels of attention, shaped by individual cognitive states [46], contextual variables [47], and personalization [48]. These major shifts necessitate a theoretical model that accounts for the interaction between users' psychological and behavioral characteristics and content delivered through more dynamic, data-driven, and real-time engagement mechanisms.

Since micro-level user variables also influence engagement and processing style, users engage with digital media differently based on their cognitive capacity at any given moment. For example, the resources required to comprehend complex content may prompt users to engage in peripheral processing, as specified by the ELM. This can lead them to favor visually appealing short-form video over complex, text-heavy material. However, this preference can quickly shift depending on the user's environment and the time spent engaging.

Moreover, content recommendations are often driven by AI that personalizes the digital experience based on a user's past behaviors and predictive analytics [49–51]. This hyper-personalization has been shown to influence sustained engagement patterns, as users develop reinforced behavioral loops shaped by algorithmic selection. In summary, digital engagement fluctuates based on the complexity and duration of each user's engagement session [52, 53].

Beyond user cognitive constraints and the appeal of personalization, media producers must also consider the effects of social feedback. Unlike traditional media, where attention to a single source (e.g., an evening newscast) was usually continuous, digital users engage in fragmented, multi-platform, and distracted task-switching [54], necessitating a more nuanced measure of engagement depth than mere exposure [55, 56]. Digital interactions are embedded in social feedback loops, where likes, shares, and comments can swiftly influence user perceptions, behaviors, and emotions in real time [57]. This feedback mechanism creates dependencies in engagement, dynamically shaping the virality and credibility [57] of content.

Traditionally, media theories focused on static message variables, such as source credibility, message appeal, and framing effects [58]. However, digital content introduced fluid, responsive, and interactive elements that fundamentally reshaped engagement, even as techniques like textual storytelling and long-form video continued to be practiced. Digital engagement is no longer limited to a two-dimensional screen. Technologies such as augmented reality (AR), virtual reality (VR), and mixed reality (MR) create spatial engagement, requiring new models to assess embodied interaction and presence-driven gratifications [59–61]. Alongside interactive formats, chatbots, AI-driven content recommendation systems, and machine learning interfaces have introduced two-way engagement mechanics, whereby content adapts to the user in real-time, fostering an evolving digital discourse rather than a static exchange of messages [62–65].

So, how have theorists kept pace with the rapid development of media channels? By the late twentieth century, some scholars had begun to recognize that traditional information-processing models needed further refinement to accurately reflect the expanding multimedia landscape. Users were now simultaneously exposed to dynamic, visual, and auditory stimuli, demanding a more complex cognitive model.

Building on the foundational work in the 1990s, Lang [66] introduced the Limited Capacity Model of Motivated Mediated Message Processing (LC4MP) to address some of the challenges in understanding digital and multimedia information processing. Rooted in media communication and psychology, LC4MP offers a dynamic framework that explains how individuals actively allocate their limited cognitive resources to encode, store, and retrieve mediated information. LC4MP conceptualized media users both as automatic and controlled processors, influenced by cognitive capacity, attention, and motivational factors.

The model assumes that human cognitive processing capacity is limited and that media messages compete for these scarce resources, using three main subprocesses:

**Encoding** (registering new information)
**Storage** (retaining information in memory)
**Retrieval** (accessing stored information for later use)

The LC4MP rejects the notion of passive media consumption and instead conceptualizes users as active processors who can selectively allocate cognitive resources for information processing. However, attention can be both automatic and intentional. Some information captures our attention without our choosing, simply due to its noticeable nature. For instance, a flashing alert on a phone or a sudden loud noise in a video can instantly draw our attention, even if we didn't plan to focus on it.

Another distinguishing feature of LC4MP is its motivational component, which emphasizes how emotion and arousal (driven by the appetitive and aversive motivational systems) influence media processing. This distinction sets it apart from models that focus solely on cognitive load. LC4MP also acknowledges the role of automatic cognitive responses, demonstrating that high-intensity sensory messages can trigger immediate encoding and/or lead to cognitive overload, which in turn affects retention and recall.

Rather than discussing individual theories in the context of engagement, the *Media Use Model* (MUM) presents a comprehensive metatheoretical framework that integrates existing theories of media processes and effects into a cohesive model [67]. MUM combines Uses and Gratifications Theory, mood management, and selective exposure for a conceptual understanding of the cognitive and motivational mechanisms that drive media selection, interpretation, and sustained media use. MUM explains how users continuously process and react to content in spontaneous and deliberate ways. It provides a conceptual framework upon which the Digital Engagement Model is built, incorporating additional user variables and content variables.

At its core, MUM presents media use as a dynamic loop that begins when a user selects content based on motivations, expectations, and cognitive predispositions. The user then interprets and evaluates the content. This interaction is not static but can shift over time as the user's cognitive and emotional states change.

MUM posits that users select media based on their motivations, expectations, and traits such as political orientation or past experiences. A second proposition is that users form impressions of content based on a match or a mismatch between the content and their mental models. A match, described as coherence, leads to a user's positive interpretations. A mismatch (incoherence) can result in confusion or rejection. Proposition 3 states that if the content aligns with the user's motivations and existing beliefs (i.e., it is coherent), the user is more likely to stay engaged or return later. If the incoherence is too strong, the user may disengage (Proposition 4). A fifth proposition states that if a user continues consuming coherent content, their impressions can become richer, even deeply ingrained. Finally, when a user disengages, the selection process resets, and new motivations can guide future choices when the six-stage loop returns.

One of MUM's novel contributions is its treatment of coherence as a continuum, not binary. That is, media content may align perfectly, moderately, or poorly with a user's mental models. This explains why users can have different interpretations of the same content, depending on their prior knowledge, values and attitudes, emotional state, and social identity.

Several of the theories discussed here view engagement through a collection of broad concepts that include motivations, though no model fully accounts for the role of interest in shaping user engagement. Interest is a complex construct than many acknowledge, as it operates beyond intentional selection, where users actively seek specific content or engage with material in which they had no prior interest. How can both occur? In psychological terms, the concept of "interest" defies a single definition.

## 3.4 Theory Defines the Concept of Interest

Interest is typically referred to as a single concept. One is either interested in content or not. We argue that there are distinct categories of interest that play a major role in digital content. Drawing on educational psychology research, the DEM categorizes the four distinct types of interest as **individual, situational, epistemic, and systemic interest**. Each fosters different cognitive pathways and shapes different motivations and outcomes in digital engagement, as explored below.

Two types of interest align with the DEM to explain a critical juncture of whether a user is motivated to seek and/or select target content or scan incidental content (e.g., social media) and engage based on how interesting they find the content to be. To the DEM, interest is a key modulator of engagement, influencing both sustained attention (attention momentum) and the depth of cognitive processing. By integrating these interest types into the model, engagement is redefined as a relational process in which users co-construct meaning based on prior knowledge, curiosity-driven exploration, or emotional triggers.

**Individual interest** is the "I" in a users DIET. It means a user's stable, long-term preferences or values, and it is tied to that user's identity [68, 69]. Individual interest can promote consistent engagement, as users seek specific content (e.g., sports, political, entertainment news, etc.) that aligns with their previous experience, knowledge, values, or beliefs. In other words, it is domain-specific and typically develops over time through repeated exposure to and interaction with subject matter [70].

From a cognitive engagement perspective, individual interest also enhances selective exposure to information [71], which we detail in the following chapter. Once an individual develops an interest in a specific domain, their cognitive system becomes attuned to seeking and processing information relating to that interest. For example, a producer or researcher of digital engagement is more likely to seek out and be reading this sentence than a ballet dancer.

Another way to amplify individual interest is through algorithmic curation. Digital platforms can enhance engagement with content by tailoring it to user preferences based on their previous interactions. And regardless of how content is presented, if a source consistently provides relevant content and fosters longer-term engagement with that content, users can form a clear preference for it. And the effect is reinforced by the lower drain on cognitive resources that this familiarity requires, as a user's prior knowledge facilitates faster comprehension and deeper analytical processing.

Conversely, **situational interest** originates ONLY from content, not the user, which explains the limited attraction to pages of text to read. Situational interest arises from spontaneous, often incidental exposure to content that temporarily attracts attention to it rather than the user's pre-existing knowledge or values [72, 73]. Situational interest is attention-driven and induced by novelty, visual appeal, or emotional intensity [74]. Unlike individual interest, which can guide intentional content selection, situational interest emerges unexpectedly when a user encounters content with compelling attributes. For instance, a non-science major might not be seeking news on climate science but could still be drawn to a social media post about climate science because it has a provocative headline, music, or visually striking animation.

In digital spaces, the sensory appeal of interactive elements, bold headlines, and video thumbnails can play a critical role in capturing users' fleeting attention. In fact, these are the attributes that help situational interest to explain why a user engages briefly with content before deciding whether to continue viewing it. The phenomenon is important because when effectively leveraged, situational interest can transition into sustained engagement.

As we will explore in the context of the DEM, it is possible for content to generate both individual interest for a target audience and situational interest for users who would otherwise ignore it. This represents the gold standard for audience analytics. However, harnessing situational interest does not just require us to present animation, photo slideshows, videos, or bold words. The DEM posits that how and where this content is placed within a cognitively friendly message structure can maximize engagement.

**Epistemic interest** is driven by curiosity and the desire to resolve specific knowledge gaps, leading to intellectual engagement with content that provides deeper insights [74]. For example, a user searching for the best way to assemble a new tool on YouTube exhibits epistemic interest because they wish to acquire new information and will view and entire video. Unlike the immediate but fleeting situational interest generated only by the content, epistemic interest extends engagement as users actively seek specific information to expand their understanding.

Epistemic interest is particularly relevant in educational and investigative contexts, where users are motivated by the need for study-specific content to pass a quiz or solve a problem. In that instance, epistemic interest can enhance critical thinking, generating higher retention and comprehension of the content. Unlike the short bursts of attention driven by situational interest, epistemic interest can also foster repeated engagement if users wish to pursue additional content. Users exhibiting epistemic interest are also more likely to evaluate whether content is credible, distinguishing between high-quality information and misinformation [74].

Finally, **systemic interest** emerges at the intersection of cognitive predispositions and media affordances [69]. In other words, it is generated by a combination of user preferences and the structural features of digital design.

Platform-driven personalization can reinforce systemic interest by tailoring content to users' prior behaviors and engagement history [75, 76]. The first way it achieves this is with the social dimension of digital engagement, such as sharing information, trending topics, and viral content. Secondly, the design of a digital interface influences systemic interest by shaping a user's experience, facilitating navigation, and avoiding information overload [77]. Finally, a user scrolling through a newsfeed may initially engage with content based on situational interest (such as an eye-catching video). Still, systemic interest, driven by algorithmic exposure and/or peer interactions, will sustain engagement over time.

We have found that these categories of interest are not widely known or addressed during media production. To address this, the DEM subdivides interest into these dimensions, positioning engagement as a multi-layered and dynamic process. The subcategories clearly demonstrate how cognitive, technological, and social factors can shape user interactions with digital content, necessitating a new model to be designed around them.

It is important to note that while any interest can be a key driver of engagement, a lack of interest can also be a powerful influence. Crucially, the DEM also recognizes that disinterest in, avoidance of, or disengagement with content is just as important.

## 3.5 A Lack of Interest Can Also Signify Avoidance

In the digital age, much of the conversation surrounding news consumption focuses on increasing engagement. By this, we mean helping audiences stay informed, access credible sources, and consume news efficiently. However, at some point during engagement, all users reach an interest threshold, where their interest wanes and engagement ceases due to a combination of cognitive, emotional, or contextual factors. Studying these patterns is crucial for identifying the potential triggers that prompt users either to ignore certain content entirely, disengage before finishing, or actively avoid it altogether. Note that this should not be confused with Disengagement Theory introduced in the 1960s, which postulates that people gradually disengage from social life as they grow older.

In the context of digital media, disengagement is not merely the absence of a user's interest, but an active decision-making process influenced by various cognitive and psychological mechanisms, physical distractions, or time constraints. For example, situational interest might initially draw a user to content they were not seeking but may then fail to generate further triggers, resulting in disengagement. This is just one scenario among many in which the DEM provides guidance on creating content that captures attention and sustains engagement for users who rely on situational interest.

Alternatively, users with strong individual interest in content may choose to skip it if they find it to be cognitively overwhelming or redundant. This latter example is addressed by unique DEM structures that can prevent redundancy (especially in news) and enable users to select only the content of interest.

Avoidance also plays a role in the information-filtering process [78]. Users frequently scroll past, mute, or block content that they find too negative, unappealing, irrelevant, disturbing, or in conflict with their worldview [79]. This behavior aligns with theories of selective exposure [71] and motivated reasoning, which show how users actively avoid news based on pre-existing beliefs and emotional responses, or engage with little to no news overall [71, 80].

If content creators, educators, and media professionals want to extend engagement, they must consider not only what captures attention but also what terminates it. By addressing both engagement and disengagement, the DEM aims to provide them with a more comprehensive framework for understanding this digital behavior. We elucidate the known elements, features, and designs that quickly terminate a user's attention, beyond the simple fading of their interest. Recognizing these dynamics paves the way for effective content strategies that can strike a balance between intrigue, cognitive ease, and emotional relevance to stimulate meaningful engagement.

In the context of news, media creators must navigate strong disincentives among users. The first of these is news fatigue, whereby individuals feel emotionally drained by constant exposure to negative headlines. Not only can this lead to disengagement from news, but also from social and political discourse.

Secondly, news consumption, particularly on digital platforms, has been linked to numerous psychological concerns, including anxiety, depression, and increased stress levels [81, 82]. In particular, research published in 2017 found that younger users were actively avoiding the news due to its overwhelmingly negative and distressing nature [83]. Seven years later, young users were still reporting that constant exposure to crisis-driven headlines contributed to a sense of helplessness and anxiety, prompting them to disengage altogether [84].

A third disincentive is the overconsumption of news, which can lead to cognitive overload, where the brain becomes overwhelmed with information, thereby decreasing productivity and increasing distress [24, 85]. Similarly, an overemphasis on staying informed can cause users to give up, leading to avoidance as a chosen counterbalance. The inevitable result of these negative factors is the avoidance of news, along with possible serious emotional and psychological consequences. For this reason, news avoidance can serve as a protective measure for users, allowing them to manage their mental well-being by controlling their exposure to potentially distressing content.

There is more to news avoidance than just an aversion to negative content. The 24-hour news cycle also fosters a culture of reactive consumption, which can impair critical thinking and analytical skills [86]. If there is a constant influx of breaking news stories that prioritize speed over accuracy, this can lead to misinformation, sensationalism, and cognitive fatigue among consumers [87]. Studies indicate that people who reduce their exposure to fast-paced news media and instead engage with in-depth, long-form analysis demonstrate improved critical thinking skills and better retention of information [88]. Strategic news avoidance, therefore, supports cognitive clarity and enhances an individual's ability to process information more meaningfully.

A further benefit lies in news avoidance's ability to foster more meaningful and less contentious interpersonal interactions by reducing exposure to emotionally charged or biased narratives. Families and individuals who practice news-free periods report stronger relationships and improved communication skills [89].

## 3.6 A New Model Presents New Propositions

Rather than concentrating solely on abstract individual differences or the broad affordances of traditional media theories, the DEM emphasizes common patterns in user behaviors. This perspective acknowledges that, despite individual variability, users often exhibit similar responses to media stimuli, as evidenced by studies on distractibility and cognitive load [90], spatial text processing [91], and media multitasking behaviors [92].

The DEM achieves this by looking beyond macro-level engagement variables, such as motivations and expectations, [67] to include micro-level cognitive processes [93]. The model helps transform the effects of traditional content structures [72, 94] into a new collection of variables [95, 96] that can significantly influence attention [97, 98].

As future news consumers, young adults may now signal how digital content could be structured and presented for maximum engagement [99, 100]. This could be leveraged to shift media theory from earlier user behaviors [40, 101] to more individualized, context-driven engagement experiences, where media is seen as a fluid, dynamic interactive space offering a range of technical affordances and user preferences [49, 102–104]. By incorporating psychological [105], technological [106], and mobile algorithmic influences [107, 108], the DEM seeks to establish a more predictive framework for understanding the future of engagement with hyper-personalized and interactive content [105, 109, 110].

Based on the theoretical roots in ecological psychology, affordances refer to the actionable properties between an object and an organism [111]. When applied to media, affordances describe the capabilities that facilitate specific actions by users [112]. In the context of the DEM, media affordances are conceptually distinct from content, with each playing a different role in shaping user behaviors and experiences. Social media, for example, affords interactivity with content [113]. However, not all social media content is appealing to every user, and we should ask ourselves why this is the case.

Let's start by considering the affordances of digital technology, which optimize the technological capabilities of the user interface to enhance user experience and engagement. Separating these affordances from the structures of content challenges producers to consider more innovative digital strategies for presenting content. The challenge is to simultaneously appeal to and satisfy the needs of scanning users who have time limitations, as well as those with more time and interest in reading paragraphs of text. Catching a user's attention and motivating a click is no longer enough to satisfy content teams looking to increase audience analytics. It is retaining the user's attention that is the challenge.

Drawing from foundational cognitive theories and concepts, the DEM focuses on the micro-level processes of attention and engagement. Unlike previous models that address broad engagement concepts or user motivations at macro- or meso-levels, the DEM sheds light on the micro-level processing that occurs second by second during the critical exposure to content. A key feature is the DEM's emphasis on interest as a fundamental cognitive driver. By integrating insights from psychology and media studies, the DEM acknowledges that well-written tests or well-produced videos are not the sole drivers of engagement. Rather, it also involves an active but complex cognitive process. Some factors that can also influence engagement include:

- The ability to quickly infer useful information when one is constrained by time
- Feeling that the content is personally relevant
- A perception of manageable levels of interactivity in content
- Situational interest curated by the content
- Emotion, when it is applicable

A key distinction to note concerns the varying preferences of different user groups for specific sources. For example, multimodal content is qualitatively different on Facebook than on Instagram. Research has shown that social media users who frequently watch short videos tend to fail to engage in deep processing in both formal and informal learning environments [98]. Some users navigate multiple information streams across various physical environments and have varying amounts of time to devote to content they are seeking or exposed to incidentally. Moreover, the distractions for mobile users, especially from short videos, are significantly higher, which reduces comprehension and memory retention [114].

Accounting for at least a portion of the complexity in the scenarios above could help communicators and journalists increase the probability that more users would attend to more content for extended periods, especially content they would typically ignore if it seemed "boring" [115]. There appears to be little downside to testing new content structures if they are the only way to inform some users about important issues. As AI-generated content continues to proliferate, designing algorithms with cognitive factors in mind may help reduce the spread of misinformation [63, 64].

Mainstream production strategies and standard structures of content often assume that users:

1. Are exposed to the content
2. Are interested enough to consume all of the content produced
3. Process all the content
4. Understand the content in the context of their prior knowledge

Research shows that pursuing maximum reach to large audiences is not always the most effective strategy for user engagement. An extensive follower count may actually reduce meaningful engagement, as demonstrated by an inverted U-shaped relationship between follower numbers and user interaction [116]. When compared to influencers with the most followers, researchers found that influencers with fewer followers tend to generate the most interactive likes, shares, and comments. This might suggest users are more likely to engage with content from influencers who seem more authentic and accessible, rather than those with massive followings. For these influencers, this may place even more importance on how digital content is more authentic and accessible.

The Digital Engagement Model sits at the intersection of evolving analytical paradigms. It incorporates postmodern insights about individualized media experiences, metamodern recognition of structured yet fluid engagement, and cognitive science's understanding of brain-based attention processes. Since user experiences and attention can define the success or failure of digital content, our model adds a cutting-edge, interdisciplinary perspective on how individuals seek, select, and interact with information in rapidly evolving technological environments.

Empirical evidence of and assumptions about the effects of content also depend on users' behaviors and their desire to consume content. Perceptions can be influenced not only by users' motivations and individual differences, but also by the amount of attention they pay to content and the structures they interact with. Audience analytics based solely on time spent on content do not distinguish between users who scan content versus those who read or view part or all of it. Eye-tracking cannot always determine how well content is comprehended, since it has been shown that longer fixation durations can be associated with complex information that requires more time to process [117].

The DEM aims to address some of the gaps in previous media effects theories by providing a more granular analysis of how the shared traits of digital users intersect with their motivations for consuming content. While previous theories acknowledge that users who produce content can also consume it [18], the theory does not adequately account for the behaviors and needs of users as they seek and consume digital content. Mobile users, for example, frequently and randomly consult their devices in different environments of distraction, challenging any assumption that consistent, self-directed selectivity of content always occurs.

Even users who do not interact with content by clicking likes or shares might still derive value from scanning and passively consuming information. The DEM addresses the limitations of audience analytics, which are unable to measure the passive consumption of incidental content. We aim to better understand why some users do not interact with content or actively avoid specific types of content, a gap in contemporary media that warrants further investigation. However, by recognizing the habitual behaviors of users and focusing on specific micro-level cognitive processes, the model offers a deeper understanding of user engagement with content. Any gratification from content follows the first critical seconds of exposure. This framework aims to more accurately represent the dynamics and evolving nature of users' attention, including their decisions to disengage prior to or during exposure to content, and whether certain content structures could pre-empt disengagement. This is particularly relevant when engagement is fragmented, varied, and often driven by instantaneous interactions with incidental content on social media.

The Digital Engagement Model contains six propositions, which we will cover in the chapters that follow:

*Proposition 1* Every user brings four core variables to digital content that shape engagement decisions: demographics, individual interests, environment (physical and technological), and available time.

*Proposition 2* A user's motivation is reflected in behaviors such as searching, scanning, reading, interacting, and passively viewing, or skipping content.

*Proposition 3* Users with prior interest in a topic are more likely to engage with content about that topic (i.e., sports). For users without such interest, content must generate situational interest by featuring scannability, personalization, interactivity, curiosity, and emotional appeal.

*Proposition 4* A user's environment, including physical environments with varying distractions, and a technological environment that includes interface design, device, and algorithmic delivery, influences whether users engage with it and, if so, how.

*Proposition 5* A user's time availability affects the duration of engagement. Even highly interested users may disengage if they lack sufficient time.

*Proposition 6* Users disengage when content is too long, complex, irrelevant, or poorly structured.

## References

1. Katz, E., J. G. Blumler, and M. Gurevitch. 1973. Uses and gratifications research. *The Public Opinion Quarterly* 37 (4): 509–523.
2. McCombs, M., and D. E. Shaw. 1977. *The emergence of American political issues: The agenda-setting function of the press.* St. Paul: West Publishing Co.
3. Noelle-Neumann, E. 1984. *The spiral of silence: Public opinion—Our social skin.* Chicago: University of Chicago Press.

4. Noelle-Neumann, E. 1974. The spiral of silence a theory of public opinion. *Journal of Communication* **24** (2): 43–51.
5. Fu, W.-T., and P. Pirolli. 2007. SNIF-ACT: A cognitive model of user navigation on the World Wide Web. *Human-Computer Interaction* **22** (4): 355–412.
6. Pirolli, P. 1998. Exploring browser design trade-offs using a dynamical model of optimal information foraging. In *Proceedings of the SIGCHI conference on human factors in computing systems.*
7. Pirolli, P., and S. Card. 1995. Information foraging in information access environments. In *Proceedings of the SIGCHI conference on Human factors in computing systems.*
8. Kahneman, D. 2011. *Fast and slow thinking.* New York: Allen Lane and Penguin Books.
9. Petty, R. E., and J. T. Cacioppo. 1986. The elaboration likelihood model of persuasion. In *Advances in experimental social psychology*, ed. L. Berkowitz, 123–205. New York.: Academic.
10. Thaler, R., and C. Sunstein. 2009. *Nudge: Improving decisions about health, wealth and happiness*, 312. Penguin Publishing Group. Amsterdam Law Forum; HeinOnline: Online.
11. Thaler, R. H., and C. R. Sunstein. 2021. *Nudge: improving decisions about health, wealth, and happiness*, 384. Penguin Publishing Group.
12. Boczkowski, P. J., and I. Siles. 2014. Steps toward cosmopolitanism in the study of media technologies. *Information, Communication & Society* **17** (5): 560–571.
13. Pavlik, J. V. 2013. Innovation and the future of journalism. *Digital Journalism* **1** (2): 181–193.
14. Deuze, M. 2007. *Media work.* Polity Press.
15. McQuail, D. 2000, 2005, 2010. *McQuail's mass communication theory.* Sage publications.
16. Wahl-Jorgensen, K., and T. Hanitzsch, eds. 2020. *The handbook of journalism studies.* 2nd ed. New York, NY: Routledge.
17. Kuhn, T. 1970. *The nature and necessity of scientific revolutions, from the structure of scientific revolutions.* Vol. 2, 148–157. Cambridge, USA: The Philosophy of Science, MIT Press/University of Chicago Press.
18. Livingstone, S. 2003. The changing nature of audiences: From the mass audience to the interactive media user. In *A companion to media studies*, eds. J. Curran & D. Morley, 337–359. Blackwell Publishing.
19. Bryant, J., and D. Miron. 2004. Theory and research in mass communication. *Journal of Communication* **54** (4): 662–704.
20. Shoemaker, P. J., and S. D. Reese. 2013. *Mediating the message in the 21st century: A media sociology perspective.* Routledge.

21. Jenkins, H., S. Ford, and J. Green. 2013. Spreadable media: Creating value and meaning in a networked culture. In *Spreadable media*. New York University Press.
22. Carlson, M. 2015. Introduction: The many boundaries of journalism. In *Boundaries of journalism*, 1–18. Routledge.
23. Hermida, A., and M. L. Young. 2019. *Data journalism and the regeneration of news*. Routledge.
24. Arnold, M., M. Goldschmitt, and T. Rigotti. 2023. Dealing with information overload: A comprehensive review. *Frontiers in Psychology* **14**:1122200.
25. Chomsky, N. 1957. Logical structure in language. *Journal of the American Society for Information Science* **8** (4): 284.
26. Newell, A., J. C. Shaw, and H. A. Simon. 1957. Empirical explorations of the logic theory machine: A case study in heuristic. In *Papers presented at the February 26–28, 1957, western joint computer conference: Techniques for reliability*.
27. Shiffrin, R. M., and R. C. Atkinson. 1969. Storage and retrieval processes in long-term memory. *Psychological Review* **76** (2): 179.
28. Miller, G. A. 1956. The magical number seven, plus or minus two: Some limits on our capacity for processing information. *Psychological Review* **63**:81–97.
29. Newell, A., and H. A. Simon. 1972. *Human problem solving*. Vol. 104. Englewood Cliffs, NJ: Prentice-Hall.
30. McQuail, D. 1983, 1987, 1994. *Mass communication theory: An introduction*. Sage Publications, Inc.
31. Sheldon, P., and K. Bryant. 2016. Instagram: Motives for its use and relationship to narcissism and contextual age. *Computers in Human Behavior* **58**:89–97.
32. Krause, A. E., A. C. North, and B. Heritage. 2014. The uses and gratifications of using Facebook music listening applications. *Computers in Human Behavior* **39**:71–77.
33. Smock, A. D., et al. 2011. Facebook as a toolkit: A uses and gratification approach to unbundling feature use. *Computers in Human Behavior* **27** (6): 2322–2329.
34. Mull, I. R., and S.-E. Lee. 2014. "PIN" pointing the motivational dimensions behind Pinterest. *Computers in Human Behavior* **33**:192–200.
35. Malik, A., A. Dhir, and M. Nieminen. 2016. Uses and gratifications of digital photo sharing on Facebook. *Telematics and Informatics* **33** (1): 129–138.
36. Haridakis, P., and G. Hanson. 2009. Social interaction and co-viewing with YouTube: Blending mass communication reception and social connection. *Journal of Broadcasting & Electronic Media* **53** (2): 317–335.

37. Falgoust, G., et al. 2022. Applying the uses and gratifications theory to identify motivational factors behind young adult's participation in viral social media challenges on TikTok. *Human Factors in Healthcare* **2**:100014.
38. Child, J. T., and P. Haridakis. 2017. Uses and gratifications theory: Considering media use in the context of family communication. In *Engaging Theories in Family Communication*, 337–348. New York: Routledge.
39. Wei, D., et al. 2024. Gratification and its associations with problematic internet use: A systematic review and meta-analysis using Use and Gratification theory. *Addictive Behaviors* **155**:108044.
40. Ruggiero, T. 2000. Uses and gratifications theory in the 21st century. *Mass Communication and Society* **3** (1): 3–37.
41. Gibson, J. J. 1977. *The theory of affordances.* Vol. 1(2), 67–82. Hilldale, USA: Lawrence Erlbaum.
42. Sundar, S. S. 2015. *The handbook of the psychology of communication technology*, 608. John Wiley & Sons.
43. Sundar, S. S. 2008. The MAIN model: A heuristic approach to understanding technology effects on credibility. In *Digital media, youth, and credibility*, ed. M. J. Metzger and A. J. Flanagin, 73–100. MIT Press.
44. Sundar, S. S. 2009. Social psychology of interactivity in human-website interaction. In *Oxford handbook of internet psychology*, ed. A. Joinson et al. Oxford, UK: Oxford University Press.
45. Sundar, S. S., and A. Limperos. 2013. Uses and Grats 2.0: New gratifications for new media. *Journal of Broadcasting & Electronic Media* **57**:504–525. https://doi.org/10.1080/08838151.2013.845827.
46. Leiva, L. A., et al. 2024. *Modeling user preferences via brain-computer interfacing.* arXiv preprint arXiv:2405.09691.
47. Peters, H., et al. 2024. Context-aware prediction of active and passive user engagement: Evidence from a large online social platform. *Journal of Big Data* **11** (1): 110.
48. Tam, K. Y., and S. Y. Ho. 2006. Understanding the impact of web personalization on user information processing and decision outcomes. *MIS Quarterly* **30** (4): 865–890.
49. Obiegbu, C., and G. Larsen. 2024. *Algorithmic personalization and brand loyalty: An experiential perspective*, 14705931241230041. Marketing Theory.
50. Thorson, K. 2020. Attracting the news: Algorithms, platforms, and reframing incidental exposure. *Journalism* **21** (8): 1067–1082.
51. Diakopoulos, N. 2019. *Automating the news: How algorithms are rewriting the media.* Harvard University Press.
52. Kobayashi, K., et al. 2020. Relationship between media multitasking and functional connectivity in the dorsal attention network. *Scientific Reports* **10** (1): 17992.

53. Nass, C. 2010. Thinking about multitasking: It's what journalists need to do. *Nieman Reports* 64:11–12.
54. Fisher, J. T., and J. R. Keene. 2020. Attention, working memory, and media multitasking. In *The handbook of communication science and biology*, 177–196. Routledge.
55. Holmqvist, K., et al. 2011. *Eye tracking: A comprehensive guide to methods and measures.* OUP Oxford.
56. McMillan, S. J., and J. S. Hwang. 2002. Measures of perceived interactivity: An exploration of the role of direction of communication, user control and time in shaping perceptions of interactivty. *Journal of Advertising* **31** (3): 14–29.
57. Alhabash, S., et al. 2013. Between likes and shares: Effects of emotional appeal and virality on the persuasiveness of anticyberbullying messages on Facebook. *Cyberpsychology, Behavior, and Social Networking* **16** (3): 175–182.
58. Tewksbury, D., and D. A. Scheufele. 2019. News framing theory and research. In *Media Effects*, 51–68. New York: Routledge.
59. Drigas, A., and A. Sideraki. 2024. Brain neuroplasticity leveraging virtual reality and brain–computer interface technologies. *Sensors* **24** (17): 5725.
60. Moreno, R., and R. E. Mayer. 2002. Learning science in virtual reality multimedia environments: Role of methods and media. *Journal of Educational Psychology* **94** (3): 598–610.
61. Biocca, F., and B. Delaney. 1995. Immersive virtual reality technology. In *Communication in the age of virtual reality*, ed. F. Biocca and M. Levy. Hillsdale, NJ: Erlbaum.
62. Smilkov, D., et al. 2019. Tensorflow.js: Machine learning for the web and beyond. In *Proceedings of machine learning and systems.*
63. Nguyen, A., et al. 2024. Enhancing student engagement through artificial intelligence (AI): Understanding the basics, opportunities, and challenges. *Journal of University Teaching and Learning Practice* **21** (6): 1–13.
64. Diwan, C., et al. 2023. AI-based learning content generation and learning pathway augmentation to increase learner engagement. *Computers and Education: Artificial Intelligence* **4**:100110.
65. Shanmugasundaram, M., and A. Tamilarasu. 2023. The impact of digital technology, social media, and artificial intelligence on cognitive functions: A review. *Frontiers in Cognition* **2**:1203077.
66. Lang, A. 2000. The limited capacity model of mediated message processing. *Journal of Communication* **50**:46–70.
67. Hoewe, J., and D. R. Ewoldsen. 2024. The media use model: A metatheoretical framework for media processes and effects. *Human Communication Research* **50** (2): 254–263.

68. Renninger, K. A., and S. Hidi. 2011. Revisiting the conceptualization, measurement, and generation of interest. *Educational Psychologist* **46** (3): 168–184.
69. Krapp, A., and M. Prenzel. 2011. Research on interest in science: Theories, methods, and findings. *International Journal of Science Education* **33** (1): 27–50.
70. Schiefele, U. 1990. The influence of topic interest, prior knowledge, and cognitive capabilities on text comprehension. In *Learning environments*, ed. J. M. Pieters, K. Breur, and P. R. J. Simons, 323–338. Heidelberg: Springer-Verlag.
71. Knobloch-Westerwick, S. 2015. The selective exposure self-and affect-management (SESAM) model: Applications in the realms of race, politics, and health. *Communication Research* **42** (7): 959–985.
72. Yaros, R. 2006. Is it the medium or the message? Structuring complex news to enhance engagement and situational understanding by non-experts. *Communication Research* **33** (4): 285–309.
73. Schraw, G., and S. Lehman. 2001. Situational interest: A review of the literature and directions for future research. *Educational Psychology Review* **13**:23–52.
74. Hidi, S. E., and K. A. Renninger. 2019. Interest development and its relation to curiosity: Needed neuroscientific research. *Educational Psychology Review* **31** (4): 833–852.
75. Bucher, T. 2018. *If… then: Algorithmic power and politics.* Oxford University Press.
76. Pariser, E. 2011. *The filter bubble: How the new personalized web is changing what we read and how we think.* Penguin.
77. Sweller, J. 1988. Cognitive load during problem solving: Effects on learning. *Cognitive Science* **12** (2): 257–285.
78. Carbone, M., S. Soroka, and J. Dunaway. 2024. The psychophysiology of news avoidance: Does negative affect drive both attention and inattention to news? *Journalism Studies* **25** (12): 1460–1475.
79. Volk, S. C., et al. 2024. Selecting, avoiding, disconnecting: A focus group study of people's strategies for dealing with information abundance in the contexts of news, entertainment, and personal communication. *Information, Communication & Society*: 1–20.
80. Betakova, D., H. Boomgaarden, S. Lecheler, and S. Schäfer. 2024. I do not (want to) know! The relationship between intentional news avoidance and low news consumption. *Mass Communication and Society* **28**:413–440. https://doi.org/10.1080/15205436.2024.2304759.
81. Yang, Z. J., and L. Kahlor. 2013. What, me worry? The role of affect in information seeking and avoidance. *Science Communication* **35** (2): 189–212.

82. Ksiazek, T. B., E. C. Malthouse, and J. G. Webster. 2010. News-seekers and avoiders: Exploring patterns of total news consumption across media and the relationship to civic participation. *Journal of Broadcasting & Electronic Media* **54** (4): 551–568.
83. Edgerly, S. 2017. Seeking out and avoiding the news media: Young adults' proposed strategies for obtaining current events information. *Mass Communication and Society* **20** (3): 358–377.
84. Reuters. 2024. Digital news report 2024.
85. Ophir, E., C. Nass, and A. Wagner. 2009. Cognitive control in media multi-taskers. *Proceedings of the National Academy of Sciences* **106** (37): 15583–15587.
86. Carr, N. 2010. *The shallows*, 278. New York: W.W. Norton & Company.
87. Pennycook, G., and D. G. Rand. 2019. Lazy, not biased: Susceptibility to partisan fake news is better explained by lack of reasoning than by motivated reasoning. *Cognition* **188**:39–50.
88. Berman, M. G., J. Jonides, and S. Kaplan. 2008. The cognitive benefits of interacting with nature. *Psychological Science* **19** (12): 1207–1212.
89. Turkle, S. 2015. Stop googling. Let's talk. *The New York Times* 27.
90. Forster, S., and N. Lavie. 2014. Distracted by your mind? Individual differences in distractibility predict mind wandering. *Journal of Experimental Psychology: Learning, Memory, and Cognition* **40** (1): 251.
91. Haenggi, D., M. A. Gernsbacher, and C. M. Bolliger. 1993. Individual differences in situation-based inferencing during narrative text comprehension. In *Naturalistic text comprehension: Vol. LIII. Advances in discourse processing*, ed. H. V. O. R. A. Zwaan, 79–96. Norwood: Ablex.
92. Sidnam, M. E., and P. Monge. 2024. Individual differences and technology affordances combine to predict mobile social media distraction behaviors and consequences. In *Proceedings of the CHI conference on human factors in computing systems.*
93. Hamilton, K. A., J. K. Yamashiro, and B. C. Storm. 2023. Special issue of applied cognitive psychology: Rethinking cognition in a digital environment. *Applied Cognitive Psychology* **37** (4): 683–685.
94. Wise, K., et al. 2009. When words collide online: How writing style and video intensity affect cognitive processing of online news. *Journal of Broadcasting & Electronic Media* **53** (4): 532–546.
95. Risko, E. F., and M. O. Kelly. 2023. Thinking in the digital age: Everyday cognition and the dawn of a new age of metacognition research. *Applied Cognitive Psychology* **37**:785–788.
96. de Barros, E. C. 2024. Understanding the influence of digital technology on human cognitive functions: A narrative review. *IBRO Neuroscience Reports* 17:415–422.

97. Takano, M., et al. 2021. Effects of incidental brief exposure to news on news knowledge while scrolling through videos. *IEEE Access* **9**:37,772–37,783.
98. Chen, Y., et al. 2023. The effect of short-form video addiction on users' attention. *Behaviour & Information Technology* **42** (16): 2893–2910.
99. Yaros, R. 2009. Digital natives: Following their lead on a path to a new journalism. In *Nieman Reports*. Nieman Foundation for Journalism at Harvard University.
100. Sutcliffe, A. 2010. *Designing for user engagement: Aesthetic and attractive user interfaces*, 47. Springer Cham.
101. Eveland, W. P., and S. Dunwoody. 2001. Applying research on the uses and cognitive effects of hypermedia to the study of the World Wide Web. In *Communication yearbook*, ed. W. B. Gudykunst, vol. 25, 79–113. Mahwah: Erlbaum.
102. Yaros, R. 2012. Social media and education: Do personalization and interactivity facilitate learning? In *Social media: Usage and impact*, ed. H. S. Noor Al-Deen and J. A. Hendricks, 57–74. Lexington Books.
103. Kim, N. Y., and S. S. Sundar. 2012. Personal relevance versus contextual relevance. *Journal of Media Psychology* **24** (3): 89–101.
104. Bennett, W. L., and A. Segerberg. 2011. Digital media and the personalization of collective action. *Information, Communication & Society* **14** (6): 770–799.
105. Wilson, T. D. 2024. Curiosity and information-seeking behaviour: A review of psychological research and a comparison with the information science literature. *Journal of Documentation* **80** (7): 43–59.
106. Newman, N. 2024. Technology trends and predictions 2024. https://reutersinstitute.politics.ox.ac.uk/journalism-media-and-technology-trends-and-predictions.
107. Gençer, M., et al. 2013. A new framework for increasing user engagement in mobile applications using machine learning techniques. In *Design, user experience, and usability. Web, mobile, and product design: Second international conference, DUXU 2013*. Las Vegas, NV: Springer.
108. Thorson, K., et al. 2021. Algorithmic inference, political interest, and exposure to news and politics on Facebook. *Information, Communication & Society* **24** (2): 183–200.
109. Faverio, M., and O. Sidoti. 2024. Teens, social media and technology 2024.
110. Omar, B., et al. 2024. Unlocking young people's engagement with online news: affective or cognitive? *Online Information Review* 48 (5): 944–958.
111. Gibson, J. J. 1979. The theory of affordances. In *The people, place, and space reader*, 56–60. Routledge.
112. Norman, D. A. 1999. Affordance, conventions, and design. *Interactions* **6** (3): 38–43.

113. Treem, J. W., and P. M. Leonardi. 2013. Social media use in organizations: Exploring the affordances of visibility, editability, persistence, and association. *Annals of the International Communication Association* **36** (1): 143–189.
114. Chu, J., et al. 2021. Attention or distraction? The impact of mobile phone on users' psychological well-being. *Frontiers in Psychology* **12**:612127.
115. Westgate, E. C., and T. D. Wilson. 2018. Boring thoughts and bored minds: The MAC model of boredom and cognitive engagement. *Psychological Review* **125** (5): 689–713.
116. Wies, S., A. Bleier, and A. Edeling. 2023. Finding goldilocks influencers: How follower count drives social media engagement. *Journal of Marketing* **87** (3): 383–405.
117. Yaros, R., and A. Cook. 2013. Attention versus learning of online content: Preliminary findings from an eye-tracking study. In *Evolving Psychological and Educational Perspectives on Cyber Behavior*, ed. R. Z. Zheng, 132–154. Hershey, PA: IGI Global.

CHAPTER 4

# Your Mind on Media

- Neuroscience defines attention.
- Attention differs from engagement.
- Continuous partial attention is ubiquitous.
- There are two types of attention.
- A new model counters disengagement.

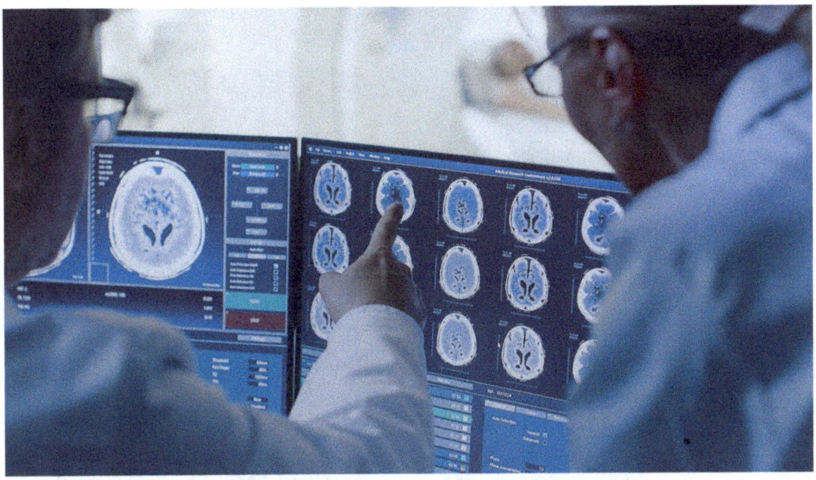


R. Yaros, *The Digital Engagement Model*, Palgrave Practical Guides in Communication,
https://doi.org/10.1007/978-3-032-03822-7_4

## 4.1 Your Attention Please

Despite clear connections, the fields of communication and journalism have been slow to address empirical evidence demonstratings how digital content can incorporate cognitive and neuroscientific perspectives. Some users may be tempted by clickbait, but is their attention sustainable? Retaining attention is the gold standard for meaningful engagement, yet it is a complex process influenced by psychological, neurological, and technological factors. When a user reads content, the brain deciphers words and retains their meaning long enough to evaluate the relevance. Consuming digital content amplifies this process, with mobile devices challenging attention spans by generating endless, algorithm-driven streams ofcontent. Younger users are particularly vulnerable to social media's cognitively driven reward system and, as detailed in this chapter, they can exhibit altered brain activity linked to addiction-like behaviors. We explain how sustained engagement with any form of content depends on more than users' motivations and the affordances of technology. The content's structure, interactive features, and neurological responses cannot be ignored. By the time you finish reading this sentence, you will have decided whether to continue reading (Fig. 4.1).

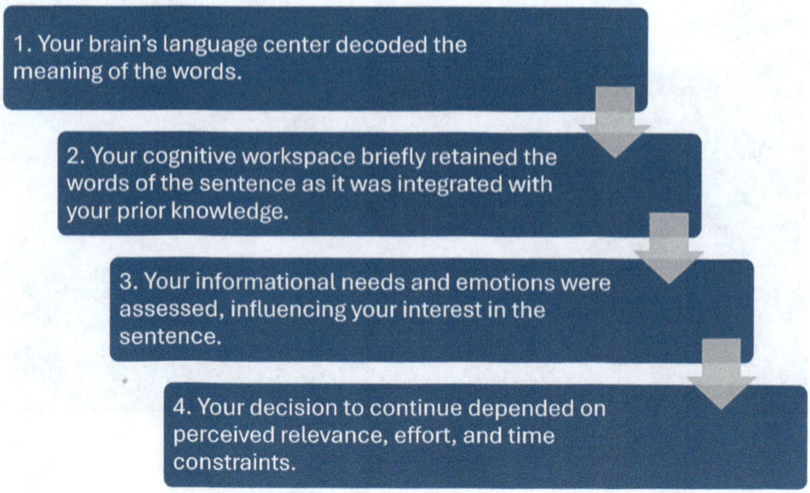


**Fig. 4.1** Your processing sequence

This sequence highlights the significance of the first seconds of exposure, as a user must decide within seconds whether to continue engaging. Attention is the gateway to meaningful engagement, and engagement is more than simply viewing content. The Digital Engagement Model (DEM) is the first to detail the critical relationship between five important user variables and five influential content variables. The framework helps to explain when and why different users allocate their attention following exposure to digital content. Importantly, these theoretical variables are generalizable across all users and any content, as the model is based on a collection of researched concepts, some of which have been established over the years, that can significantly influence attention.

Attention is an important finite resource but neuropsychology is not typically covered in textbooks on communication. Instead, these books focus more on target audiences, production skills, and the effects of media.

The concept should be included because neuropsychological insights into how, when, and why users engage with digital content can help us to benefit from the newest digital technologies and changing patterns of media consumption.

This chapter is not intended to be a lengthy lesson about the brain, peppered with neuroscientific jargon. Nonetheless, having some familiarity with three key regions of the brain will help to explain and support some of the goals for producing content, guided by the Digital Engagement Model.

At the same time, it is important to avoid the temptation to think that any one region of the brain is solely responsible for each cognitive or emotional process. Neuroscientists argue that the brain's architecture provides the computational flexibility to support complex, ever-changing environments, going beyond previous terminology that suggested different cognitive processes originate in only one portion of the brain [1].

Terms such as attention, memory, cognition, and emotion, by themselves, do not provide meaningful explanations of how the mind functions. Each one helps to describe general mental processes, but without further scientific context, they do not advance our understanding of the underlying mechanisms.

The goal of examining specific brain regions and their related cognitive functions in the context of this chapter is to support a comprehensive framework that connects the way digital content is currently created to the way the human mind processes it. By understanding how the brain facilitates attention, memory, and perception in relation to digital media, we aim to bridge the gap between content production and user engagement.

Producing content that effectively engages today's digital media consumers requires us to transcend traditional concepts, such as motivations, individual differences, and uses and gratifications. We can also integrate cognitive processes, such as how users allocate attention, manage cognitive load, and experience sustained engagement with multimedia in dynamic digital environments, to offer unique and more precise strategies for designing content that aligns with the way that the brain naturally processes information. Ignoring these cognitive processes would result in an incomplete and less effective engagement model.

Research indicates that longer-form narratives significantly enhance memory and comprehension by providing contextual and emotional frameworks that facilitate deeper engagement with the information [2]. Unlike expository texts, which often present facts in a fragmented or abstract manner, narratives offer a structured flow that mirrors how people naturally process and retain information. Stories activate brain regions involved in language, emotion, and sensory experience, leading to stronger mental representations and more enduring recall.

Let's briefly review three primary regions of the brain (Fig. 4.2), before exploring how each region interacts in the mental processes governing digital engagement.

1. **Prefrontal Cortex**: This region helps manage executive functions, including decision-making, attention control, and goal-directed activities such as searching for information. It plays a role in filtering and prioritizing content, sustaining focus, and processing it, utilizing the available cognitive resources that are available [3].
2. **Parietal Lobe**: This region facilitates attention shifting, spatial awareness, and the integration of sensory information, helping users to navigate screens, track moving elements, and engage with multimedia. It also contributes to the coordination of actions such as scrolling, clicking, and maintaining focus on relevant digital stimuli, enhancing a user's interaction with and experience of digital environments [3].
3. **Amygdala**: This small, almond-shaped brain structure plays an important role in processing emotions and forming emotional memories. It influences users' emotional responses to digital con-

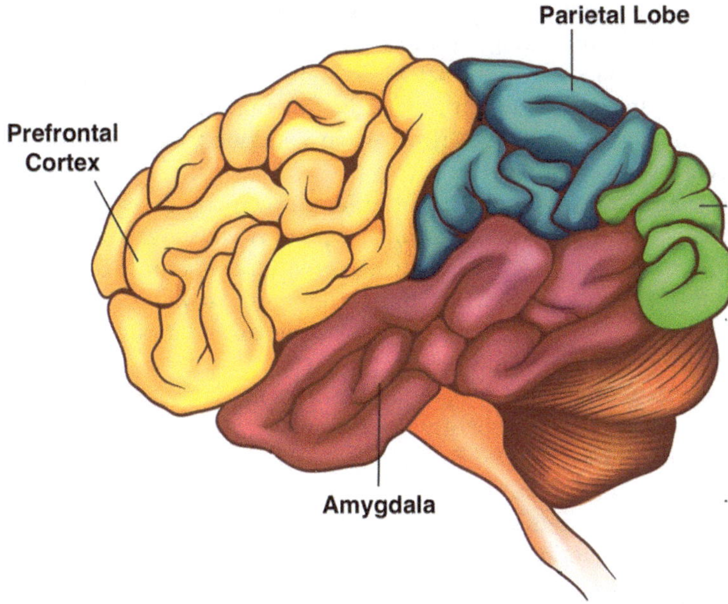


**Fig. 4.2** Regions of the brain

tent, particularly those designed to evoke fear, urgency, or excitement. Research suggests that heightened amygdala activation can enhance attention to emotionally charged digital stimuli, thereby shaping user engagement patterns and information [4] retention.

While all these regions and their associated contributions help to describe cognitive processing of digital content, it is equally important to consider the fundamental, hard-wired limitations of a user's ability to process content at any given moment. The rapid evolution of content distribution and user access has far outpaced the brain's natural capacity to process information efficiently. This imbalance makes cognitive load—the mental effort required to process information—a critical factor in determining whether content will engage or overwhelm. When digital content exceeds a user's cognitive capacity, it can create disengagement rather than meaningful interaction. Cognitive load and reward-driven behaviors help to explain why short-form content dominates many engagement behaviors.

**Cognitive Load Theory** (CLT) posits that the human brain has a limited capacity for processing information. Overloading this capacity impairs comprehension [5, 6]. In the fields of communication and journalism, this theory can and should aid in the production and distribution of content that minimizes cognitive overload when combined with other effective strategies.

Clear and concise language in breaking down complex information is just the first step, as that strategy may help inform users who are interested in the content, but overlook other users who lack the time or interest in reading. A page of concise text and bullet points is still a page of text to users not attracted to text with perhaps a photo, but a photo's ability to retain users isn't always enough to get users to read accompanying text. This phenomenon is particularly evident in today's multi-platform environment, where users frequently switch between apps, articles, and videos, without sustained attention to any one source.

In the field of communication, extensive research has been devoted to understanding how the brain's limited capacity to process information affects attention and audience engagement. Scholars emphasize that cognitive constraints are not just theoretical concerns but practical limitations that content producers should acknowledge when designing digital media. Ignoring these constraints can lead to information overload, reducing comprehension, retention, and overall engagement.

Lang's Limited Capacity Model of Motivated Mediated Message Processing (LC4MP) demonstrates that human attention has finite resources, implying that when content demands more cognitive resources than a user has available, meaningful engagement decreases [7]. Potter and Bolls [8] argue that media producers must account for cognitive and emotional processing constraints if they want to create content that resonates with users. As digital content consumption accelerates and becomes increasingly fragmented, integrating cognitive load considerations into content design is essential for maximizing its impact and effectiveness.

Digital platforms often increase extraneous cognitive load by presenting too much fragmented information within attention-grabbing formats. Online landing pages often overwhelm users with more choices than they can realistically process in a short amount of time. Such pages assume that users can quickly evaluate and select from many options, but cognitive research suggests otherwise. We have known for some time that the amount of information on a web page negatively correlates with users' decision-making and engagement [9].

Providing users with abundant choices for news stories, for example, does not guarantee that they will identify and engage with the most relevant content, even though this is the goal for most digital platforms. Effective content design prioritizes structured navigation, cognitive-friendly layouts, and relevant information to facilitate decision-making and sustained engagement. And while the ability to endlessly scroll on mobile apps provides users with a continuous influx of new content, scrolling can limit the time a user spends processing any single portion of the content.

As digital platforms increasingly shape what information people consume and how their brains process it, neuropsychological principles have contributed new insights into concepts that define the way we seek, select, and engage with content. Our model uniquely combines concepts to address the needs and behaviors of a broader user base, not just a small target audience. This is not to say that there aren't target audiences for specific information on health, cooking, exercise, and so on. There are. Or that a new structure for digital content guarantees the content will engage all users. It does not. Instead, the new model seeks to attract users' attention, especially on social media, who would not typically have sought or selected content that was presented for readers with the interest and the time to consume it.

A new model for producing digital content supported by the ways we process information could help in crafting content in new structures that align with the cognitive realities, ensuring the reach of content not just through channels such as social media, but more meaningful engagement that can simultaneously satisfy the requirements for short- and long-form consumption. Producers must assume that all their digital content could be exposed to users who will ignore it if consuming it requires more time than they have or overloads them with too much information.

The digital world has become a cognitive battleground. We argue that there can be no downside to a model that synthesizes related concepts from neuropsychology, communication, journalism, marketing, and advertising to create content that sustains the attention of more users. This depends, however, on how we define attention.

## 4.2 Neuroscience Defines Attention

According to neuroscience, attention is a finite cognitive resource that operates within the complex neural mechanisms, enabling individuals to focus on relevant content while filtering out the rest. While researching sustained attention in infants, Dr. John wrote,

> Attention may be characterized by its selectivity and intensity. The selective aspect of attention narrows the focus of information processing from a wide range of available stimuli, thoughts, and responses to a single aspect of the environment, or a selected set of stimulus activities. The intensity aspect of attention improves the quality of information processing once the information processing focus is narrowed. [10] (p. 342)

On this basis, the Digital Engagement Model turns to neuroscience to identify two modes of attentional responses that describe users' motivations. They are either seeking specific information (e.g., Google) or casually browsing random content (e.g., Instagram). Both "bottom-up" and "top-down" processing can guide a user's attention to content and eventually determine how long that attention will be sustained.

*"Attention is the rarest and purest form of generosity"*
*-Simone Weil*

**Bottom-up attention** is stimulus-driven and is an automatic process triggered by content such as short videos, to which a user has been exposed incidentally while scrolling. Bottom-up attention is impactful because incidental exposure to emotionally charged or novel content can generate attention to content users would not typically seek. This is because bottom-up attention is partly governed by the brain's emotion center, or amygdala, which plays a pivotal role in rapidly identifying salient stimuli [11]. Attention generated by a user's eye movements toward unexpected visual stimuli is also controlled by a structure in the midbrain [12]. This helps to explain why even producing content well about a given topic does not always determine how much attention it will generate.

**Top-down attention** is goal-directed and associated with intentional user behaviors, such as seeking specific information. For example, a user might search for the steps to complete a task and find them on a YouTube video. Top-down attention involves cognitive control and can be associated with a target audience that consumes content based on users' prior knowledge, experience, and expectations. The brain's prefrontal cortex and parietal lobe together allow such users to sustain focus on specific information while suppressing irrelevant content and distractions [13]. Not only this, but the prefrontal cortex is also involved in maintaining a user's working memory and so facilitates top-down attention [14]. MacDonald and colleagues used functional magnetic resonance imaging (fMRI) to examine brain activity during a task that requires working memory and cognitive control. They found that the dorsolateral prefrontal cortex (DLPFC) was active during the maintenance of task-relevant information, suggesting that this brain region plays a crucial role in sustaining working memory that guides top-down attentional control.

**Working memory** is a cognitive system that temporarily holds and processes information for immediate use. It is essential for decision-making, reasoning, and learning. Unlike long-term memory, which stores information for extended periods, working memory is limited in capacity and duration, typically holding specific information for approximately 20 to 30 seconds [15].

Working memory helps a user keep relevant details accessible for short-term tasks, such as comprehending content, remembering a phone number, performing mental calculations, and solving problems. Working memory also helps users filter distractions and focus on content perceived as critical at that moment. Content that overloads an individual's working memory with too much information, too many choices, or that is overly complex impairs working memory. Conversely, structured, scannable, and cognitively optimized content can help working memory to process and comprehend it.

Research employing psychophysiological measures, such as heart rate, also determined that the pace of videos can affect working memory and attention. Fast-paced and arousing video content generally increased users' self-reported arousal levels, despite eliciting different patterns of physiological arousal. Fast-paced content increased heart rate and skin conductance, indicating heightened physiological arousal, while arousing content alone did not produce the same effects. The researchers concluded that the pacing of content and its potential for arousal play an important role in how viewers process video messages and how media content design can effectively capture and maintain attention [16].

At the same time, certain design elements that capture users' attention do not continually improve comprehension. For example, research into how the structures of online content affect working memory, attention, and learning found that eye fixations on visually prominent features did not always enhance understanding [17]. These findings underscore the importance of aligning content design with cognitive processing principles.

Neuroscience also explains why maintaining attention in digital environments is increasingly complex. The prefrontal cortex is responsible for focus and decision-making, yet it competes with the limbic system, which drives reward-seeking behaviors. When faced with the choice between a page of text requiring more time and cognitive effort than shorter, visually appealing videos, many users gravitate toward the latter. That means important and well-written text, for example, might never be consumed by many of the users exposed to it. The reason is that factual information, such as news, must compete with entertaining storytelling that stimulates a key neurotransmitter in the brain, dopamine.

The effects of dopamine on engagement are widely known. Neuroscientists have shown that dopamine is released when individuals encounter unexpected or rewarding information, increasing their motivation to engage with it [18].

When users engage with easily digestible content, their brains reward them with small dopamine releases, which reinforce a user's need for more of that content. An obvious example is how social media platforms exploit dopamine-driven reward systems, with some users becoming dependent on the social validation of likes and shares [19]. MRI brain scans have confirmed that the brain's reward centers respond to social media likes, reinforcing habitual use [20]. This can be particularly pronounced in adolescents because the brain's dopaminergic mechanisms reinforce social media's so-called low-effort content trap [21].

At the same time, repeated exposure to rapid, low-effort digital content can make high-effort, longer-form content feel less rewarding. Social media interactions activate neural reward circuits, reinforcing behaviors that include scrolling and liking. This feedback loop keeps users superficially engaged but does not necessarily promote deep cognitive processing or knowledge retention. Going further, the algorithms that personalize content for a user amplify this process by reinforcing the compulsive behaviors that undermine deeper engagement [22]. Ultimately, the immediate gratification these short interactions provide can condition users to prioritize short-term rewards.

Sustainable digital engagement strategies require us to move beyond dopamine-driven tactics by delivering engaging content after capturing initial attention by other means. This might be an eye-catching photo or a great headline. If we understand the differences between curiosity-driven and knowledge-driven attention, we can create more effective strategies for producing digital content, as this book explores later. Such strategies optimize content for sustained user engagement following initial attention. This encourages further exploration and deep learning, utilizing personalization that aligns with users' interests while striking a balance between emotional appeal and information density.

As the speed of information and its consumption accelerates, content must address the way that users frequently shift between multiple sources rather than engaging with pages of text only. This is known as cognitive switching, and it taxes the brain's executive function while reducing a mobile user's ability to focus for extended periods.

Despite concerns about what some have called an attention crisis, researchers argue that attention spans aren't necessarily diminishing but merely adapting to a more stimulating digital landscape. Others point to the affordances offered by the technology to argue that overload can be avoided [23]. Gibson introduced the concept of affordances to denote actions offered by an environment. In the context of technology, affordances refer to the ways in which technology provides or limits user interactions to shape engagement. For example, a mobile device allows for swiping and tapping of content, while hyperlinks facilitate navigation to other content. Gibson's ecological approach laid the foundation for later research that applied technological affordances to media interaction and interpretation [24], shedding light on how technological features can be used to enable or constrain user attention.

What is clear is that digital media that demands bottom-up attention creates overstimulation through notifications, rapid content shifts, and algorithm-driven engagement, which can weaken top-down attentional control. By recognizing the interplay between bottom-up and top-down attention, as well as the brain regions involved in sustained focus, we offer content producers new strategies to enhance sustained attention in later chapters, rather than relying on brief interactions and superficial engagement. The goal of these strategies is to attract a large, generalist audience while still catering to the selective exposure of the target user.

**Selective exposure** occurs when users prefer to consume information that aligns with their pre-existing beliefs while avoiding content that contradicts them [25]. This tendency is deeply rooted in the cognitive and neurological mechanisms that shape perception, decision-making, and engagement. To understand the implications of selective exposure in the digital age, it is necessary to investigate the brain's reward systems, cognitive dissonance, and the role of algorithmic reinforcement in media consumption.

At the core of selective exposure is the brain's response to congruent and incongruent information. Research suggests that encountering information that matches our beliefs activates the brain's reward centers [26]. These areas and the dopamine they produce are associated with a user's pleasure and motivation. That explains why users can experience satisfaction when exposed to entertaining videos or sports events.

The benefits for the user are twofold. Not only does familiarity engender pleasure, but the preference for familiarity is an evolutionary adaptation that streamlines cognitive processing. By prioritizing information that aligns with pre-existing schemas, such as recognizing family members, the brain conserves energy and reduces the cognitive load required for processing new or challenging information.

This tendency is exploited by digital media, which leverage a user's selective exposure to preferred content to maximize their engagement. Algorithms personalize content based on a user's previous interactions, creating information ecosystems that cater to individual preferences. This process creates social media feeds, search engine results, and news aggregators that prioritize content that aligns with specific preferences and behaviors. This can reinforce existing beliefs but also limit a user's exposure to alternative perspectives [27].

Personalized content can have profound implications for information diversity and democratic discourse. While personalized content might enhance a user's experience, it also fosters ideological polarization by reducing cross-cutting exposure. When individuals regularly encounter information that confirms existing biases, their perspectives can become more rigid, making constructive dialogue and critical thinking more challenging [28, 29].

Selective exposure is, by its nature, a product of selective attention, the cognitive process by which the brain filters relevant stimuli while ignoring extraneous information. Social media exploits this mechanism with short bursts of content that capture attention. Broadly speaking, the key factors that influence selective attention include:

**Visual and sensory cues.** Bright colors, high-contrast imagery, and motion elements draw immediate focus. Lang's Limited Capacity Model explains how vivid sensory features—such as bright colors, movement, and rapid scene changes—automatically capture users' attention [7, 30].

**Emotional triggers**. Content that elicits strong emotional reactions, such as fear, anger, or joy, is more likely to capture and maintain attention. Headlines optimized for clickability, often featuring provocative language or emotionally charged phrases, capitalize on emotions to attract attention (Bucher and Schumacher, 2006). Research indicates that emotionally evocative information enhances memory retention, reinforcing selective exposure tendencies by making confirmatory content more memorable [26].

**Algorithmic curation**. Personalized recommendations based on past engagement patterns make it more likely that users will encounter content aligned with their interests [31]. This continuous reinforcement strengthens selective attention, making it less likely that individuals will engage with contradictory viewpoints [32]. Others outlined how algorithmic personalization on social media platforms can tailor content based on prior user behavior [33]. This reinforcement loop increases exposure to ideologically or interest-consistent material, reducing incidental exposure to opposing views and contributing to selective attention and confirmation bias.

While selective exposure to content can determine initial attention, the critical transition from **selective** to **sustained attention** depends on several cognitive and contextual factors, including:

**Continued personal relevance.** Information that a target audience perceives as personally significant is more likely to hold their attention over time. Studies suggest that relevance enhances cognitive engagement, making individuals more willing to process and retain content that aligns with their values and experiences (Bucher and Schumacher, 2006).

**Environmental context.** Distraction-free settings facilitate deeper engagement. In contrast, multitasking, such as browsing social media while watching television, reduces the ability to sustain focus, reinforcing the brain's reliance on algorithmically curated, low-effort content.

**Cognitive state**. Motivation and emotional arousal significantly impact the ability to transition from selective to sustained attention. High motivation, such as needing to solve a problem, enhances cognitive persistence, making individuals more likely to engage with complex or challenging information [26].

The shift from selective to sustained attention occurs in milliseconds to seconds, depending on the nature of the content and the user's cognitive resources at that given moment. Digital platforms are optimized for immediate engagement, often at the expense of deep cognitive processing. This explains why long-form content often struggles for attention in environments dominated by rapid, algorithmically driven information cycles (see Chap. 2).

When addressing a target audience, the omnipresence of digital media and its larger population of users is often overlooked. This is a mistake because digital media ensures that larger populations of users are exposed to the content, often without deliberate intent. That is called incidental exposure. To help content producers maximize this untapped resource, the variables and strategies suggested by our digital engagement model prioritize users who have also been incidentally exposed to unexpected content. You can read more about them in Chap. 7.

**Incidental exposure** represents an increasingly dominant mode of information acquisition, particularly where content is algorithmically curated and seamlessly integrated into social media feeds, news aggregators, and entertainment platforms [34]. Understanding incidental exposure and its implications for behavior, cognition, and engagement is critical when attention is both fragmented and persistently redirected.

As with selective exposure, incidental exposure stimulates cognitive mechanisms that influence how information is processed, stored, and retrieved. Unlike active engagement, where users purposefully seek information, incidental exposure relies on implicit learning instead. This type of learning involves an unconscious process in which users absorb patterns, associations, and meaning without explicit awareness [35]. This phenomenon is particularly relevant in social media, where rapid scrolling and fleeting interactions with content characterize user behaviors [36].

Well-researched cognitive effects related to incidental exposure also include the mere exposure effect [37]. When users encounter content multiple times, even passively, they can develop a heightened sense of familiarity and emotional connection to the content.

This mechanism can play a crucial role in shaping public perception, brand recognition, and even ideological reinforcement. However, it also presents challenges: repeated exposure to misinformation can foster a false sense of its credibility, reinforcing beliefs without requiring analytical scrutiny [38].

Understanding the stages through which information is processed during incidental exposure sheds light on its influence on engagement and retention. The progression from passive exposure to cognitive imprinting follows a structured process:

*Initial selection*: Content that is visually or emotionally salient captures attention within milliseconds [39]. In digital contexts, elements such as striking images, headlines, and dynamic features (e.g., autoplay videos) facilitate this selection. The interplay between bottom-up (stimulus-driven) and top-down (user-driven) attention mechanisms determines whether incidental content will be retained in working memory.

*Engagement transition*: If, at first, the content appears to align with a user's interests, concerns, or social context, it transitions from mere exposure to minimal cognitive engagement. For example, a news headline glimpsed during scrolling may prompt further reading if it is coherent and resonates with existing knowledge or emotional states. However, if its relevance is not immediately apparent, the exposure remains peripheral and susceptible to being rapidly forgotten [40].

*Cognitive investment*: Repeated encounters with similar content reinforce recognition, even if engagement remains passive. Over time, this contributes to the formation of implicit memory, which in turn influences future recall and decision-making. Studies on incidental learning demonstrate that individuals can internalize complex information structures without conscious effort, highlighting the role of repeated, passive exposure in shaping perceptions and behaviors [41].

The increasing reliance on incidental exposure as a primary means of news consumption has profound implications. Algorithmic content delivery systems amplify incidental exposure by optimizing engagement, as measured by metrics such as time spent on platforms and interaction frequency. Personalized recommendations prioritize content based on previous behaviors, increasing the likelihood that users will encounter familiar content, such as recommended news articles [32]. While this potentially enhances user experience by aligning content with user preferences, it can also foster filter bubbles and echo chambers, wherein exposure to diverse perspectives is limited.

While personalized algorithms are often praised for tailoring content to individual interests, not all users appreciate this level of curation. Some users find that algorithmic assumptions are intrusive or inaccurate, particularly when they are based on brief or incidental interactions. For example, briefly scanning an article about another country for informational or academic purposes can lead to travel ads, even when the user has no intention of traveling. This type of "false relevance" can frustrate users, giving them a sense of being misunderstood or surveilled. Eslami et al. [42] found that users often perceive algorithmic systems, such as Facebook's News Feed, as manipulative, particularly when the feed delivers unexpected content.

Similarly, Rader and Gray [43] found that some users are unaware of how algorithms work and are surprised when systems make incorrect assumptions about their preferences. These misfires not only diminish user trust in the platform but also highlight the limitations of using past behaviors as a proxy for future intent.

Engagement-driven algorithms can also favor emotionally charged content, as emotional arousal correlates with a higher likelihood of retention and sharing [44]. Research indicates that many users acquire political and scientific knowledge passively through social media, rather than through direct engagement with traditional news sources [45]. This raises concerns regarding the amplification of sensationalist or misleading information, as content designed to elicit strong reactions spreads more efficiently than neutral or purely informational material.

To address this, practitioners can design emotionally engaging content that maintains factual accuracy, using narrative and multimedia strategies that attract attention without resorting to distortion. Research by Berger and Milkman [44] demonstrates that emotionally arousing content, especially that which evokes anger or anxiety, is more likely to be shared. This suggests the effects of emotionally resonant yet truthful information. Media literacy efforts, particularly "prebunking" techniques that expose users to manipulation tactics before they encounter misinformation, have been shown to increase resistance to false information [46]. Additionally, publishers can adjust algorithmic ranking systems to prioritize source credibility or constructive engagement rather than mere virality.

Interface design changes, such as prompts encouraging users to read articles before sharing them, can reduce the impulsive distribution of misleading content [47]. Finally, curating content that periodically introduces users to high-quality, contrasting perspectives can help mitigate filter bubbles and enhance cognitive flexibility, thereby supporting more balanced information and informed engagement in digital environments [48].

As digital landscapes evolve, incidental exposure will continue to shape how large populations of users engage with information. While offering opportunities for serendipitous learning and exposure to new ideas, incidental exposure can still present challenges related to cognitive overload. Future research is needed into how incidental exposure to content interacts with differences in users' attention spans and digital habits.

## 4.3 Attention Differs from Engagement

The concepts of attention and engagement, though closely related, remain two distinct cognitive processes. While attention is a prerequisite for engagement, it does not guarantee comprehension, retention, or meaningful interaction. Moreover, brief attention can be driven by any external stimulus, whereas sustained attention is more selective in its focus. In the digital world, we might attend to our phone during a face-to-face conversation, then quickly switch attention back to the person in front of us when they pose a question. A user might be briefly distracted by an annoying pop-up window that they quickly close, an animated advertisement that they quickly ignore, or a photo of a celebrity that needs no additional attention. We know that attention can be fleeting.

On the other hand, sustained attention facilitates deeper cognitive processing, comprehension, and knowledge gain. This distinction is crucial in a landscape where platforms and content often prioritize capturing a user's attention over fostering comprehension, understanding, and retention of content.

Another division between attention and engagement is, as stated previously, cognitive load. Imagine attending to content that is filled with unfamiliar words. Our first response might be to view it as a page filled with text, and therefore uninteresting or confusing. Despite assigning attention to it, we might ultimately decide not to engage with it.

Since we know that the limited capacity of a user's working memory can constrain processing, attention can be quickly overwhelmed when too much information is presented. In their LC4MP model, Lang suggests that individuals have finite cognitive resources for encoding, storing, and retrieving information [7]. When digital environments present excessive or complex information too rapidly, cognitive overload occurs, reducing the likelihood of both sustained attention and meaningful engagement.

To define digital engagement, the DEM identifies two separate dimensions: cognition and interactivity.

**Cognitive engagement** occurs at a passive level in a digital environment. Users consume content without necessarily interacting with or deeply processing it. Examples include watching videos, reading headlines, or perusing a feed. Cognitive engagement can be either surface level, where attention is momentary, or deeper, where users actively reflect on the content. However, the former is far more common in digital environments (see Chap. 2).

**Interactive engagement** involves active participation, such as commenting, sharing, or responding to content. It suggests a higher level of cognitive investment, as users not only consume the information but also react to and interact with it. However, interactive engagement does not always imply comprehension; users may share content based on emotional triggers rather than critical analysis.

Understanding these two dimensions is crucial for designing and implementing a cognitive content model that fosters sustained engagement, rather than merely momentary attention. While attention is a finite resource, engagement is a cultivated process—one that requires thoughtful design, strategic structuring of content, and a commitment to foster users' attention and understanding.

The distinction between attention and engagement poses significant implications for education, journalism, and digital marketing. For educators, it underlines the importance of structuring lesson content to go beyond attention-grabbing techniques and support deeper learning. For journalism, the distinction highlights the risks of clickbait-driven strategies that prioritize momentary attention over informed discourse. The DEM specifies why new structures are needed for information that is exposed to a user following a click. In digital marketing, the distinction suggests that sustainable brand engagement requires more than just eye-catching ads; it demands content that fosters lasting and meaningful interaction.

While short-form content and rapid information consumption cater to modern attention spans, they also shape them by reinforcing cognitive habits that may discourage deep engagement. Understanding how digital consumption patterns shape the brain can help individuals and institutions develop strategies that foster sustained attention, critical thinking, and meaningful learning. The principle of **neuroplasticity** suggests that the human brain can continuously adapt to its environment, and the digital landscape is no exception.

## 4.4 Neuroplasticity Shapes Engagement

The modern digital landscape prioritizes brevity. Platforms such as TikTok, Instagram Reels, and YouTube Shorts have conditioned users to expect highly condensed content that delivers multimedia within seconds. The rise of short-form content exemplifies how consumption patterns, including scanning and snacking, continually reshape the ways users are entertained and informed [49]. This reshaping is made possible by neuroplasticity, or the brain's ability to reorganize itself by forming new neural connections [50].

Neuroplasticity plays a crucial role in users' shifting behaviors as they seek, select, and share content. This enacts our brain's inclination toward efficiency, eventually reinforcing neural pathways that favor rapid processing over sustained engagement [51]. When individuals habitually consume bite-sized digital content, the brain reinforces the circuits associated with scanning, multitasking, and instant gratification. Over time, this adaptation can make it more challenging for a user to engage in deep reading, extended concentration, and complex problem-solving. The decline in sustained attention and an increased propensity to cognitive overload mean that the brain struggles to process excessive amounts of rapidly presented information.

Content producers should note that the effects of neuroplasticity aren't confined to social media. Eye-tracking studies have found evidence that readers spend fewer than 15 seconds on average on digital news before shifting their attention to other sources [52]. The researchers referred to this pattern as "news snacking"—or when individuals rely on heuristic processing to engage superficially with information, rather than critical analysis. Instead of reading full articles, users skim headlines and social media summaries, absorbing fragmented pieces of information without fully understanding the context or nuances of a topic.

While such changes reflect the brain's remarkable adaptability, they also raise concerns about the long-term implications for attention to and retention of content presentations [53]. Might these cognitive shifts discourage deep analytical thought? They appear particularly pronounced in younger generations, who have grown up in a digital ecosystem that prioritizes immediacy over depth. Our collective ability to critically evaluate sources, recognize bias, and synthesize information may have been compromised.

For efficiency, the brain relies on heuristics or mental shortcuts to make decisions quickly. While these tools can help users filter information rapidly, they can also increase susceptibility to misinformation and cognitive bias. For instance, some users might assume that highly shared or frequently encountered information is more credible, even when it lacks factual accuracy. As previously explored, that effect is exacerbated by algorithm-driven content curation, which reinforces pre-existing beliefs and limits exposure to diverse perspectives.

Heuristic processing can also affect the retention of information. It is widely known that when users engage with digital content superficially, they encode less information into long-term memory. Unlike deep learning, which requires users to make connections between new and existing knowledge, rapid consumption of content can mean that information is quickly forgotten rather than integrated into a user's broader cognitive framework.

As detailed in the following chapters, new content structures could promote deeper cognitive engagement. To achieve this, we must facilitate the heuristic processing of longer-form content by strategically placing interactive multimedia within the text and making it more scannable, thereby challenging users to think critically rather than passively consuming the information.

In classrooms, activities that require sustained focus, such as reading long texts and engaging in extended discussions, can facilitate neuroplasticity in students' brains, promoting deeper analytical thinking. Neuroplasticity allows the brain to adapt positively when consistently challenged with cognitively demanding tasks [54].

As digital media continues to evolve, maintaining a balance between efficiency and depth will be essential if we want to enjoy robust user engagement. Despite an increasing amount of research on information processing, several gaps remain, including the teaching and application of a new production mindset with new production skills, as well as a better understanding of the long-term effects of digital technology [55]. In the meantime, some argue that the common practice of multitasking as users attempt to be more productive has been replaced by a cognitive state that persists throughout the day. That state is continuous partial attention.

## 4.5 Continuous Partial Attention Is Ubiquitous

In today's hyperconnected world, continuous partial attention (CPA) has become an unavoidable reality. Since 1998, CPA has described a state in which individuals split their focus across multiple sources or streams of information, never fully engaging with any one task [56]. Unlike the term multitasking, which essentially means switching between specific tasks with the intention to complete both tasks with 100% efficiency, CPA represents an ongoing but fragmented mode of user cognition that significantly reduces efficiency and impairs learning.

Continuous partial attention is driven by technological advancements, particularly mobile devices that supply social media on demand alongside real-time notifications. It affects not only personal productivity but also broader societal domains such as schools, universities, and workplaces. Communication specialists and journalists face the challenge of capturing and maintaining users' attention amid a constant influx of digital distractions. While CPA enables individuals to stay connected, it is yet another barrier to sustained attention. Research found that continuous partial attention overactivated the prefrontal cortex and related systems governing decision-making, attention regulation, and memory formation [57]. Such over-activation can limit the brain's ability to encode and retrieve information effectively.

In a state of continuous partial attention, a user almost always perceives a need to check their device at idle moments throughout the day, often shifting between multiple stimuli. CPA is common among users who are frequently bombarded with notifications, emails, and social media updates. Several studies have shown that students who frequently switch between digital distractions and academic tasks exhibit poorer retention and comprehension compared to those who engage in focused, uninterrupted study sessions [58].

Furthermore, CPA has implications for professional work environments. Employees who frequently check their devices for emails, text messages, notifications, and news and sports updates have been shown to experience cognitive overload, which reduces their ability to complete problem-solving and other complex tasks efficiently [59]. Their inability to sustain attention and work without interruption leads to decreased productivity and increased stress levels.

Newport [60] introduced the concept of "deep work" to refer to the ability to focus on cognitively demanding tasks without distraction. The author maintains that CPA is one of the primary reasons why some individuals struggle more to engage in deep work now than they did in previous years. The constant barrage of notifications and digital stimuli forces individuals into a state of perpetual fragmentation, where attention is constantly diverted. This erosion of deep work has implications not just for users of digital resources but also for the creative professionals, researchers, and writers who rely on extended periods of uninterrupted focus when creating content.

For journalists, users' continuous partial attention presents a growing challenge. Media outlets strive to capture fragmented audience engagement, often relying heavily on clickbait titles and teasing headlines, combined with sensationalist reporting [53]. And content producers themselves are not immune. The need to monitor multiple information sources, social media platforms, and breaking news can compromise their ability to produce compelling content or conduct in-depth reporting. Beyond these cognitive inefficiencies, the continuous state of partial attention has social and psychological ramifications. It can affect interpersonal relationships by reducing the quality of communication and connection. Researchers have found that the mere presence of a smartphone during face-to-face interactions can diminish perceived empathy and conversational depth [61].

It is not only interpersonal communication that suffers in the presence of a smartphone. Even when a device is not in use, it can reduce cognitive capacity by diverting a user's attentional resources. Through a series of experiments, participants completed cognitive tasks while their smartphones were placed either in another room, in their pocket or bag, or face down on their desk. Results showed that participants performed poorly on tasks requiring sustained attention and working memory when their smartphones were in the other room compared to when it was in a bag or pocket in the room. The poorest performance occurred when the phone was left silently on the desk. This persistent distraction taxes cognitive resources even when not actively in use. However carefully producers assemble and present content, users who are constantly distracted by their device and its content will struggle to process and retain it.

Continuous partial attention can also contribute to heightened stress and mental fatigue. The brain's continuous toggling between multiple stimuli consumes a user's cognitive resources, eventually leading to mental exhaustion. Social media platforms can exacerbate continuous partial attention by encouraging frequent device checking. Upon viewing content, infinite scroll interfaces, push notifications, and algorithmically curated feeds can compel users to stay connected at all times [62]. This contributes to compulsive use of devices, reinforcing the cycle of fragmented attention and reducing opportunities for focus and reflection.

## 4.6 Attention Momentum Is the Goal

Given the constant challenges to avoid overloading users with information, capturing attention is no longer enough to sustain it. The Digital Engagement Model introduces the concept of **attention momentum,** which refers to the ability of all content, regardless of its length, to maintain attention following initial exposure. Without sustained attention, digital fleeting distractions will continue to interrupt interactions, preventing valuable engagements. Building attention momentum in content beyond an initial click increases the probability that more users will consume more of it for longer periods of time.

The influence of attention momentum depends on whether a user's attention is top-down (goal-directed) or bottom-up (triggered by content). In either case, all content needs to be:

**Relevant and useful.** Content that aligns with user interests and real-world applications sustains engagement more effectively.

**Novel and surprising.** Unexpected elements provided in a stream of creative storytelling can maintain users' curiosity and sustain attention, much as a full-length movie can.

**Easily assimilated.** Replacing content structures that are too dense or complex with structures that strike a balance between simplicity and depth will sustain engagement.

**Interactive** Users are more likely to stay engaged when they actively participate rather than passively consume. There is, however, a point when too much interactivity overloads cognitive processing. Producers should be guided by neuroscience to avoid the temptation to include as much information as possible.

While the Digital Engagement Model focuses on the moments of exposure to content to build attention momentum, examples exist where content has transformed passive readers into active participants. We have found that producing all text with brevity and bullet points is not one of them. This is because the users who respond to the Digital Engagement Model still view a page of short sentences and bullet points as a page of text. Unlike traditional linear narratives, new interfaces enable users to tailor their content experience by making choices that cater to their needs and interests. This technique fosters emotional and cognitive investment, making information more memorable.

We demonstrate how compelling storytelling encompasses interactive data visualizations that are cognitively manageable, embedded graphics that tell a story, and simple polls that personalize the effects of the reported content. This does not yet include augmented reality (AR) and virtual reality (VR), but the Digital Engagement Model will continue to evolve with more research. These are immersive environments that quickly engage users on a multisensory level, but AR and VR are not yet part of a typical user's daily routine for accessing digital content.

Subsequent chapters will be guided by **progressive disclosure**. Progressive disclosure is a structure that reveals information to users gradually, rather than overwhelming them with excessive detail all at once. The DEM suggests that this approach can enhance usability and maintain engagement by keeping more users curious and motivated to explore further.

A preview of techniques for implementing progressive disclosure includes layering content, which involves organizing information into tiers that allow users to access deeper layers as desired. We also outline how dynamic loading displays additional content only when users show interest, such as by clicking a button labeled with specific content. Finally, *Adaptive Learning Paths* adjusts content based on a user's behavior and prior knowledge.

In summary, the Digital Engagement Model advocates for a structured approach to digital content, fostering attention momentum by optimizing the interplay between textual, visual, and interactive elements. DEM structures aim to balance cognitive load while maximizing retention through the intentional design of content. The DEM sequence includes designing content to:

(1) Capture users' attention by being visually appealing and contextually relevant.
(2) Be for both short- and long-form consumption.
(3) Encourage deeper exploration through interactivity and layered storytelling.
(4) Enhance memory and learning.

Subsequent chapters outline how to balance visual and textual elements to create a visually appealing layout that can help reduce cognitive fatigue.

Presenting content, such as news stories, with an interface of cognitively digestible chunks leverages micro-engagements and considers diverse user intent, ranging from casual browsing to deep exploration.

Sustaining engagement beyond the initial click will be an evolving challenge that requires a flexible approach to strategic content design. By addressing the cognitively driven aspects, techniques, and principles of the Digital Engagement Model, digital content can foster longer-term cognitive investment, rather than forcing users to decide whether the content consists of brief bullet points or pages of storytelling. The future of digital engagement lies in continuously adapting to technological advancements while prioritizing user experience, ensuring that attention momentum remains a central goal in content creation.

## 4.7 The New Model Counters Disengagement

With unprecedented access to digital content, it is reasonable to assume that more users are engaging with more news than ever before. Research suggests the opposite. Whether it is the cognitive load of content or the affordances of technology, constant temptations to check devices and frequent navigation around digital platforms can eventually lead to information fatigue and disengagement [63]. This presents a paradox. While users are more connected than ever, they are also more likely to experience cognitive overload, reducing the depth of processing and retention of the information to which they are exposed.

Avoiding a user's disengagement with content is just as important as facilitating engagement with information when developing strategies to reach diverse populations. Despite the constant availability of digital media, information avoidance is significant. A 2022 Reuters Institute study reported that respondents avoided news because it negatively impacted their mood and mental health. This pattern was particularly pronounced among younger users, who often cite mental well-being as a reason for limiting news consumption. "On days where I really want to relax, I avoid political news because it gets me anxious sometimes," one 24-year-old female participant stated [64] (p. 44). By 2024, Reuters found that nearly 40% of surveyed individuals reported feeling "worn out" by the sheer volume of news, an increase from the 28% cited in the Institute's 2019 report.

Studies of heuristic thinking and decision fatigue reveal why some users tend to skim headlines rather than thoroughly process news. The research found that exposure to distressing news, particularly stories related to crises, conflict, or injustice, can increase stress and anxiety [65].

Symptoms prompting disengagement from digital news are not related only to emotions; they also have physiological underpinnings. Research suggests that frequent digital media consumption can lead to structural and functional changes in the brain, particularly in areas related to attention control, memory, and decision-making [66].

This sustained negative state serves as a protective mechanism against emotional contrast, where a sudden shift from a neutral or positive state to a negative one could be more distressing. Users may worry or ruminate to maintain a state of sustained negative affect, thereby avoiding sudden negative emotional shifts [67]. Newman and Llera proposed that individuals, particularly those with anxiety, often use worry to sustain negative emotions to prevent experiencing sharp increases in negative affect in response to adverse events. If individuals withdraw from sources that provide essential and factually accurate information about topics such as science, health, or the economy, their ability to make informed decisions diminishes, and democratic discourse weakens. Understanding why information avoidance occurs is critical when developing strategies to re-engage users. Key drivers of avoidance, such as emotional exhaustion, cognitive dissonance, and algorithmic reinforcement of content, should be addressed if we are to combat disengagement and improve users' information retention.

Supporting neuroscientific research suggests that repeated exposure to distressing content activates the amygdala, the brain region responsible for processing emotions, particularly fear and anxiety [26]. When users repeatedly encounter digital content that evokes stress, such as news about political instability, climate disasters, or economic downturns, their brains can perceive these threats as immediate dangers [68]. This chronic stress response results in emotional burnout, prompting some users to disengage from consuming news altogether.

To combat emotional exhaustion, media organizations might rethink how they present distressing content. Constructive journalism, which balances reporting on problems with potential solutions, has been proposed to sustain user engagement while reducing emotional burnout [69]. It is possible that integrating positive psychology techniques into news reporting could lead to more engaging coverage. This practice could counteract the adverse effects of traditional journalism's focus on only conflict and problems, which can lead to user fatigue and disengagement. By highlighting possible solutions, constructive journalism can inform and empower audiences, potentially mitigating some of the anxiety and burnout associated with news consumption. In short, curating hopeful narratives within complex stories could encourage sustained engagement without overwhelming audiences.

Another major contributor to disengagement is cognitive fatigue, which occurs when individuals are overloaded with excessive stimuli. Many digital platforms present an overwhelming array of content, ranging from providing more choices than a user can consume in a visit to social media feeds flooded with trending topics. Even brief content must still compete with the overwhelming amount of content that accompanies it. A constant influx of information challenges the limited capacity of working memory, which is responsible for processing and retaining new information [70]. Cooper [71] noted that many high-tech products are designed by engineers, rather than individuals who prioritize usability and user experience. Cooper argues that this can lead to products that are often overly complex, frustrating, and difficult for ordinary users to navigate. There is also what some call "cognitive friction."

**Cognitive friction** refers to the mental effort required when interacting with a system or interface that does not align with a user's expectations or prior knowledge. This misalignment can increase cognitive load if an interface or feature forces users to stop and think [71]. Research has explored the impact of cognitive friction on user behavior and performance. When users encounter unexpected interface challenges, it can lead to increased error rates and decreased efficiency. Conversely, a manageable degree of cognitive friction can be beneficial, as it encourages users to engage more deeply with content, leading to learning and retention. Therefore, designers must carefully balance cognitive friction to enhance user engagement without causing undue frustration.

Other factors that can drive disengagement are algorithmic reinforcement, which prioritizes low-effort, high-reward content over substantive journalism. Social media platforms are designed to maximize engagement time with machine-learning algorithms that prioritize content likely to generate clicks and interactions. This can result in a feedback loop, whereby emotionally charged or sensationalist content dominates in-depth information and reporting. While promoting content that requires minimal cognitive effort, research has shown that personalized recommendation algorithms also significantly reduce the diversity of content individuals encounter, reinforcing confirmation bias and ideological polarization [33].

In sum, avoidance of and disengagement from digital media are not simply issues of user behavior; they are deeply intertwined with the way content is designed and presented. Emotional exhaustion, cognitive fatigue, cognitive friction, and algorithmic reinforcement all contribute to the declining engagement with substantive journalism.

To counteract this, media strategies could focus on producing high-quality content that is more accessible, easier to process, and retain. Platforms should also be transparent, allowing users to adjust algorithmic settings for more diverse information. This is just another reason why rethinking the presentation of digital information benefits from knowledge about cognitive science and neuroscience, so that content aligns with how the human brain processes and users engage with information.

Digital consumption habits will continue to evolve with the introduction of new technologies and sources. Although the streams of digital content won't slow down, new efforts can be made to reorient quick or passive consumption of information toward sustained attention and deeper engagement. By addressing the underlying cognitive and psychological barriers to information consumption and retention, a more informed and critical-thinking society could emerge.

Forthcoming research suggests that newer technologies such as artificial intelligence (AI), augmented reality, and adaptive learning systems could be leveraged to create more personalized engagement experiences. AI-driven recommendation systems could be optimized to prioritize content that balances user interest with cognitive load management, reducing the tendency toward superficial consumption or cognitive fatigue.

Moreover, digital literacy programs can continue to equip users with the skills needed to navigate information-dense environments effectively. Teaching individuals how to assess and manage their digital interactions critically could help mitigate the adverse effects of constant cognitive switching. Merely claiming attention spans are shorter today is not as powerful as the empirical evidence that shows how technology can modify learning and habitual behaviors. The future of digital engagement depends on our ability to strike a balance between efficiency and depth, ensuring that attention is not only momentarily seized but also meaningfully sustained.

## References


1. Pessoa, L., L. Medina, and E. Desfilis. 1844. Refocusing neuroscience: Moving away from mental categories and towards complex behaviours. *Philosophical Transactions of the Royal Society B* 2022 (**377**): 20200534.
2. Mar, R. A., et al. 2021. Memory and comprehension of narrative versus expository texts: A meta-analysis. *Psychonomic Bulletin & Review* **28**:732–749.
3. Culham, J. C., P. Cavanagh, and N. G. Kanwisher. 2001. Attention response functions: Characterizing brain areas using fMRI activation during parametric variations of attentional load. *Neuron* **32** (4): 737–745.
4. Zadra, J. R., and G. L. Clore. 2011. Emotion and perception: The role of affective information. *Wiley Interdisciplinary Reviews: Cognitive Science* **2** (6): 676–685.
5. Sweller, J. 1994. Cognitive load theory, learning difficulty, and instructional design. *Learning and Instruction* **4** (4): 295–312.
6. Sweller, J. 1988. Cognitive load during problem solving: Effects on learning. *Cognitive Science* **12** (2): 257–285.
7. Lang, A. 2000. The limited capacity model of mediated message processing. *Journal of Communication* **50**:46–70.
8. Potter, R. F., and P. Bolls. 2012. *Psychophysiological measurement and meaning: Cognitive and emotional processing of media*. Routledge.
9. Dvir, N., and R. Gafni 2018. *How content volume on landing pages influences consumer behavior*. arXiv preprint arXiv:1806.00923.
10. Richards, J. 2014. *Cognitive neuroscience of attention: A developmental perspective*. Routledge.
11. Corbetta, M., and G. L. Shulman. 2002. Control of goal-directed and stimulus-driven attention in the brain. *Nature Reviews Neuroscience* **3** (3): 201–215.
12. Fecteau, J., and D. Munoz. 2006. Salience, relevance, and firing: A priority map for target selection. *Trends in Cognitive Sciences* **10** (8): 382–390.
13. Miller, E. K., and J. D. Cohen. 2001. An integrative theory of prefrontal cortex function. *Annual Review of Neuroscience* **24** (1): 167–202.
14. MacDonald, A. W., et al. 2000. Dissociating the role of the dorsolateral prefrontal and anterior cingulate cortex in cognitive control. *Science* **288** (5472): 1835–1838.
15. Johnson, J. 2020. *Designing with the mind in mind: Simple guide to understanding user interface design guidelines*. Morgan Kaufmann.
16. Bolls, P. D., et al. 2019. Media psychophysiology and neuroscience: Bringing brain science into media processes and effects research. In *Media effects*, 195–210. Routledge.
17. Yaros, R., and A. Cook. 2013. Attention versus learning of online content: Preliminary findings from an eye-tracking study. In *Evolving psychological and*

*educational perspectives on cyber behavior*, ed. R. Z. Zheng, 132–154. Hershey, PA: IGI Global.
18. Bunzeck, N., & E. Düzel. 2006. Absolute coding of stimulus novelty in the human substantia nigra/VTA. *Neuron* **51** (3): 369–379. https://doi.org/10.1016/j.neuron.2006.06.021.
19. Wachler, B. B. 2022. *Influenced: The impact of social media on our perception*, 322. Rowman & Littlefield.
20. Sherman, L. E., et al. 2016. The power of the like in adolescence: Effects of peer influence on neural and behavioral responses to social media. *Psychological Science* **27** (7): 1027–1035.
21. Meshi, D., C. Morawetz, and H. R. Heekeren. 2013. Nucleus accumbens response to gains in reputation for the self relative to gains for others predicts social media use. *Frontiers in Human Neuroscience* 7:57063.
22. Kardaras, N. 2022. *Digital madness: How social media is driving our mental health crisis—And how to restore our sanity*. St. Martin's Press.
23. Gibson, J. J. 1979. The theory of affordances. In *The people, place, and space reader*, 56–60. Routledge.
24. Sundar, S. S. 2008. The MAIN model: A heuristic approach to understanding technology effects on credibility. In *Digital media, youth, and credibility*, ed. M. J. Metzger and A. J. Flanagin, 73–100. MIT Press.
25. Knobloch-Westerwick, S. 2014. *Choice and preference in media use: Advances in selective exposure theory and research*. Routledge.
26. Petersen, S. E., and M. I. Posner. 2012. The attention system of the human brain: 20 years after. *Annual Review of Neuroscience* **35** (1): 73–89.
27. Bucher, H.-J., & P. Schumacher. 2006. The relevance of attention for selecting news content. An eye-tracking study on attention patterns in the reception of print and online media. *Communications* **31** (3): 347–368. https://doi.org/10.1515/COMMUN.2006.022.
28. Levy, G., and R. Razin. 2019. Echo chambers and their effects on economic and political outcomes. *Annual Review of Economics* **11** (1): 303–328.
29. Zhu, J., et al. 2021. Influence maximization problem with echo chamber effect in social network. *IEEE Transactions on Computational Social Systems* **8** (5): 1163–1171.
30. Kanuri, V. K. 2024. *High color complexity in social media images proves more eye-catching, increases user engagement* [cited 2025 November 15, 2024]. https://news.nd.edu/news/high-color-complexity-in-social-media-images-proves-more-eye-catching-increases-user-engagement/.
31. Bustanur, B., K. Hafizi, and N. Yuhelman. 2022. Analysis of the filter bubble algorithm in the search for information on the internet. *Jurnal Teknologi dan Open Source* **5** (2): 136–141.
32. Bakshy, E., S. Messing, and L. A. Adamic. 2015. Exposure to ideologically diverse news and opinion on Facebook. *Science* **348** (6239): 1130–1132.

33. Pariser, E. 2011. *The filter bubble: What the Internet is hiding from you.* Penguin UK.
34. Lee, J. K., and E. Kim. 2017. Incidental exposure to news: Predictors in the social media setting and effects on information gain online. *Computers in Human Behavior* **75**:1008–1015.
35. Reber, A. S. 1989. Implicit learning and tacit knowledge. *Journal of Experimental Psychology: General* **118** (3): 219.
36. Thorson, K. 2020. Attracting the news: Algorithms, platforms, and reframing incidental exposure. *Journalism* **21** (8): 1067–1082.
37. Zajonc, R. B. 2001. Mere exposure: A gateway to the subliminal. *Current Directions in Psychological Science* **10** (6): 224–228. https://doi.org/10.1111/1467-8721.0015.
38. Fazio, L. K. 2020. Repetition increases perceived truth even for known falsehoods. *Collabra: Psychology* **6** (1): 38.
39. Itti, L., and C. Koch. 2001. Computational modelling of visual attention. *Nature Reviews Neuroscience* **2** (3): 194–203.
40. Sparrow, B., J. Liu, and D. M. Wegner. 2011. Google effects on memory: Cognitive consequences of having information at our fingertips. *Science* **333** (6043): 776–778.
41. Cleeremans, A., A. Destrebecqz, and M. Boyer. 1998. Implicit learning: News from the front. *Trends in Cognitive Sciences* **2** (10): 406–416.
42. Eslami, M., et al. 2015. "I always assumed that I wasn't really that close to [her]" reasoning about invisible algorithms in news feeds. In *Proceedings of the 33rd annual ACM conference on human factors in computing systems.*
43. Rader, E., and R. Gray. 2015. Understanding user beliefs about algorithmic curation in the Facebook news feed. In *Proceedings of the 33rd annual ACM conference on human factors in computing systems.*
44. Berger, J., and K. L. Milkman. 2012. What makes online content viral? *Journal of Marketing Research* **49** (2): 192–205.
45. Mitchell, A., et al. 2020. *Americans who mainly get their news on social media are less engaged, less knowledgeable*, 30. Pew Research Center.
46. Van der Linden, S., et al. 2017. Inoculating the public against misinformation about climate change. *Global Challenges* **1** (2): 1600008.
47. Mosleh, M., G. Pennycook, and D. G. Rand. 2020. Self-reported willingness to share political news articles in online surveys correlates with actual sharing on Twitter. *PLoS One* **15** (2): e0228882.
48. Garrett, R. K., and N. J. Stroud. 2014. Partisan paths to exposure diversity: Differences in pro-and counterattitudinal news consumption. *Journal of Communication* **64** (4): 680–701.
49. Ohme, J., and C. Mothes. 2023. News snacking and political learning: Changing opportunity structures of digital platform news use and political knowledge. *Journal of Information Technology & Politics* **22** (1): 1–15.

50. Choudhury, S., and K. A. McKinney. 2013. Digital media, the developing brain and the interpretive plasticity of neuroplasticity. *Transcultural Psychiatry* **50** (2): 192–215.
51. de Barros, E. C. 2024. Understanding the influence of digital technology on human cognitive functions: A narrative review. *IBRO Neuroscience Reports* 17:1–512.
52. Dunaway, J., et al. 2018. News attention in a mobile era. *Journal of Computer-Mediated Communication* **23** (2): 107–124.
53. Carr, N. 2010. *The shallows*, 278. New York: W.W. Norton & Company.
54. Drigas, A., and A. Sideraki. 2024. Brain neuroplasticity leveraging virtual reality and brain–computer interface technologies. *Sensors* **24** (17): 5725.
55. Office of the Surgeon General. 2023. Social media and youth mental health: The US Surgeon General's Advisory [Internet].
56. Rose, E. 2010. Continuous partial attention: Reconsidering the role of online learning in the age of interruption. *Educational Technology* **50** (4): 41–46.
57. Foerde, K., B. Knowlton, and R. Poldrack. 2006. Modulation of competing memory systems by distraction. *Proceedings of the National Academy of Sciences* **103** (31): 11778–11783.
58. Junco, R., and S. R. Cotten. 2012. No A 4 U: The relationship between multitasking and academic performance. *Computers & Education* **59** (2): 505–514.
59. Mark, G., D. Gudith, and U. Klocke. 2008. The cost of interrupted work: more speed and stress. In *Proceedings of the SIGCHI conference on Human Factors in Computing Systems.*
60. Newport, C. 2016. *Deep work: Rules for focused success in a distracted world.* Hachette UK.
61. Przybylski, A. K., and N. Weinstein. 2013. Can you connect with me now? How the presence of mobile communication technology influences face-to-face conversation quality. *Journal of Social and Personal Relationships* **30** (3): 237–246.
62. Alter, A. 2017. *Irresistible*, 354. New York: Penquin Random House, LLC.
63. Ducharme, J. 2023. *Why everyone's worried about their attention span—And how to improve yours* [cited 2023 August 13, 2023]. https://time.com/6302294/why-you-cant-focus-anymore-and-what-to-do-about-it/.
64. Newman, N., et al. 2022. *Digital news report 2022.* Reuters Institute for the Study of Journalism.
65. Kellerman, J. K., et al. 2022. The mental health impact of daily news exposure during the COVID-19 pandemic: Ecological momentary assessment study. *JMIR Mental Health* 9 (5): e36966.
66. Kondo, H., N. Osaka, and M. Osaka. 2004. Cooperation of the anterior cingulate cortex and dorsolateral prefrontal cortex for attention shifting. *Neuroimage* **23** (2): 670–679.

67. Newman, M. G., and S. J. Llera. 2011. A novel theory of experiential avoidance in generalized anxiety disorder: A review and synthesis of research supporting a contrast avoidance model of worry. *Clinical Psychology Review* **31** (3): 371–382.
68. Lang, A., J. E. Newhagen, and B. Reeves. 1996. Negative video as structure: Emotion, attention, capacity, and memory. *Journal of Broadcasting & Electronic Media* **40**:460–477.
69. Mast, J., R. Coesemans, and M. Temmerman. 2019. Constructive journalism: Concepts, practices, and discourses. *Journalism* **20** (4): 492–503.
70. Miller, G. A. 1956. The magical number seven, plus or minus two: Some limits on our capacity for processing information. *Psychological Review* **63**:81–97.
71. Cooper, A. 1999. *The inmates are running the asylum: Why high-tech products drive us crazy and how to restore the sanity*. Sams Publishing.

CHAPTER 5

# Social Media Uniquely Builds Attention

- Social media's reach differs from engagement.
- Novel content grabs users' attention.
- Algorithms shape how long users stay engaged.
- AI can increase engagement, but not always credibility.
- This leads to the introduction of a "digital DIET."

R. Yaros, *The Digital Engagement Model*, Palgrave Practical Guides in Communication,
https://doi.org/10.1007/978-3-032-03822-7_5

This chapter discusses the characteristics of social media, including unique algorithmic filtering, the viral sharing of social media posts, and the reasons why short videos are key to social media engagement. These extend beyond the best practices that content producers, including those in social media, are already familiar with. What may not be as familiar in social media formats is the concept of attention momentum, as defined by the digital engagement model. Understanding why users focus on social media content and its ability to retain. This also explains why a chapter on social media is presented before discussing in-depth explanations of how the digital engagement model.

## 5.1 Engagement Extends Beyond Shares and Likes

Let's start by setting out a vision for this chapter. First, this chapter doesn't review all the well-known benefits of social media for engagement. Instead, it examines why social media does not always represent ***meaningful*** engagement. Secondly, instead of detailing the prevalence of algorithms, this chapter focuses on what producers can or need to do to maximize engagement with AI.

We will examine how social media algorithms can affect engagement in the sections that follow. For that reason, we have reserved discussion of how algorithms can capture attention to those sections. There, you will find more information on how to deploy them to increase engagement with novel content while simultaneously limiting exposure to other content.

You may recall that Chapter four outlined how certain hard-wired cognitive processes can predict users' habitual behaviors and reactions to digital content. However, it is no secret that the delivery and consumption of short videos on mobile social media apps radically differ from those of longer-form storytelling on the web. Therefore, before we detail the key user and content variables of the digital engagement model in the next chapters, it is important that this chapter acknowledges the unique effects of social media and algorithms.

We already know that algorithms have transformed the ways individuals interact with digital information. One significant change has been to optimize content for the interactive metrics that track users' views, clicks, and time spent viewing specific content [1, 2].

This shift has emphasized metrics such as views, clicks, and viewing duration, not merely as passive indicators of popularity, but as inputs into ongoing algorithmic decision-making. While some scholars have noted that algorithmic systems influence user engagement by surfacing content aligned with past behavior patterns, these processes often occur without transparency, raising concerns about visibility, personalization, and bias [2].

In the context of digital platforms, algorithms also serve as invisible guides for user experiences. They curate personalized news, social media, and video recommendations into users' feeds. Moreover, certain ads are exposed to potential customers based on their previous online shopping habits. As these algorithms continue to grow in sophistication, the way they present certain content and the order in which content is presented to specific users will change. The benefits of this algorithmic personalization, however, must be balanced with trade-offs.

For example, **filter bubbles** emerge when users repeatedly engage with similar information, which limits their exposure to diverse perspectives [3]. This can lead to ideological polarization as users consume a limited range of sources [4]. In addition, algorithms that have been optimized for engagement can prioritize emotionally charged or misleading content, increasing the probability of that content being shared with like-minded contacts or provoking strong reactions [5].

**Algorithms** also raise ethical questions about transparency. Most platforms do not explain to users how their algorithms work or why certain content appears [6]. This can make it more difficult for users to discern whether digital engagement is self-directed or guided by computational outcomes. What is clear is that algorithms can't be neutral when they are designed to privilege certain content over other content [1].

> *If you're not paying for the product, you ARE the product.*
>
> *-Andrew Lewis*

Vast amounts of data are gathered from user activity on platforms that track each user's logins, page views, and clicks, all contributing to a digital footprint. However, platforms need to go further if they want to extract value from this data. Constructing these extensive databases of user behaviors necessitates intricate programming and data processing [7].

Despite concerns about bias or echo chamber effects, algorithms offer undeniable utility in managing the otherwise overwhelming information streams produced by users' digital engagement. They can assist users by filtering and then presenting content that's more likely to appeal to them directly. In this way, algorithms can enhance discovery, support learning, and ultimately improve the overall digital experience. The challenge lies in aligning them with the human values of fairness, diversity, and emotion.

Leaving aside the variables of the Digital Engagement Model for now, social media and its personalized algorithms are tailored to past user behaviors. The benefit is more efficient delivery of interesting content to the user, but how does it work? To use an everyday example, a recipe for baking a cake provides you with a list of ingredients, plus step-by-step instructions on what to do with those ingredients and in what order. In the digital world, computer code for algorithms instantly accesses prior user data (ingredients) and then executes the necessary steps (instructions) to process and output specific content (the cake) to the user (Fig. 5.1).

Understanding how algorithms structure a user's content and the extent to which they deliver selected content is therefore critical to producers. Users who open their Instagram or TikTok app do not see a random collection of posts because an algorithm has already selected and organized the content. Future visits reflect what the algorithm has learned, and content will prioritize posts or ads that align with their interests.

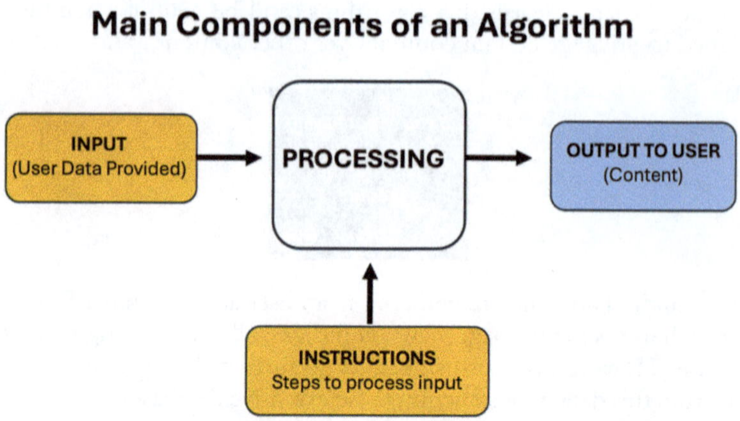


**Fig. 5.1** Main components of an algorithm. Credit: Digital Engagement Lab

Not all algorithms function in the same way. Some are simple instructions, such as showing a user's posts in reverse chronological order. Others are complex, using artificial intelligence not only to track and learn a user's online behaviors, but also to predict what would appeal most to that user in the future.

Some worry that the use of algorithms can lead to what some refer to as "agency hacking." In other words, algorithms make curated information so appealing that it is nearly impossible for the user to ignore, assuming they have the time to consume it. In response, scholars have offered a framework for assessing the content that algorithms provide and strategies to avoid agency hacking [8]. But a paradox emerges. While algorithms can overwhelm users by continually surfacing irresistibly tailored content, content creators often struggle to get their material included in that curation. So, in practice, the challenge lies not only in resisting the influence of algorithmic design but also in ensuring that meaningful content reaches its intended audience.

While algorithms may seem unpredictable, there are strategic approaches producers can adopt. The most effective approach is to align content with the core principles guiding algorithmic prioritization and to adapt planning based on user behavior. Most algorithms favor content that maximizes relevance, engagement, and retention. As a result, material that is compelling, clearly structured, and contextualized for the platform is more likely to be surfaced and promoted.

Successful content typically captures attention quickly. To illustrate this point, the algorithms of TikTok, Instagram Reels, or YouTube Shorts are designed to detect early indicators of engagement, including whether a user watches for more than the first few seconds. This suggests that digital content should begin with a visual or, at the very least, a surprising fact, question, or visually dynamic element that evokes curiosity. As detailed later, however, that does NOT mean posting clickbait that assumes all users have the time and desire to pursue more information. Most users tend to focus on emotional content, especially if it provokes laughter or controversy. We know this because it performs better in line with the algorithmic preference for shareable content [9]. Structuring a post to create a narrative payoff at the end also increases watch time, another key factor measured by algorithms [10].

On platforms such as Facebook or Instagram, posts with clear visuals, readable text, and informative captions will support accessibility and increase "dwell time" (the pause when a user views content of interest).

Both have been shown to influence algorithmic favorability because algorithms reward behavior that signals value. Additionally, content that invites users to share their thoughts can foster meaningful engagement, which platforms interpret as the signal to distribute that content widely. Ultimately, success is less about outsmarting the algorithm and more about creating content that aligns with the psychological and behavioral patterns that algorithms recognize and reward.

Does the curated content really align with every user's interests? One study, for example, explored the sociological implications of algorithms by identifying six dimensions of public relevance related to political content [2]. The dimensions included patterns of inclusion, cycles of anticipation, evaluation of relevance, promise of algorithmic objectivity, entanglement with practice, and the production of calculated publics. The results provided important insights into how algorithms can shape public discourse and interactivity, implying that algorithms help us to understand what there is to know, participate in social discourse, and familiarize us with the publics in which we engage.

## 5.2 Interactivity Is Only One Dimension of Engagement

There is a common misconception that social media likes and shares reflect the same level of engagement as actually consuming and understanding the full message or story. Meaningful cognitive engagement—crucial to both producers and advertisers—requires time and lasting impressions, not the split-second it takes to click a button. A click does not always equal consumption.

Another important distinction to make is between reach, interactivity, and engagement. The number of followers on a social media account represents the *potential* reach of content. But the *actual* reach also depends on the viewing duration. The number of likes or shares after a user takes a second to click represents **interactivity**. At the same time, interactivity does not always equal meaningful engagement. A "like" requires only a tap, and a share can be motivated by the appeal of only a headline. Researchers found that while social influence suggests that "likes" for a headline or title tend to attract additional likes, they do not significantly increase the number of users who continue viewing or reading the subsequent content [11].

To illustrate why the *potential reach* of social media content does not translate to all users consuming it, imagine walking into a large grocery store. Of course, just entering the store does not mean you will notice every item before you depart. In the limited time you have, you will notice only a fraction of the selections available to you. Perhaps you specifically sought an item on your shopping list or were incidentally exposed to an item placed at the end of an aisle. All the other products had the *potential* to be noticed by you but were not. Similarly, content posted online has the *potential* to reach all followers of an account, but that doesn't mean all content will be noticed, clicked, read, or watched by all the followers.

One might also assume that all 100,000 followers of a social media influencer will see, read, or view all of the influencer's posts. The combination of algorithmic selection and the behaviors of users located in different environments on various devices with varying engagement times is a significant barrier to meaningful engagement with all content by all followers. Each influencer's post is evaluated by a combination of algorithms on a platform that tracks the quantity of views, likes, comments, and shares. The algorithms then determine the potential reach of the content in users' feeds [12].

This also explains how Instagram's multiple algorithms assess the relationship between users, content, and engagement history to personalize feeds [13]. Based on this, an influencer's posts will reach only some of their followers. Some users will have the time and interest to consume all of the posts, but a larger population will scroll past them unless they instantly generate situational interest. Instagram and Facebook deploy algorithms that present content to a portion of an individual's followers, unless that content gains quick traction. On X (FKA Twitter), where feeds are presented chronologically, the sheer volume of content means many posts will be missed.

These processes are important to understand when conducting research, since the same assumptions must be applied to achieve reliable results. Assuming all of the content "scraped" from a social network has widespread influence based on the number of followers or likes and shares alone ignores the important distinction between the *potential* reach of content and its *actual* reach, which may or may not be consumed long enough for any effects on users. We'll look next at why the number of likes and shares on content does not always correlate with engagement with that content.

## 5.3 Headlines Are Often Shared Without Consuming Their Message

A large-scale analysis of more than 35 million public Facebook posts between 2017 and 2020 found that approximately 75% of the news links shared occurred without users first reading the content [14]. The researchers attributed the virality of political content, including misinformation, as the driver of what they call the "superficial processing" of headlines or blurbs before they are shared, rather than engaging with the facts. The researchers also noted the implications of the findings for the design and discourse in digital content.

Other studies support the existence of this rapid sharing behavior. Ward et al. [15] found that sharing on social media can lead users to believe they are as knowledgeable as their posts suggest. In a series of six studies, the researchers demonstrated correlational and causal links between sharing and inflated self-perceptions of knowledge. Specifically, many users shared articles without reading them, allowing researchers to isolate the act of sharing from the consumption of content. Their findings revealed that merely sharing content, even if it is unread, can lead some users to feel more informed about a topic than they genuinely are. This effect is driven by a psychological process in which people internalize the expert identity signaled by public sharing, blurring the line between appearing informed and being informed.

It's a similar story for video content. Videos posted to YouTube and Facebook may count as "viewed" after just a few seconds. That means producers cannot conclude that all viewers who clicked the video were deeply engaged with it. Even if most or all of the video was played, there is no guarantee that the viewer was 100% attentive without interruptions while the video played, especially for long videos that span several minutes. Metrics from the site *Wistia* indicate that the average consumption rate of social media videos one minute or less in duration is 45%. It drops to 43% for 1–3 minute videos, increases to 44% for 3–5 minutes, then decreases to 32% for videos lasting 5 and 30 minutes [16].

## 5.4 Unexpected Content Can Instantly Engage Users

We know that unexpected or novel content on social media posts can go viral and break through the content clutter. Unexpected content can interrupt a user's routine scrolling when it sparks curiosity. Curiosity of novel content can be a key driver of attention that interrupts expected flows of content, despite algorithms' ability to generate an impressive number of users quickly. With hours of video being uploaded to YouTube every second, the platform's recommendation algorithms must be responsive enough to balance newly uploaded video with users' most recent interactions.

This helps explain why the Digital Engagement Model emphasizes the impact of unexpected or novel content from previously unfollowed sources. Even before the first website was published, psychological literature positioned curiosity as a cognitive driver that motivates individuals to explore unfamiliar content or resolve uncertainty [17]. A user's natural inclination to seek novel and unexpected information is an important mechanism in the engagement process. Given overwhelming amounts of digital information, algorithmic content curation, and social media, continued curiosity following initial exposure has become central to meaningful engagement.

Social media content can spark curiosity when the information is ambiguous, headlines provide limited information, thumbnails provoke surprise, or posts create a gap between what users know and what they want to know [18]. The effectiveness of these strategies illustrates how and why social media stimulates so much curiosity and attention, often applying carefully engineered information gaps that draw some users deeper into content streams. Instagram, TikTok, and Facebook all capitalize on this by algorithmically amplifying content that elicits emotions and leverages curiosity to boost engagement. The intended effect, of course, is to prolong session times and reinforce return visits.

To model such mechanisms, scholars and engineers have turned to computational methods to simulate curiosity-driven behaviors in artificial agents. This work draws on psychological theories to design algorithms that mimic human responses to novelty, uncertainty, and learning [19, 20]. Here, curiosity is operationalized to help artificial agents detect and adapt to new inputs, make aesthetically relevant decisions, and guide functions that mirror human behavior.

Building on this foundation, some have developed various forms of computational curiosity to equip artificial agents with human-like capabilities, such as detecting and adapting to novel stimuli, making aesthetically guided decisions, and supporting pedagogical goals. For example, Wu and Miao [21] proposed a two-step psychological framework for modeling curiosity computationally. Detecting novelty or uncertainty is the first step, followed by responding to it based on internal goals or constraints. This structure applies psychological theory to analyze curiosity and test diverse computational approaches. By aligning algorithmic design with cognitive principles, these models can not only inform human-computer interaction but also support the development of more adaptive and cognitively realistic artificial agents.

This dual-process model can also be valuable for interpreting how users interact with novel content on social media, where algorithmic personalization must strike a balance between reinforcing known preferences and introducing novel stimuli that spark curiosity and sustain engagement. Wu and Miao [21] identified four research challenges in the development of computational curiosity. They are (1) defining and modeling curiosity computationally, (2) identifying appropriate stimuli for eliciting curiosity, (3) managing curiosity-driven behavior in artificial agents, and (4) evaluating the effectiveness of such systems. Addressing these challenges assists in the design of algorithms that simulate curiosity in ways that align with patterns in human cognition. The researchers also outlined ten applications, ranging from education and entertainment to decision support systems that aid human judgment, and where computational curiosity could have a significant impact.

This intersection of psychological theories, user curiosity, and computational modeling represents a robust framework for understanding how users interact with novel content. However, strategies are still evolving that could leverage computational curiosity to maximize users' attention in ways that support more meaningful engagement and educational psychology.

One of the applicable psychological theories is the Information-Gap Theory, which posits that curiosity arises when individuals perceive a gap between what they know and what they want to know [17, 22]. This perceived gap can create psychological discomfort that motivates a user to seek information that closes the gap. This framework has been adopted across disciplines to explain and enhance user engagement in digital environments, education, journalism, and marketing.

In the production of digital content, the theory supports strategies such as headline framing, selective disclosure, and "teaser" content, which intentionally reveal just enough information to highlight what the user doesn't yet know, activating their curiosity and increasing engagement. Studies show that headlines prompting questions or implying missing knowledge (e.g., "You won't believe what happened next") can increase interaction for some but not all users. The ethical use of such tactics has been debated [23].

In instructional design, the Information-Gap Theory informs the sequencing of content to expose knowledge gaps that stimulate curiosity-driven learning. Adaptive learning systems leverage this approach by adjusting content difficulty to maintain learners in a state of optimal uncertainty, neither too familiar to be boring nor too novel to be confusing [18]. By synthesizing psychological theories with computational approaches, the authors demonstrate the value of harnessing curiosity as a driving force for exploration and creativity in both humans and artificial systems. By understanding how perceived knowledge gaps can stimulate interest and motivate information-seeking behavior, content producers can design materials that intentionally provoke curiosity. This extends into our analysis of social media, as we consider how the concept of curiosity also applies to videos [24].

## 5.5 Short Videos Fuel Attention Momentum

Beyond its motivational role, curiosity can serve as a mechanism that helps prioritize attention in video environments overloaded with information, such as social media. In this context, curiosity can also serve as a cognitive filter, guiding users to content that promises to resolve uncertainty or offer novel insights. Understanding how curiosity also operates in video is essential for explaining patterns of user engagement and for designing content that sustains interest, defined by our model as attention momentum, over time.

On its twentieth anniversary in 2025, YouTube was the most widely used online platform in the United States. About 85% of US adults reported using YouTube, surpassing Facebook (70%) and Instagram (50%) [25]. YouTube's popularity is concentrated among younger users, with nine in ten US teens aged 13 to 17 saying they use YouTube and 73% claiming to visit YouTube daily (73%). YouTube's immense library of user-generated videos and the network's availability in more than 100 countries, with support in more than 80 languages, make YouTube the premier video platform for diverse populations.

For news alone, the Pew Research Center reported that about a third of US adults regularly obtain their news from YouTube, up from 23% in 2020 [25]. This skew is particularly pronounced among men who consume news, with 57% considering YouTube their regular news source, compared to 42% of women. The tenets of credibility and balanced reporting do not seem to be the main concerns for 24% of YouTube users who say they regularly obtain news from influencers.

The platform's continuous evolution and features that enhance the user experience have played a significant role during its 20 years of growth. Additional features, such as YouTube Shorts, have outcompeted other short-form video platforms, highlighting YouTube's adaptability to changing user needs and behaviors. That is one example in support of new models proposing changes in content that is presented in response to changes in audience preferences. Beyond a comprehensive suite of video tools, YouTube offers performance and audience behavior analytics, as well as monetization opportunities. YouTube also utilizes discovery algorithms to assist users in finding content tailored to their interests.

Similar to other social networks, YouTube's algorithm analyzes the number of likes, shares, viewing time, and comments to personalize videos that increase their relevance. This ecosystem of creation, discovery, and personalization helped to position YouTube as a popular hub in the media landscape.

Regardless of a video's topic, the first three seconds are critical for capturing and retaining attention. Several explanations have been proposed for why the first seconds are most important [26]. For example, starting with dramatic visuals, music, animation, and promises of valuable information can reduce disengagement. This suggests that users who remain engaged during the initial seconds of a video are more likely to continue watching. A pattern of sustained viewership signals to YouTube's algorithm that the video is valuable, thereby increasing its promotion [27, 28].

The average daily time spent viewing YouTube is an important metric to track. Americans spend an average of about 48 minutes per day viewing videos. For mobile US users alone, the average increases to 52 minutes [29]. To account for variations in video length, engagement is measured using the average duration as a proportion of the video's total length. Short-form videos sustain attention through seamless user interfaces that encourage attention. Videos shorter than five minutes have an average viewing duration of between 50% and 70% of the total video. For longer videos, most consider a viewing duration of 40% to 60% of the content to be successful. This raises a key question. How many users complete the longer videos they start watching?

Despite the relatively low proportion of consumers who finish watching full videos online, the demand for video has made it a fast-growing market. However, creating high-quality videos takes time, energy, resources, and skill, leading some to leverage the assistance of artificial intelligence for video production. Conversational AI tools can transform the passive consumption of information into real-time interactivity, offering personalized videos that mimic human conversation. But there are two dimensions to this technology.

## 5.6 AI Can Increase Engagement, but Not Credibility

The relationship between artificial intelligence and digital communication began with the emergence of the World Wide Web in the 1990s. That led to the evolution of digital journalism and social media [30]. By the early twenty-first century, machine learning and natural language processing were helping AI to curate digital news feeds and personalize user experiences [2]. Facebook and YouTube accelerated that personalization as algorithms shaped what users saw. The effect was to moderate public discourse, with users primarily exposed to information and perspectives with which they agreed [3]. Despite some objections, public opinion toward AI has softened, and its techniques have become widely accepted, especially when used in conjunction with video.

For example, a large-scale field experiment tested the impact of AI-generated video titles on a platform in Asia, involving nearly one million users. The results showed that videos using AI-generated titles received slightly more engagement. Specifically, a 1.6% increase in valid views and a 0.9% increase in total watch time suggested that AI helped better align content with user interests [31]. By the end of the experiment, the number of videos using AI-generated titles had grown by 41%, indicating that more content creators adopted the tool over time.

An earlier study investigated the impact of AI-generated voices on viewer engagement in human-produced videos. Researchers used audio and video analysis algorithms to detect the presence of AI voices in nearly 429,000 TikTok videos created by over 4000 users [32].

They found that while AI voices made it easier for creators to produce a higher volume of shorter videos, these videos typically received less user engagement. This suggests a trade-off. AI voices may boost production efficiency, but at the cost of reduced audience interaction. Further research will be necessary as AI technology continues to advance, but these effects have already been translated into practical applications in marketing campaigns.

Another study examined whether AI-generated content could enhance social media interactions, including likes, shares, and comments, compared to user-generated content [33]. Results suggest that while AI-generated content can enhance engagement metrics such as likes, shares, and comments, it also presents challenges related to authenticity and brand voice. The authors suggest that integrating AI-generated content with user-generated content could leverage the strengths of both approaches, combining the efficiency of AI with the authenticity of user contributions. This aligns with other empirical studies in advertising, social media, and digital marketing, which consistently show that AI-generated content can enhance engagement by improving personalization and optimizing content delivery.

A qualitative study interviewed marketers and creative directors to explore the differences in consumer engagement between human- and AI-generated ads [34]. Perhaps counterintuitively, the results suggest that AI-generated ads were more effective than human-generated content in terms of consumer engagement and increased purchasing, likely due to the creativity in the AI-generated ads. Others employed multiple studies to investigate the impact of disclosing AI use in ads on consumer attitudes. While an initial disclosure of AI-generated content led to unfavorable attitudes toward ads [35], the research also found that participants who perceived AI as more human-like than machine-like were less negative about a subsequent AI disclosure.

In journalism, a Cornell study asked nearly 600 participants to evaluate the credibility, readability, and expertise of news either written by journalists, revised by AI, or entirely written by AI. Interestingly, all the articles were perceived to be of equal quality [36]. But when participants who read the AI news were informed about AI's role, they were more willing to continue reading the articles, but were not more willing to read more AI-generated news in the future. The researchers concluded that any aversion to AI use in news media may not be influenced by a perceived lack of quality but by factors such as trust or transparency. At the same time, disclosing the use of AI could increase short-term engagement with stories.

A similar 2025 study investigated how readers' awareness of AI versus human authorship affected their engagement with news [37]. Participants were told whether the content was AI-generated or human-written before evaluating the articles. The findings revealed that AI-generated news received lower ratings of perceived liking compared to human-written news after participants were informed that AI generated the content. This effect was mediated by the article's perceived credibility, not its perceived authenticity. Unlike previous research suggesting that disclosing AI authorship could increase short-term engagement, this study found that such disclosure had the potential to reduce perceived credibility and result in lower engagement. However, the negative impact was mitigated when the AI-generated content appeared human-like, indicating that the design and presentation of AI content can influence reader response. These insights underscore the importance of transparency and content design in the use of AI-generated news, suggesting that while disclosure is crucial, the way AI content is crafted and presented plays a significant role in audience engagement.

This research in the rapidly evolving world of AI and its uses in news, social media, and advertising uncovered that some emerging user responses and behaviors are increasingly predictable. Whether a user is exposed to content fed by algorithms, sparked by surprising content, or driven by the attention momentum of short videos on social media, algorithms and AI are demonstrating that human behaviors and preferences can be predictable. It's not that human creators are not preferable, but algorithms and AI tools can do it much faster.

Predictable user responses could guide the evolution of a new model for structuring digital content that can better serve the needs of diverse user populations. In the next chapter, we detail the model's new "digital DIET" of variables that explain how and why different types of users share similarities even though they may have different needs from content. Producers can expand their traditional skills for producing content that serves audiences not imagined when printed newspapers were at their peak. The model's goal is to attract, retain, and educate the largest possible population with unique strategies that social media, algorithms, and AI alone cannot easily replicate.

## References


1. Bucher, T. 2018. *If... then: Algorithmic power and politics.* Oxford University Press.
2. Gillespie, T. 2014. The relevance of algorithms. In *Media technologies: Essays on communication, materiality, and society*, 167. Cambridge, Massachusetts: MIT Press.
3. Pariser, E. 2011. *The filter bubble: How the new personalized web is changing what we read and how we think.* Penguin.
4. Spohr, D. 2017. Fake news and ideological polarization: Filter bubbles and selective exposure on social media. *Business Information Review* **34** (3): 150–160.
5. Vosoughi, S., D. Roy, and S. Aral. 2018. The spread of true and false news online. *Science* **359** (6380): 1146–1151.
6. Tsamados, A., et al. 2021. The ethics of algorithms: Key problems and solutions. In *Ethics, governance, and policies in artificial intelligence*, 97–123.
7. Stalder, F., & C. Mayer. 2012. *The second index search engines, personalization and surveillance.* Routledge.
8. Lazer, D., B. Swire-Thompson, and C. Wilson. 2024. A normative framework for assessing the information curation algorithms of the Internet. *Perspectives on Psychological Science* **19** (5): 749–757.
9. Cingi, C. C., N. Bayar Muluk, and C. Cingi. 2023. Harnessing the power of visuals and positive presenting. In *Improving online presentations: A guide for healthcare professionals*, 167–176. Springer.
10. RealSubscribers. 2025. How to increase your watch-time on YouTube videos. https://www.realsubscribers.com/blogs/youtube-watch-time.html.
11. Huang, S., and S. Lin. 2024. Do more "likes" lead to more clicks? Evidence from a field experiment on social advertising. *Journal of Marketing*. https://doi.org/10.1177/00222429241307608.
12. Lauron, S. 2025. *2025 Facebook algorithm: Tips and expert secrets to succeed* [cited 2025 March 3, 2025]. https://blog.hootsuite.com/facebook-algorithm/.
13. Gagliardi, A. 2025. *How the Instagram algorithm works in 2025 (and how to make it work for you).* February 27, 2025 [cited 2025 March 5, 2027]. https://later.com/blog/how-instagram-algorithm-works/.
14. Sundar, S. S., E. C. Snyder, M. Liao, J. Yin, J. Wang, and G. Chi. 2025. Sharing without clicking on news in social media. *Nature Human Behaviour* **9** (1): 156–168.
15. Ward, A. F., J. Zheng, and S. M. Broniarczyk. 2023. I share, therefore I know? Sharing online content-even without reading it-inflates subjective knowledge. *Journal of Consumer Psychology* **33** (3): 469–488. https://doi.org/10.1002/jcpy.1321.

16. Wistia. 2025. *2025 State of video report* [cited 2025]. https://wistia.com/for/thanks-state-of-video?submissionGuid=6bf2fedd-ea48-42c7-89c1-eedb4cd712c6.
17. Loewenstein, G. 1994. The psychology of curiosity: A review and reinterpretation. *Psychological Bulletin* **116** (1): 75–98.
18. Kang, M. J., et al. 2009. The wick in the candle of learning: Epistemic curiosity activates reward circuitry and enhances memory. *Psychological Science* **20** (8): 963–973.
19. Oudeyer, P. Y. 2018. *Computational theories of curiosity-driven learning*. arXiv preprint arXiv:1802.10546.
20. Oudeyer, P. Y. 2018. Computational theories of curiosity-driven learning. In *The new science of curiosity*, ed. G. Gordon. Nova Science Publishers.
21. Wu, Q., and C. Miao. 2013. Curiosity: From psychology to computation. *ACM Computing Surveys (CSUR)* **46** (2): 1–26.
22. Loewenstein, G., and Z. Wojtowicz 2023. *The economics of attention*. Available at SSRN 4368304.
23. Blom, J. N., and K. R. Hansen. 2015. Click bait: Forward-reference as lure in online news headlines. *Journal of Pragmatics* **76**:87–100.
24. Hsiung, A., et al. 2023. Curiosity evolves as information unfolds. *Proceedings of the National Academy of Sciences* **120** (43): e2301974120.
25. Dannebaum, C. 2025. 5 Facts about Americans and YouTube.
26. Vyrill. 2023. *The importance of the first 3 seconds in your video* [November 3, 2024]. https://www.vyrill.com/blog/the-importance-of-the-first-3-seconds-in-your-video.
27. Wu, S., M.-A. Rizoiu, and L. Xie. 2018. Beyond views: Measuring and predicting engagement in online videos. In *Proceedings of the international AAAI conference on web and social media*.
28. Park, M., M. Naaman, and J. Berger. 2016. A data-driven study of view duration on YouTube. In *Proceedings of the international AAAI conference on web and social media*.
29. Jowarth, J. 2025. Worldwide daily social media usage.
30. Castells, M. 2002. *The Internet galaxy: Reflections on the Internet, business, and society*. Oxford University Press.
31. Zhang, X., et al. 2024. *The value of AI-generated metadata for UGC platforms: Evidence from a large-scale field experiment*. arXiv preprint arXiv:2412.18337.
32. Zhang, X. 2023. *How does AI-generated voice affect online video creation?: Evidence from TikTok*. University of British Columbia.
33. Shantatula, S., Z. Lei, and J. Wiredu. 2024. The effect of artificial intelligence generated content and user generated content on. *International Journal of Development Research* **14**:65318–65321.
34. Ratta, A. A., S. Muneer, and H. ul Hassan. 2024. The impact of AI generated advertising content on consumer buying behavior and consumer engagement. *Bulletin of Business and Economics (BBE)* **13** (2): 1152–1157.

35. Baek, T. H., J. Kim, and J. H. Kim. 2024. Effect of disclosing AI-generated content on prosocial advertising evaluation. *International Journal of Advertising*, 1–22.
36. Fabrizio, G., et al. 2025. Willingness to read AI-generated news is not driven by their perceived quality.
37. Lee, D. C., J. Jhang, and T. H. Baek. 2025. AI-generated news content: The impact of AI writer identity and perceived AI human-likeness. *International Journal of Human-Computer Interaction:* 1–13. https://doi.org/10.1080/10447318.2025.2477739

CHAPTER 6

# All Users Have a "Digital DIET"

- Users bring similarities to content, not only "individual differences."
- Demographics are associated with preferences.
- Interests that are long term dictate specific information seeking.
- Environment, both physical and technological, affects engagement.
- Time that a user has to engage, regardless of interest, is often overlooked.





R. Yaros, *The Digital Engagement Model*, Palgrave Practical Guides in Communication,
https://doi.org/10.1007/978-3-032-03822-7_6

## 6.1 There's a Time and Place for a Target Audience

With digital technology deeply embedded in our daily lives, individual differences are evident in how people use, interpret, and engage with online content. The digital environment amplifies individual differences, representing more diverse patterns of information-seeking, social interaction, and media consumption.

This chapter contrasts individual differences with the four user variables in the digital engagement model's "digital DIET," namely, demographics, interests, environment, and time. These four variables provide an expanded framework for producers wishing to broaden the appeal of their content beyond their target audience. This means appealing to other users who share group. Specific information and products will still be addressed to a select audience only, but in a media ecosystem dominated by algorithmic delivery and incidental exposure to content via social sharing, defining a target audience only limits the content's potential reach. If the goal is to reach the maximum number of users, content can be designed with other variables in mind to address the differing needs and behaviors of larger and more diverse user populations. Therefore, producing content that can appeal to users beyond the target audience expands its potential reach and impact.

## 6.2 Add Individual Similarities to Individual Differences

The Digital Engagement Model (DEM) posits that a shared interest in content is not the only defining attribute of a *target audience*. While the model acknowledges that individual differences always play a role in how users seek and process content, it introduces a new set of variables that all digital users share, regardless of the content they pursue or encounter. The model's four *Digital DIET* variables represent four shared user variables. It follows that if we attend to these four variables when producing content, we can increase the likelihood that more of our content will appeal to a broader audience.

The concept of individual differences has been central to social science research for over a century. Francis Galton (1822–1911), a pioneer in statistics and a cousin of Charles Darwin, used the term "individual differences" to refer to a wide range of cognitive, emotional, social, and biological traits, explaining why individuals respond differently to the same experience [1]. Galton's early work with large datasets laid the foundation for psychometrics, and over time, the field evolved to include studies of intelligence and personality [2, 3].

Specifically, individual differences mean that no two people experience, interpret, or interact with the world in the same way. These differences are shaped by a mix of biological, psychological, and social factors, including genetics, education, culture, personal experiences, and age [4].

In the digital era, individual differences can shape how users interact with technology and engage with media. It's obvious that different users will have distinct cognitive styles and behaviors. Some may only typically skim headlines, for example, while others focus on visuals or delve into the details. However, early research in psychology suggested that individual differences can be accounted for, to some extent, by the way that content is presented [5–7]. More recent research has demonstrated how content that is designed to support multiple modalities can cater to specific user preferences and behaviors [8–11].

There is a growing tension between the varying responses of users to content and the variables that can predict when, how, and why media is processed. In response, the Differential Susceptibility to Media Effects Model (DSMM) attempts to explain how users vary in their responses to media [12]. The model identifies three moderators of media effects:

- *Dispositional* (e.g., personality, mood)
- *Developmental* (e.g., age-related cognitive capacity)
- *Social* (e.g., culture, peers)

Dispositional dimensions, such as gender, personality, attitudes, beliefs, motivations, and moods, predispose users' selections of and responses to media. The authors note, however, that dimensions such as personality and temperament are more stable across time than mood and motivations [13]. Stable personality traits can change in response to the environment [14], while moods can last for only hours or days, reflecting cognitive and affective traits.

The DSMM suggests that developmental effects depend on a user's age and stage of cognitive development. For example, children may lack the cognitive tools to critically interpret advertising, while adolescents are more sensitive to social comparisons on social media such as Instagram or TikTok. Social susceptibility refers to the way cultural norms, peer influence, and family dynamics combine to shape users' responses to media. This means, for example, that two users may interpret the same video differently. At the same time, the digital environment, with its unlimited availability of information on demand, has revealed some predictable user needs that also depend on users' interests, physical and technological environments, and the time users have to consume information. Often overlooked by producers are these traits that influence the content selected, the duration of its consumption, and the effects of consuming it.

By accounting for the real-time emotional or physiological reactions that mediate media experiences, the DSMM's strength lies in noting that media effects are not entirely content-driven. They are also shaped by the user's identity and their developmental and social status. While it's true that the model emphasizes variations between individuals, in this chapter, we will argue that digital content itself can level the playing field across larger populations. Regardless of a user's personality or developmental stage, digital platforms clearly create shared environmental conditions that shape the needs and behaviors of all users. For example, briefly checking a smartphone for travel or weather details is essentially the same process regardless of who is doing it. Other influences include how content is presented and the device used to access it, but the finite amount of time that all users have to pursue content cannot be ignored.

While the long-term effects of content may differ between individuals, users' initial reactions to content that grabs their attention, as well as what is scanned or skipped, can be the result of how that content is presented. The structure and context of that content also have a bearing on this early stage of attention, not just the user's traits. Otherwise, the popular social media features of sharing and liking content would fail to motivate other users to interact with it [15–18]. Recognizing the other shared freedoms or constraints that shape user behavior can therefore yield more effective content that appeals to a broader user base.

In a fast-paced, feed-driven digital world, the DEM posits that there are variables that all users share. We advocate adding them to the lists of broader individual differences because shared variables can influence the behaviors of user populations as they seek and select specific content. This can in itself lead to the formation of everyday user needs and predictable user behaviors based on those needs, all of which reflect deep-rooted cognitive and behavioral traits.

All users' attention, memory, and decision-making are constrained by the pressures of limited time. These pressures lead users to take shortcuts when scanning headlines, favoring bold visuals, and reacting to emotionally charged content. Regardless of individual differences, mobile users with limited time will tend to engage in fast-paced, surface-level processing of content.

Table 6.1 summarizes some variables that can shape how users process digital content, and which are separate from the standard collection of "individual differences." These variables shape when and how users engage with content, not based on who they are, but on the combination of their needs and the way that content is structured.

These variables are especially evident in social media feeds, video platforms, or mobile apps. It can take only seconds for a user to scan content that took hours for producers to prepare. Whether a user is an extroverted teen or an introverted adult, both can navigate the same interface and face the same constraints, level of distraction, and design logic.

**Table 6.1** Universal variables that influence all users

| *Variable* | *Description* |
|---|---|
| Cognitive load | Users process so much at once; simpler, clearer content is favored |
| Time constraints | Limited time pushes users into fast, surface-level processing [5] |
| Device and format | Mobile screens restrict field of view, encouraging scanning over reading |
| Feed-based browsing | Content is encountered passively, not sought out intentionally |
| Platform norms | Platforms teach users expectations and behaviors (e.g., swiping, skipping) |
| Attention momentum | Content that continues to generate curiosity after the first second or click is more likely to sustain attention. |

## 6.3 Bridging Individual Differences with User Similarities

Despite some of the differences established above, the Differential Susceptibility to Media Effects Model and the digital DIET variables of the Digital Engagement Model are not in conflict. They describe different parts of the same media experiences. The Media Effects Model explains how content affects people differently in the long term, while the Digital DIET variables demonstrate that content can appeal to a broader audience and satisfy their needs, even those outside its stated target. For content creators, educators, and media researchers, this means addressing both the individual differences and shared user variables that influence attention. A robust engagement model must address both. Digital users exhibit individual differences, yet they also share surprisingly similar needs and behaviors.

Any notion of shared user similarities inevitably has significant implications for how content can and should be designed to appeal to a broader audience. Although individual differences exist, some also become flexible within a digital environment. Under certain conditions, such as limited time, mobile interfaces, or the algorithm-driven feeds users are served, those users may process content in more similar ways than one would expect. Instead of assuming that only individual differences can determine a certain proportion of engagement, content can be designed to address shared user traits. It is these commonalities that can produce predictable moments when users, regardless of their individual differences, share specific needs from and perceptions of content. This can include the ways that text is read, photos are viewed, and videos are scrolled. Individual differences never disappear, but the digital environment can transform some of them into recognizable similarities.

Take, for example, personality traits. Research suggests that extroverts are more likely to engage actively with social media, post content online, and interact with others, while introverts are more likely to consume information than participate [19]. Users with analytical cognitive styles tend to prefer long-form articles, academic papers, and detailed content. In contrast, users with experiential cognitive styles tend to engage more with videos, social media snippets, and visually stimulating content [20]. Moreover, cultural background influences social media usage, privacy preferences, and trust in online sources. Users from collectivist cultures have been found to engage more in group-based online discussions, while users from individualistic cultures may prioritize personalized content and independent exploration [21].

Nevertheless, some universal similarities that all users bring to any digital content are often overlooked during the production process. Although digital engagement can often be deeply personal, the Digital Engagement Model acknowledges that patterns exist, enabling researchers and producers to assume some universality in digital experiences. Identifying the variables shared by large populations of users provides insights into how the fixed aspects of digital technology can shape human interaction. These variables are crucial for creating more engaging and effective content for the largest possible audience, not just a target audience with an inherent interest in the given content.

## 6.4 Defined Motivations Stem from Individual Similarities

The variables in the users' "Digital DIET" include their demographics, personal (long-term) interests, their current physical and technological environments, and the time they have available to consume content. All of these factors contribute to a user's motivation, whether to search for specific information or casually scroll through engaging yet unexpected social media content. Individual differences notwithstanding, the digital engagement model proposes that users engage with content for four primary reasons:

1. Problem-Solving. Users seek information to address immediate needs, such as troubleshooting an issue, finding health advice, or researching a topic. This motivation applies across all demographics, as individuals universally turn to online resources for answers and solutions.
2. Social Connection. Users engage with platforms to maintain social relationships, participate in communities, and stay informed. Whether through social media, messaging apps, or discussion forums, this shared motivation highlights the predictable degree of universality in online social interactions.
3. Knowledge and Curiosity. Many users access digital content for intellectual enrichment, education, or professional growth. Online courses, news sites, and research tools cater to users who share a fundamental drive for knowledge, regardless of their backgrounds.
4. Entertainment. Users turn to online content for leisure and escapism by engaging with videos, games, and streaming services. The universal appeal of digital entertainment underscores how technology fulfills a shared human need for relaxation and enjoyment.

Among the four motivations for digital information-seeking—problem-solving, social connection, knowledge and curiosity, and entertainment—problem-solving is one of the most prominent across all demographics [22]. For example, younger individuals often turn to TikTok, Instagram, YouTube, and peer-led forums to troubleshoot issues related to technology, education, and finances. Many value community-driven insights over institutional guidance [23]. On the other hand, older users often consult Facebook and Reddit for expert recommendations to solve problems, particularly in areas such as healthcare, financial planning, and home maintenance [24]. At the same time, teachers, students, and journalism practitioners know that, to be effective, content must be well-researched for accuracy, well-written for comprehension, and well-structured for coherence.

New writers are taught how to reach a target audience. However, the unlimited streams of digital content available to a global population on demand add a degree of complexity in achieving this. Recognizing that similarities exist across large populations (for example, Gen Z on Instagram versus Baby Boomers on Facebook) complicates the definition of a target audience for important content. In the case of critical information about science, health, or the economy, it is essential that campaigns are agnostic about platform, device, demographics, and other variables, because they are frequently intended for—and could benefit—both populations.

For this reason, users' demographics, long-term interests, physical and technological environments, and limited time define the "Digital DIET" framework. Our framework not only explains how and why a target audience engages with content, but it also helps differentiate why users outside a defined target audience can still engage with unexpected content, even when not actively searching for it.

## 6.5 Demographics Provide Opportunities to Personalize

In the DIET framework, demographics represent a universal variable that all users bring to their content experience. However, rather than treating demographics as vague or solely individual traits, the DEM posits that demographics can be predictive indicators of content preferences and behaviors that are cohort-specific.

In other words, while demographic traits like age, gender, education, and cultural background vary among individuals, they also reflect a key variable of shared patterns within groups that should be considered as content is produced. These predictable patterns are now increasingly evident in the ways different cohorts engage with digital content, allowing for more targeted personalization based on predictable cohort preferences and behaviors. For example, generational differences in digital news consumption.

Prior to the smartphone era, it was already observed that so-called "digital natives" were more likely to consume headlines or brief summaries without context, grazing content rather than deeply engaging with it. Since the advent of smartphones, these digital behaviors have become even more distinct across generations [25].

Examples of variances within the shared DIET variable of demographics are that younger users prefer visually engaging, fast-paced content, such as entertaining videos on social media. They respond strongly to content that triggers emotional or interactive engagement [26]. Even within a cohort, research found that college freshmen and sophomores engage with their devices differently than juniors and seniors [27]. Younger students were more inclined to use mobile phones for completing writing assignments and reported higher comfort levels with mobile technology and multitasking. Older students preferred traditional methods, such as using laptops or desktops, citing concerns about screen size and typing efficiency on mobile devices. Some students appreciated the flexibility and convenience that mobile devices offered, while others expressed concerns about distractions, which they felt could hinder the quality of their writing.

On the other hand, older users are more likely to have the time and interest for more detailed, informative content, including investigative journalism and government reports. This content is often tied to work, family, or financial responsibilities that older users face. The same principle applies in the health and wellness sector. Younger users are more likely to turn to mental health content, wellness apps, and influencers, often via social media. Older adults prioritize information on chronic illness, aging, and traditional medical sources [28]. In addition, platforms such as Reddit skew more male, while Pinterest attracts more female users. Even neurological research indicates that different demographic groups process content in measurably different ways.

In summary, these patterns illustrate that demographics are not just general traits, but variables that can be systematically linked to predictable content needs and preferences. The DEM emphasizes that demographic differences should not be treated as generic "individual differences," but rather as functionally significant content variables within the DIET framework. Recognizing the cohort-based nature of demographics, for example, enables content producers to anticipate content that will resonate with different groups and estimate their likelihood of engagement.

When it comes to staying abreast of current affairs, most younger users tend to avoid regular engagement with news or pursue alternative forms of news [29]. In particular, most Gen Z users report that their primary news interests relate to entertainment [26]. While millennials have been found to seek investment tips, news about the economy, and career advancement strategies through social media, older professionals tend to focus on financial planning, retirement strategies, industry-specific insights, or expert-driven financial news [30]. When browsing interactive content, younger users tend to gravitate toward video streaming and gaming, while older users spend more time on news-based entertainment, documentaries, and traditional streaming shows [31].

Age is not the only factor. A user's perception of engaging content may be influenced by its relative complexity, which can be linked to their level of education. An expert in a topic may seek more in-depth analysis, while users without specialized training in the same topic might prefer straightforward, easily digestible content. Similarly, education levels influence digital literacy, with more highly educated individuals often displaying greater proficiency in information retrieval and critical analysis. Digital skills are linked to various aspects of digital engagement, such as social media use, health tracking, and feeling included in the information society [32].

The demographics of race and cultural background have also been shown to influence how content is perceived and consumed [33]. Cultural norms and values influence what is considered interesting, appropriate, or relevant [34]. And this works both ways, because race can determine which stories and topics are covered or not covered by content producers [35]. Black audiences who tend to prefer news stories featuring Black individuals spend more time on that content compared to news featuring white individuals. In contrast, white audiences showed no preference based on the race of the characters in news stories [36].

Once a user starts consuming content, research has found evidence that the structure of news affects cognition differently in men versus women [37]. In tests of task reaction times, recall, recalled accuracy, and comprehension, women's reaction times were slower than men's across news stories, but their cognitive resources were affected less by story structure.

In short, given that all users bring demographic preferences to content, often with predictable preferences and behaviors, our model's Digital DIET posits that producers could attract more users to their content by accounting for the preferences and behaviors of various demographic groups. But in the Digital DIET, demographics are just the beginning. A user's interest—or more specifically, individual interest as defined in the previous chapter—is one of the most influential DIET variables because it defines the target audience. This chapter illustrates the role of individual interest, which helps differentiate it from another critical type of interest described in the next chapter.

## 6.6 Individual Interest Defines a Target Audience

Another DIET similarity in a target audience is the longer-term individual interest in a topic based on a user's experience, prior exposure, training, or expertise.

The field of educational psychology has defined individual interest, and there is strong evidence to suggest that this can be usefully applied to the disciplines of communication and journalism [38, 39]. For the purposes of this discussion, we focus on how a user's long-term interests shape their attention, information-seeking behaviors, and sustained engagement with content. The Digital Engagement Model aligns such interests with a target audience—an audience to which the topic takes precedence, rather than how the content is presented. And indeed, search results are typically organized in order of semantic relevance.

One key difference with a user's engagement with digital content on websites is that it is not as incidental as it is when scrolling through videos on social media. The motivation for engaging with specific content can be guided by deep-rooted values that determine the sources a user trusts, the platforms they frequent, and the information they prioritize, even when scanning a stream of content. On social media, an individual's interest in specific content can determine why a user might follow an influencer who shares an interest in the same topics [40]. A user who is passionate about technology and artificial intelligence, for example, will follow or subscribe to information about the latest AI developments, while another user who is committed to regular fitness will forgo AI news and frequent health-related content and fitness apps. Digital platforms capitalize on these interest-driven behaviors through recommendation algorithms, ensuring that personalized content reaches users regardless of their individual differences.

As personalized content and algorithms continue to affect the ways in which users engage with online content, content that taps into a user's pre-existing interests can translate into longer viewing times. That means individual interest alone can profoundly influence a user's attention to topics as diverse as news, sports, marketing, education, political discourse, and entertainment when the goal is to deliver detailed information about a specific topic.

When seeking information online, individuals employ different search strategies depending on their level of interest in a topic. Highly invested users use specialized search tools, academic databases, and niche online communities to access expert knowledge. At the same time, more casual users without an individual interest in a topic rely on search engines, social media trends, and mainstream news to obtain general information [41]. For example, a medical student researching a disease will turn to peer-reviewed journals and medical forums, whereas a casual reader interested in a health-related symptom may rely on lifestyle blogs, social media influencers, or generic health websites (e.g., WebMD) for information.

Users' long-term interests also dictate which platforms they use for information gathering. Professionals and academics rely on Google Scholar, ResearchGate, or LinkedIn. By contrast, entertainment, lifestyle, or gaming enthusiasts might prefer Reddit, YouTube, or Twitch. Studies show that user engagement increases when a platform caters to specific interests, such as *WhatsApp* groups for professional networking or subreddits dedicated to niche hobbies [42].

Users tend to gravitate toward information that aligns with their interests, a phenomenon known as selective exposure, which was addressed in previous chapters. And it is selective exposure to content about an individual interest that motivates users to seek confirmation of their existing beliefs rather than exploring opposing views. As a result, these users may continue to develop expertise in specialized topics while ignoring those they consider less relevant [43]. For example, only users who are very interested in cryptocurrency may frequently visit crypto news sites and financial analysis blogs, while ignoring traditional stock market news.

Long-term interests can not only shape what users choose to read but also how well they retain the information. Topics that relate to a user's individual interest have a greater probability of deeper cognitive engagement, provided the user has the time to consume them and their environment supports that. Conversely, a user encountering text about a topic in which they have little to no individual interest will typically ignore it or, at best, reading will be shallow and retention rates will be low [44]. As detailed in the next chapter, this is when the structure of content can play a role.

In addition to the four motivations for information-seeking—problem-solving, social connection, knowledge, curiosity, and entertainment—individual interest is a second variable that all users share. It is not that everybody shares an interest in a single topic, but that every user brings their longer-term individual interests to content. Individual interests determine why and how users use keywords to search for specific information. A third variable, which is more important than ever to mobile engagement, is the environment that every user brings to content.

## 6.7 A User's Environment Includes Physical and Technological Factors

When content is produced, the environment in which it will be accessed and consumed is often overlooked, especially in the case of text-based content. The result is that only readers in specific environments have the option of consuming long-form texts. Understanding a user's environment through the dimensions of the physical and technological environment provides a producer with new insights into how and why the structure of content matters.

Early research by Smith, Glenberg, and Bjork [45] showed that context—such as physical surroundings and situational cues—plays a significant role in memory encoding and retrieval, suggesting that external environments systematically shape internal cognitive processing. Other research, conducted before the advent of digital technology, demonstrated that in a time-pressured environment, individual differences in cognitive style tend to collapse, with most participants employing a faster, more uniform mode of processing [5]. That description also applies to today's mobile users. In our fast-paced digital environment, mobile users are forced to process content in similar ways: quickly, intuitively, and often superficially. While individual differences still exist, digital environments reduce variability between individuals and instead promote certain user similarities.

> ***Don't design for everyone. Design for someone.***

Just as all users bring individual interests to specific content, all users encounter content within a given environment. To help us understand the impact of the environment, the DEM categorizes it into two dimensions: a physical environment and a technological environment. The physical environment includes a user's level of distraction, surrounding noises, sensory input, and social interactions. The technological environment is defined by the type of device used, its screen size, and the speed of the internet or mobile network. Together, these two environments have a significant influence on a user's attention, interactions, and cognitive processing. Neither of these factors is typically addressed in journalism or communications textbooks; however, but understanding them is crucial to designing accessible content that engages the maximum number of users. Content creators, journalists, web and mobile app developers, business owners, and educators can optimize user experiences by considering context-specific variables, such as the environment [46].

The technological and physical environments that all users bring to any content can also influence their motivations and subsequent digital experiences. A physical environment featuring distractions, with or without social interaction, can affect the amount of attention a user devotes to mobile content. Highly distracting physical environments, such as live sports events, concerts, noisy bars, and shared workspaces, promote fragmented engagement sessions where users scan most of the content rather than engaging deeply with it [47].

On the other hand, low-distraction physical environments, such as quiet rooms, libraries, or private offices, provide users with the opportunity to engage with longer-form content with minimal distractions. These are the physical and technological environments some producers assume that all users are when consuming their content. Challenging this assumption means that content could and should be optimized for short-form consumption in both high- and low-distraction environments to engage the broadest range of users. That requires structures of content that can satisfy both short-term and longer-term consumers, which the model addresses.

Social interactions within a user's physical environment also influence attention and engagement. For example, collaborative tools can facilitate team engagement [48]. The presence of friends, family, and colleagues can influence how and when users engage with certain content, indicating that social interactions can either facilitate or hinder attention and engagement. A user physically within a group of friends may prefer shareable content, including memes or short videos. When the user is alone, they might use delve into more detailed material. In sum, a user's physical environment encompasses the tangible, spatial, and sensory aspects that surround them, including workspace, social context, and geographical location.

The interplay between physical and technological environments highlights the need for flexible content structures that can be consumed in varying environments. Users can adjust their behaviors to their technological environment. Therefore, both a user's physical and technological environment must be considered if content is to adapt to users' needs and behaviors.

### *The Technological Environment*

Is your content structured so that users can consume it on different devices? Technology forms the building blocks of a user's environment in the form of smartphones, tablets, laptops, and watches, not to mention the connectivity options for those devices by way of different operating systems, browsers, or apps. It is not just the quality or length of content that shapes users' attention, engagement, and their digital experience. The type of device they are using is also a significant factor.

On-the-go mobile users view smaller screens that are easy to scroll. However, while mobile devices afford portability and convenience, they can also lead to distracting environments and shorter periods of engagement [49]. This explains why mobile engagement can be sporadic but more frequent, often driven by mobile notifications and quick access to content on demand. Researchers have found that users in mobile environments tend to consume short-form content, including text alerts, social media videos, and quick reads. Users often overlook text-heavy content in favor of shorter or more visually appealing elements [50].

Compared with smartphones, a tablet's larger screen size supports users who prefer visually rich and longer-form content, such as interactive e-books. The use of tablets in more private and relaxed environments (e.g., at home) can lead to longer periods of engagement, illustrating the interaction between physical and technological environments on a user's experience. Tablet users are more likely to engage in digital reading, online shopping, and media streaming, as they benefit from a larger display that still offers mobility [51].

Laptops and desktops facilitate even longer-term tasks, including research, content creation, and interactive digital experiences, making larger screens ideal for consuming longer-form content, participating in virtual meetings, and undertaking professional tasks. These users engage with more complex, task-oriented content compared with phone users, including writing detailed reports, data analysis, and designing interfaces for content. Even designing for small mobile app screens can be easier on larger desktop screens. Larger desktops and smart TV screens enable multi-window interactions, side-by-side comparisons, and extended content consumption [52].

The simultaneous use of multiple devices of different sizes is commonly referred to as "media multitasking." Attempting to use more than one device will influence how they consume content. For example, sports events, especially, are often consumed on a smart TV screen while users post related comments on social media [53]. This study also found that the type of content viewed, the technological environment, and individual user characteristics can affect the level of multitasking. Users are also more prone to multitasking when they are alone, as opposed to when they are with others.

Immersive audio and visuals enhance the multitasking experience. Research on the impact of audio on media multitasking presents conflicting findings, depending on the nature of the audio and the user's environment. One positive finding was that music can enhance attentional focus and reduce mind-wandering during sustained attention tasks [54].

In contrast, irrelevant background speech can disrupt cognitive performance by dividing a user's linguistic attention [55].

In addition to hardware, Internet connectivity, reliability, and security are critical components of the technological environment. The quality of a user's technological environment, especially Internet connectivity and access to updated devices, plays a pivotal role in shaping digital engagement [3]. For instance, poorly connected environments often create significant barriers to user participation, including delayed access, limited interactivity, and heightened frustration. These constraints can undermine even the most well-designed content by impeding seamless interaction and deterring sustained engagement.

Conversely, users in robust technological environments benefit from smooth, uninterrupted digital experiences that enhance their ability to consume, interact with, and respond to content effectively. This suggests that the technological environment is not merely a background condition but a central determinant of how users will engage with digital media.

While the Digital Engagement Model recognizes that every user has a physical and technological environment when exposed to content, variations between environments mean that one size of content does not fit all. Any content producer who wishes to tailor digital content and experiences to a broader audience must start by understanding how physical and technological environments influence user engagement and how to structure content accordingly. Ensuring content has the potential to adapt to varied environments, especially physical environments, can enhance attention, engagement, and user satisfaction.

Finally, the environmental mix now includes the way that AI can regulate the appeal of content in real-time environments and through adaptive video quality, adjusting the resolution of a video based on the strength of a user's Internet connection. This helps prevent video buffering and ensures smooth video playback for users. For example, streaming platforms automatically adjust video quality based on available bandwidth to ensure a continuous viewing experience [56]. Similarly, location-based services provide information that is tailored to a user's physical location. Mobile tracking techniques are employed to provide users with pertinent information at the right time, based on their current location [57]. This capability allows content to be tailored to meet users' needs and personal preferences.

One study investigated how ChatGPT-related videos performed in terms of audience engagement on YouTube [58]. By analyzing 100 ChatGPT-focused videos that had together amassed over 65 million views and comparing them with 200 other videos from the same creators, researchers found that ChatGPT content attracted significantly higher engagement, measured by views, likes, comments, and new subscribers, than non-ChatGPT content. These findings suggest that timely, innovative content, such as ChatGPT-produced videos, can enhance audience interaction, offering valuable insights for content creators and AI developers seeking to boost user engagement.

Increasing our understanding of how physical and technological environments can significantly influence attention to, and consumption of, digital content is crucial for enhancing the user experience. To create more accessible, adaptive, and engaging content, it is essential to understand how distractions in a user's physical environment and the device, screen size, and internet speed in their technological environment interact to influence their behavior. Content creators who adopt this approach can expect to maximize user satisfaction and efficiency compared to more rigid and traditional production practices.

Looking to the future, AI-powered content and personalization, faster speeds, and multi-device synchronization will continue to refine how users in similar physical and technological environments interact with seamless, immersive, and dynamic content structures. In most cases, the time a user has to engage within a given environment represents the fourth and final DIET variable that all users bring to any content.

## 6.8 Time Affects Engagement, Even for Interested Users

The "T" in a user's "DIET" reminds us to consider how the amount of time a user has to pursue and consume content affects their engagement with content. There is no shortage of online examples of content that ignores the varying times users have to engage. As Simone Weil observed decades ago, human attention is constrained by gravity-like forces that pull thought toward immediacy and necessity rather than reflection [59]. Pages of longer-form textual storytelling and videos assume that interested users will always have the time to consume content that interests them. This is not the case. When you have only a couple of minutes and see content stating, "an eight-minute read," why would you start consuming it? Time constraints influence decisions on what to consume and how the brain processes information. Users who skim content when they have limited time engage in different neurological responses compared to when they have time to consume detailed content.

Time-constrained users prefer bite-sized content, including factual headlines that inform, not clickbait that forces users to devote more time to pursue *how* or *why* something occurs, or the "five ways to improve one's life." With endless information at their disposal, there is a growing premium on saving users' time rather than forcing it [60]. Why do some still assume all users have the time to pursue clickbait? Perhaps this explains the high bounce rates of users exposed to a page of content and then leave. Clickbait will always pique the curiosity of some users. Does it engage *the most* users?

Obviously, users with more time are more likely to consume long-form articles, documentaries, videos, and in-depth analyses. Consider, too, that the time of day can also influence consumption patterns. During a busy workday, some prefer quick and informative updates as opposed to teasing clickbait headlines. In the evening, however, users with more time will be more receptive to clickbait, such as a headline that reads, "Five reasons to improve your tech time." A user's time, not just their interest, is required to pursue details buried in the content that follows. When under time pressure, the instant availability of content may appeal to a user's cognitive state that some call *continuous partial attention* [61–64]. This state is the result of users feeling they are a "node on a network," meaning they are constantly aware of the option to check their devices at every available moment.

Other research into the effects of time on mobile behavior began with a pilot study that measured users' self-determinant behaviors [65, 66]. Respondents were asked questions such as "How often do you schedule specific times to use your phone?" Measures of non-determinant behaviors included "How often do you lose track of time while using your phone?" The results revealed that mobile users exhibit significantly less productive self-determinant behaviors and that these behaviors affect their engagement.

### *Content Can Be Produced to Support Users' Time Management and Engagement*

To win deeper cognitive investment from users, content creators and platform designers need to address the amount of time users have to devote to consuming content. One way to mitigate this is to reduce users' cognitive overload when time is limited. This can be achieved by simplifying the presentation of content. The final chapter in this book presents a new interface that instantly informs scanners, including the target audience members with various times to engage scanners who may not typically seek or select the content unless it generates situational interest. Clear typography, structured layouts, and focused messaging also help users to process information more effectively. Similarly, tailoring content to users' interests and cognitive capacity enhances the appeal of even short-form content. This implies that using adaptive algorithms that adjust the difficulty or structure of content based on user preferences can result in more meaningful interactions.

For users with more time, prompting them to reflect, question, or discuss content promotes deeper engagement. Open-ended questions, thought-provoking prompts, and interactive elements (e.g., quizzes, polls) can encourage interaction.

When users have time to engage, presenting information in a story-driven format can foster deeper cognitive engagement than quick-hit content or shallow summaries [67]. Instead of overwhelming audiences with a high volume of disconnected updates, content strategies should prioritize depth and structure to enhance engagement. This approach not only supports better retention but also fosters more meaningful connections with the material, especially for educators, journalists, and communicators seeking to inform, rather than just capture attention.

### *Interest in Content and Time to Consume Do Not Always Correlate*

Our model acknowledges an essential but often overlooked aspect of when and how digital users consume content. That is, even users highly motivated to consume certain information, which may be long-form, frequently do not, because they lack the time to do so. That leads users to either scan the content, defer engagement, or ignore it altogether [68]. How are those users served?

Time availability also influences the extent to which users interact with content. For instance, as we saw above, news consumers in mobile environments tend to read headlines and opening paragraphs only, rarely engaging with full-length stories. Mobile users typically employ micro-moment engagement, which includes brief interactions with digital content while multitasking or in transit. Research also indicates that time pressure may increase the frequency of fact-checking but reduce the depth of engagement, suggesting that users under time constraints are more likely to engage in quick, habitual behaviors rather than deep content consumption [69].

In terms of video, researchers found that social media, particularly Facebook, plays a dominant role in distribution and innovation [70]. Moreover, the short video clips commonly found on TikTok and Instagram Reels outperform long-form videos on mobile devices. Similarly, podcast snippets are more frequently consumed than full-length episodes, while social media threads get more engagement than long-form blog posts.

When time is limited, users' attention spans are more fragmented, making it difficult for them to maintain focus on long-form content to retain information. One study found that most users do not spend significant time on the majority of websites they visit and that even heavy media consumers exhibited shallow engagement across many platforms, reflecting brief, surface-level interactions rather than deep content consumption [71].

To combat this threat to producers of detailed, longer-form content, some platforms have implemented "resumable engagement" features, such as bookmarks and "read later" functions. Examples include *Pocket* and *Instapaper* [72]. Timestamps enable viewers to skip directly to key video sections, as well as podcast and audiobook chapters. These techniques pre-empt an overload of information. Our model recognizes that even users who express interest and intend to stay informed about news may avoid engaging with it when faced with time constraints. In other words, interest doesn't always guarantee engagement.

Studies have divided the concept of "time" into three temporal dimensions of patterns, structures, and context. The three dimensions draw from a diverse body of interdisciplinary research in media studies, cognitive psychology, and human-computer interaction.

Studies inform the temporal patterns of digital attention dynamics, as seen in an analysis by Yang and Leskovec [73]. The research revealed the **temporal patterns** of how media engagement unfolds in distinct periods ranging from micro-moments to prolonged interactions. **Temporal structures** reveal how users organize and regulate their media sessions, including frequency, session duration, and behaviors across various media platforms. These topics are commonly addressed in interface design studies. Finally, context stems from the psychological Temporal Context Model [74], illustrating how situational factors and user goals influence information processing and memory retrieval over time. These factors can influence a user's balance of media use with other activities and how these relate to gratifications sought. Together, these dimensions provide a more comprehensive framework for examining how digital users allocate, structure, and contextualize their time across mobile and online environments.

Mobile content available on demand gives users options for when and how they consume digital content. Many users are compelled to check their devices frequently for fear of missing new information [75]. This can lead to spending more time-consuming media than the users initially intended. To pilot-test such dimensions, our lab conducted a mobile survey of 44 participants aged 18–23. Measures addressed the challenges users face in balancing the benefits of on-demand access to information with the risks of being constantly connected and overconsumption of information.

Questions measuring self-determinant behaviors [65, 76] included "How often do you schedule specific times to use your phone?" Conversely, measures tapping non-determinant behaviors asked questions such as "How often do you lose track of time while using your phone?" Results indicated users allocated significantly more time to non-self-determinant behaviors than to self-determinant behaviors. The data also suggested that the time users had available when accessing information significantly affected the extent to which they engaged with content.

The constant variable of time in the context of user needs and behaviors demonstrates a similarity all users share. The need to check one's device can create a sense of urgency for all users, especially those who feel compelled to respond to messages immediately, regardless of the importance of the messages [77]. Mobile users who prioritize time on their devices often disrupt their daily routines and tasks to consult them. Research also found that frequent interruptions from notifications were positively related to levels of boredom and anxiety, with device interruptions associated with disruptions in daily activities [77]. Compulsive phone-checking can distort a user's perception of time, adversely affecting their overall well-being and productivity [78]. These are just some of the reasons why variations in users' time to engage motivated our model for structuring content that informs users with either limited or unlimited time to consume information.

While some individual differences shape how people consume media, this chapter introduced four individual similarities in the Digital Engagement Model that all users bring to any content. Demographic factors, as well as individual interests, contribute to a user's level of engagement with a target audience. Similarly, variables that are not yet regularly addressed by content structures are also relevant. Those variables include a user's physical and technical environments, as well as the time they have available to consume content. These variables define a user's digital DIET. Instead of differences, the model considers these shared traits as filters through which all users consume content.

Understanding why the digital DIET variables are important to how content is structured satisfies half of the equation proposed by the Digital Engagement Model. The remaining half, which is the focus of the next chapter, includes key content variables that can significantly increase user engagement. These variables may be necessary to engage a target audience, but they are crucial for attracting other users who respond to the "interestingness" of content.

## References

1. Galton, F. 1883. *Inquiries into human faculty and its development*, 387. Macmillan.
2. Lampropoulos, G., et al. 2022. The impact of personality traits on social media use and engagement: An overview. *International Journal on Social and Education Sciences* **4** (1): 34–51.
3. Chen, W., and B. Wellman. 2004. The global digital divide—Within and between countries. *IT & Society* **1** (7): 39–45.
4. Constantinidou, F., and S. Baker. 2002. Stimulus modality and verbal learning performance in normal aging. *Brain and Language* **82** (3): 296–311.
5. Smith, J. D., and D. G. Kemler. 1984. Overall similarity in adults' classification: The child in all of us. *Journal of Experimental Psychology: General* **113** (1): 137.
6. Yaros, R. 2006. Is it the medium or the message? Structuring complex news to enhance engagement and situational understanding by non-experts. *Communication Research* **33** (4): 285–309.
7. Yaros, R. 2011. Effects of text and hypertext structures on user interest and understanding of science and technology. *Science Communication* **33** (3): 275–308.

8. Cabual, R. A. 2021. Learning styles and preferred learning modalities in the new normal. *Open Access Library Journal* **8** (4): 1–14.
9. Sobel, K. V., et al. 2007. Individual differences in working memory capacity and visual search: The roles of top-down and bottom-up processing. *Psychonomic Bulletin & Review* **14**:840–845.
10. Redden, R. S., et al. 2023. Individual differences in working memory capacity and visual search while reading. *Memory & Cognition* **51** (2): 321–335.
11. Wagner, J., A. Zurlo, and E. Rusconi. 2024. Individual differences in visual search: A systematic review of the link between visual search performance and traits or abilities. *Cortex* 178:51–90.
12. Valkenburg, P. M., and J. Peter. 2013. The differential susceptibility to media effects model. *Journal of Communication* **63** (2): 221–243.
13. Gray, E. K., and D. Watson. 2001. Emotion, mood, and temperament: Similarities, differences, and a synthesis. In *Emotions at work: Theory, research and applications for management*, eds. R. Payne and C. Cooper, 21–43. John Wiley & Sons.
14. Rothbart, M. K., B. E. Sheese, and M. I. Posner. 2014. Temperament and emotion regulation. In *Handbook of emotion regulation*, ed. J. J. Gross, 305–320. Guilford Press.
15. Wu, S., M.-A. Rizoiu, and L. Xie. 2018. Beyond views: Measuring and predicting engagement in online videos. In *Proceedings of the international AAAI conference on web and social media.*
16. Nixon, L. J. 2020. Predicting your future audience: Experiments in picking the best topic for future content. In *Proceedings of the 2020 ACM international conference on interactive media experiences.* Cornella, Barcelona: Association for Computing Machinery.
17. Shao, Y. 2024. Research on prediction model of audience viewing behavior of new media driven by big data. In *2024 IEEE 2nd international conference on image processing and computer applications (ICIPCA)*. Shenyang, China: IEEE.
18. Lu, Y., et al. 2014. Integrating predictive analytics and social media. In *2014 IEEE conference on visual analytics science and technology (VAST)*. IEEE.
19. Moisescu, O. I., et al. 2025. Does one size fit all? The role of extraversion in generating electronic word-of-mouth through social media brand page engagement. *Psychology & Marketing* 42:1827–1847.
20. Hietajärvi, L., E. Maksniemi, and K. Salmela-Aro. 2022. Digital engagement and academic functioning. *European Psychologist* 27:102–115.
21. Wang, X., and Z. Liu. 2019. Online engagement in social media: A cross-cultural comparison. *Computers in Human Behavior* **97**:137–150.
22. Jacobs, W., A. O. Amuta, and K. C. Jeon. 2017. Health information seeking in the digital age: An analysis of health information seeking behavior among US adults. *Cogent Social Sciences* **3** (1): 1302785.

23. Zhitomirsky-Geffet, M., and M. Blau. 2017. Cross-generational analysis of information seeking behavior of smartphone users. *Aslib Journal of Information Management* **69** (6): 721–739.
24. Lorence, D. P., H. Park, and S. Fox. 2006. Assessing health consumerism on the Web: A demographic profile of information-seeking behaviors. *Journal of Medical Systems* **30**:251–258.
25. Palfrey, J. 2006. *How digital natives experience news* [cited 2006 November 21]. http://blogs.law.harvard.edu/palfrey/2006/05/20/how-digital-natives-experience-news/.
26. Liu, J., et al. 2022. Delineating the effects of social media marketing activities on generation Z travel behaviors. *Journal of Travel Research* **62**:1140–1158.
27. Yaros, R., and J. Misak. 2020. Completing college writing assignments on mobile phones: Comparing students' attitudes and engagement across disciplines and age. *Journalism & Mass Communication Educator* **76** (2): 216–227.
28. Lambert, S. D., and C. G. Loiselle. 2007. Health information—Seeking behavior. *Qualitative Health Research* **17** (8): 1006–1019.
29. Edgerly, S. 2017. Seeking out and avoiding the news media: Young adults' proposed strategies for obtaining current events information. *Mass Communication and Society* **20** (3): 358–377.
30. Dahl, A. J., J. W. Peltier, and G. R. Milne. 2018. Development of a value co-creation wellness model: The role of physicians and digital information seeking on health behaviors and health outcomes. *Journal of Consumer Affairs* **52** (3): 562–594.
31. Jones, A., and J. Kang. 2020. Media technology shifts: Exploring millennial consumers' fashion-information-seeking behaviors and motivations. *Canadian Journal of Administrative Sciences/Revue Canadienne des Sciences de l'Administration* **37** (1): 13–29.
32. Kappeler, K. 2024. A longitudinal perspective on digital skills for everyday life: Measurement and empirical evidence. *Media and Communication* **12**. https://doi.org/10.17645/mac.8159.
33. Mulupi, D., F. H. C. Wong, and R. A. Yaros. 2025. Investigating the effect of a physician's race and gender on user engagement with and perceived credibility of COVID-19 vaccine news. *Newspaper Research Journal* **46** (1): 96–117.
34. Beaudoin, C. E., and E. Thorson. 2005. Credibility perceptions of news coverage of ethnic groups: The predictive roles of race and news use. *The Howard Journal of Communications* **16** (1): 33–48.
35. Owens, L. C. 2008. Network news: The role of race in source selection and story topic. *The Howard Journal of Communications* **19** (4): 355–370.
36. Knobloch-Westerwick, S., O. Appiah, and S. Alter. 2008. News selection patterns as a function of race: The discerning minority and the indiscriminating majority. *Media Psychology* **11**:400–417.
37. Sternadori, M., and K. Wise. 2010. Men and women read news differently. *Journal of Media Psychology* 22:14–25.

38. Renninger, K. A. 1990. Children's play interests, representation, and activity. In *Knowing and remembering in young children*, ed. R. Fivush and J. Hudson, 127–165. Cambridge.: Cambridge University Press.
39. Renninger, K. A., S. Hidi, and A. Krapp. 1992. *The role of interest in learning and development*, xiv. Hillsdale: Erlbaum. 461 p.
40. Balabanis, G., and E. Chatzopoulou. 2019. Under the influence of a blogger: The role of information-seeking goals and issue involvement. *Psychology & Marketing* **36** (4): 342–353.
41. Martzoukou, K. 2005. A review of web information seeking research: Considerations of method and foci of interest. *Information Research* **10** (2): 215.
42. Martinez-Comeche, J.-A., and I. Ruthven. 2021. Engaging interaction and long-term engagement with WhatsApp in an everyday life context: Exploratory study. *Journal of Documentation* 77 (4): 825–850.
43. Agarwal, N. K. 2011. Information source and its relationship with the context of information seeking behavior. In *Proceedings of the 2011 iConference*, 48–55.
44. Case, D. O., and L. M. Given. 2016. *Looking for Information: A survey of research on information seeking, needs, and behavior*, 528. Emerald Group Publishing Limited.
45. Smith, S. M., A. Glenberg, and R. A. Bjork. 1978. Environmental context and human memory. *Memory & Cognition* **6** (4): 342–353.
46. Mogaji, E. 2024. *Digital consumer management: Understanding and managing consumer engagement in the digital environment*, 254. New York, NY: Routledge.
47. Oh, J., B. Saraswathi, and S. S. Sundar. 2018. Clicking, assessing, immersing, and sharing: An empirical model of user engagement with interactive media. *Communication Research* **45**:737–763.
48. Kai-Wai Chu, S., and D. M. Kennedy. 2011. Using online collaborative tools for groups to co-construct knowledge. *Online Information Review* **35** (4): 581–597.
49. Oulasvirta, A., et al. 2012. Habits make smartphone use more pervasive. *Personal and Ubiquitous Computing* **16**:105–114.
50. Huth, F., et al. 2024. Eye tracking on text reading with visual enhancements. In *Proceedings of the 2024 symposium on eye tracking research and applications.*
51. Vorderer, P., N. Krömer, and F. M. Schneider. 2016. Permanently online–Permanently connected: Explorations into university students' use of social media and mobile smart devices. *Computers in Human Behavior* **63**:694–703.
52. Saleem, J. J., and D. T. Weiler. 2018. Performance, workload, and usability in a multiscreen, multi-device, information-rich environment. *PeerJ Computer Science* **4**:e162.
53. Rubenking, B. 2016. Multitasking with TV: Media technology, genre, and audience influences. *Communication Research Reports* **33** (4): 324–331.

54. Kiss, L., and K. J. Linnell. 2024. The role of mood and arousal in the effect of background music on attentional state and performance during a sustained attention task. *Scientific Reports* **14** (1): 9485.
55. Yadav, M., and D. Cabrera. 2019. Two simultaneous talkers distract more than one in simulated multi-talker environments, regardless of overall sound levels typical of open-plan offices. *Applied Acoustics* **148**:46–54.
56. Cloudflare. n.d. *What is adaptive bitrate streaming*? https://www.cloudflare.com/learning/video/what-is-adaptive-bitrate-streaming/.
57. Mohammadi, S., A. Darzian Azizi, and N. Hadian. 2021. Location-based services as marketing promotional tools to provide value-added in e-tourism. *International Journal of Digital Content Management* **2** (3): 189–215.
58. Hussain, K., M. L. Khan, and A. Malik. 2024. Exploring audience engagement with ChatGPT-related content on YouTube: Implications for content creators and AI tool developers. *Digital Business* **4** (1): 100071.
59. Weil, S. 1952. *Gravity and grace*. Routledge & Kegan Paul.
60. Newman, N. and E. Heinrichs Seven things journalists can do to counter news avoidance. 2024.
61. LaRose, R. 2010. The problem of media habits. *Communication Theory* **20** (2): 194–222.
62. Firat, M., and I. L. Ulas. 2020. Relationship between self-control and continuous partial attention: Case of prospective teachers. *International Journal of Psychology and Educational Studies* 7 (3): 34–45.
63. Stone, L. 2005. *Continuous partial attention* [cited 2010 July 7, 2010]. http://lindastone.net/qa/continuous-partial-attention/.
64. Stone, L. Beyond simple multi-tasking: Continuous partial attention. 2009.
65. Martela, F. 2020. Self-determination theory. In *The Wiley-Blackwell encyclopedia of personality and individual differences*, ed. B. J. Carducci and C. S. Nave. Wiley-Blackwell.
66. Ryan, R. M., and E. L. Deci. 2000. Self-determination theory and the facilitation of intrinsic motivation, social development, and well-being. *American Psychologist* **55** (1): 68–78.
67. Mar, R. A., et al. 2021. Memory and comprehension of narrative versus expository texts: A meta-analysis. *Psychonomic Bulletin & Review* **28**:732–749.
68. Wang, M., and J. Choi. 2022. How web content types improve consumer engagement through scarcity and interactivity of mobile commerce? *Sustainability* **14** (9): 4898.
69. Wang, Z., and R. Yu. 2023. Effects of time pressure, reward, and information involvement on user management of fake news on a social media platform. *Perceptual and Motor Skills* **130** (4): 1433–1452.
70. García-Perdomo, V. 2024. How social media influence TV newsrooms online engagement and video distribution. *Journalism and Mass Communication Quarterly* **101** (4): 911–932.

71. Taneja, H., et al. 2012. Media consumption across platforms: Identifying user-defined repertoires. *New Media & Society* **14** (6): 951–968.
72. Boston, T. 2022. The rise of read-it later apps and the implications to content marketing. In *Rocketcontent*. www.rocketcontent.com.
73. Yang, J., and J. Leskovec. 2011. Patterns of temporal variation in online media. In *Proceedings of the fourth ACM international conference on web search and data mining*.
74. Howard, M. W., and M. J. Kahana. 2002. A distributed representation of temporal context. *Journal of Mathematical Psychology* **46** (3): 269–299.
75. Mannion, K. H., and S. A. Nolan. 2020. The effect of smartphones on anxiety: An attachment issue or fear of missing out? *Cogent Psychology* 7(1). https://doi.org/10.1080/23311908.2020.1869378.
76. Deci, E., and R. Ryan. 1985. *Intrinsic motivation and self-determination in human behavior*. New York: Plenum Press.
77. Elhai, J. D., et al. 2021. Disrupted daily activities from interruptive smartphone notifications: Relations with depression and anxiety severity and the mediating role of boredom proneness. *Social Science Computer Review* **39** (1): 20–37.
78. Elhai, J. D., et al. 2017. Problematic smartphone use: A conceptual overview and systematic review of relations with anxiety and depression psychopathology. *Journal of Affective Disorders* **207**:251–259.

CHAPTER 7

# SPICE Content Generates Situational Interest

- Scannable content supports users with time limitations.
- Personalization increases perceived relevance.
- Interactive content that is too complex discourages engagement.
- Curated curiosity after the initial kick builds attention momentum.
- Emotional content can make attending to it more urgent.



R. Yaros, *The Digital Engagement Model*, Palgrave Practical Guides in Communication,
https://doi.org/10.1007/978-3-032-03822-7_7

While it is commonly believed that all content must generate interest and shared meaning [1], there is not a comprehensive cognitive model for producing digital content. To attract and engage the most users longer than they would otherwise devote to digital content, this chapter adds the evidence for why a *combination* of five key variables matters. Facilitating engagement is no small feat in today's distracting environments where users can choose from unlimited sources of information.

If the goal is to attract, retain, and inform as many users as possible, applying the five "SPICE" variables in the Digital Engagement Model can make a significant difference because the variables can attract users who are outside a predictable "target audience."

> *The greatest problem of communication is the illusion that it has been accomplished.*

Some producers may feel they are doing all they can with one or more of the content variables presented in this chapter. However, at the time of writing this book, most digital content does not address the proposed combination of key content variables in the Digital Engagement Model. The model seeks to produce the gold standard for producing any content. Otherwise, many users will continue to ignore or avoid content, regardless of how important, accurate, thorough, or socially important it may be. By setting aside users in a traditional target audience driven by their specific individual interest in a topic, this chapter emphasizes the power of **situational interest** generated by content that can appeal to a broader range of users. Building on multidisciplinary research, we explain how and why content that is scannable, personalized, interactive, curiosity-driven, and emotional ("SPICE" variables) significantly enhances attention and attracts users who are outside the traditional target audience. Those users are defined by the millions online and on social media who are incidentally exposed to a variety of content.

To be clear, we make no claim that addressing the variables in the model will guarantee that all users will engage with all content. Previous research and models have focused on concepts that can influence media use and the long-term effects of content. However, little research has been devoted to the critical micro-seconds of initial exposure that determine the user's attention to, and sustained engagement with, the content.

The Digital Engagement Model does not eschew the value of recognizing users' motivations to consume certain content or their individual differences. Our model proposes a unique set of user and content variables not typically considered when producing content for diverse audiences. Some of the variables highlight the similarities, not just differences, that all users share when exposed to content. A model to increase attention and engagement must rely on multidisciplinary research of how different types of user interest, environments, and time respond to content varying in personalization, interactivity, curiosity, and emotion. The model's formula differs radically from the established skills used to produce content that addresses only a "target audience."

If content structures do not influence users, the popularity of sharing and liking content exposed to other users incidentally would fail to increase engagement and become a priority metric for audience analytics teams [2–5]. The growing body of empirical evidence presented in this book converges to demonstrate how and why the structure and presentation of digital content matter. A new engagement model that recognizes similarities shared by users and the potential influence of a powerful combination of content variables can be fruitful when producing and presenting content to attract more users.

If previous multidisciplinary research has demonstrated that individual content variables, such as personalization or interactivity, can enhance engagement, then a new *combination* of five such variables should have an even more powerful influence on engagement. The combined SPICE variables to be detailed in this chapter cater to the mental and situational needs of a broader range of users. The combination addresses not only users with longer-term individual interests in specific content but also the situational interest that a specific content structure generates for users who would not typically be attracted to that topic if presented mainly as text. To address both types of interest, Fig. 7.1 shows how the five content SPICE variables of the Digital Engagement Model combine to accommodate the users' DIET variables detailed in the previous chapter.

The following variables will be detailed in this chapter.

**Scannable** content responds to the variations in the *environments* and *times* that all users bring to digital information. In mobile environments that range from noisy distractions and tasks to the serenity of one's quiet room, a significant number of users cannot or do not consume all of the content to which they are exposed. Many users only scan content with the hopes of finding something appealing. A structure with detailed features

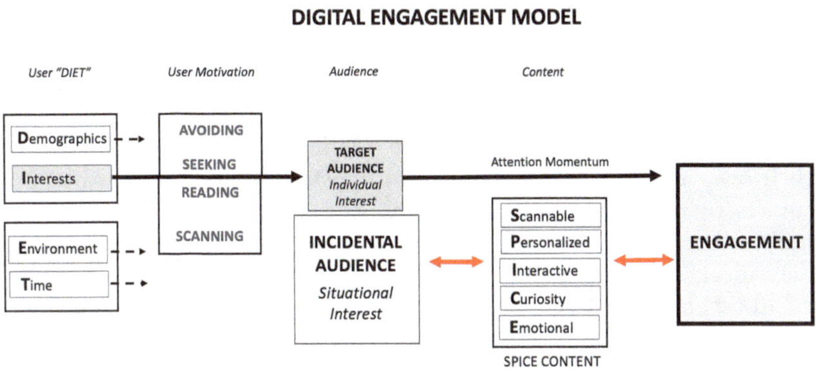


**Fig. 7.1** Digital engagement model. Credit: Digital Engagement Lab

that support scanning extends beyond just headlines, bullet points, or generic titles that merely introduce content to informative subheadings, brief summaries, bolded terms, and a specific organization of the information to make it easier for users in certain environments and with limited time to acquire the main points in the content. This doesn't suggest that SPICE variables will prompt all users to engage. It means the content will engage more users than just those with time and interest. Using clickbait or teasing open-ended titles such as "*How* to attract users," "*Why* users engage with content," or "*Five ways* to attract users to content" may motivate some users with time to pursue the specifics, but may not entice other users to at least sample and acquire more information. Many scanning users do not have the interest or time to take the clickbait. Even users with time and interest may encounter structures that overwhelm them with excessive amounts of text, media, graphics, pop-up windows, or the request to subscribe. The model's solution is to structure all content so that it can be more easily consumed and be informative in either short-form or long-form formats. That helps to addresses all users who will quickly decide whether to engage for a short time, a longer time, or move on.

**Personalized** content tailored to a user not only appeals to a user's long-term individual interest in a topic but can also generate situational interest for users who would not typically engage with the topic. That is because personalized content increases the relevance, tone, or value of the information, especially content that's important but less engaging than, say, an entertaining video or interactive graphic.

**Interactive** content can amplify engagement across all of the other content variables. While some producers define likes and shares as engagement, these represent only interactivity. They do not guarantee that the content was consumed, or if so, to what extent. Techniques such as strategically placing links, visualizations, and offering users the option to choose their own sequence of storytelling can transform users from passive consumers to active participants. Quizzes and data visualizations can also build attention. The power of interactivity lies in its ability to accommodate diverse demographics and keep pace with rapidly evolving digital environments by offering users control. Note, however, that while interactivity can give users a reason to stay and click, too many interactive features can be overwhelming and counterproductive.

**Curated curiosity** generates sustained attention, or what the model calls "attention momentum." This is the process of intelligently revealing what's next in content, rather than including links that take users to other content. If a user's first impression is that the text doesn't include anything worthy of their attention, why would they read it? For time-limited users, curating their curiosity could be the difference between disengagement and diving deeper. And if users are outside a target audience, curating curiosity after the initial click means introducing content in ways that are inviting, not overwhelming. Content combining personalized and interactive elements with curated curiosity can generate attention momentum.

**Emotional** content cuts across users' demographics, individual interests, environment, and available time to grab their attention amid a glut of information. Emotional content doesn't have to be dramatic. Humor, awe, empathy, or even quiet relevance can create a moment that is memorable.

Together, these SPICE content variables add support to the digital DIET presented in the previous chapter. By employing SPICE content, producers can create new structures that adapt to diverse user populations, taking into account who they are, where they are, and what they need in various environments. SPICE variables do not guarantee all users will attend to the content, however. SPICE variables increase the probability that more of the users who are incidentally exposed to content will find it more attractive.

## 7.1 Incidental Exposure and Serendipity Are Not Always Synonymous

A significant population of users encounters digital content passively while browsing casually or multitasking [6]. Content that is unintentionally encountered is incidental exposure [7]. A user might see a serious news headline about climate change while scrolling Instagram for entertainment news. While an environmental activist with a clear interest in the topic is more likely to engage with the information about the climate, the typical user scanning their feed may not, unless the presentation of that content excites their curiosity and *sustains* their attention.

Research indicates that many users, especially regular social media users, sporadically encounter and click on content but spend little time consuming it [8]. This is concerning, given that socially important information, such as health, politics, and science can be valuable for all users. In some cases, the explanation for the limited engagement with those topics is that they lack the appeal that drives habitual social media engagement [9]. This doesn't just mean a void of well-written text or well-edited video, but how that content generates situational interest.

The Digital Engagement Model predicts that content structure can play a pivotal role in maximizing engagement for at least some users who encounter a topic that does not typically interest them. To illustrate the point, two teachers can present the same content in different ways. One simply assigns readings that students may or may not complete. The other teacher uses scannable slides, personalized student photos, interactive graphics, challenging questions at key moments, and, when appropriate, emotion when sharing the same information. Unlike the first teacher, the second teacher transforms the class from passive students to active participants. The same effect can be achieved by integrating SPICE variables into virtually any digital content, even text that would otherwise be passively consumed. This doesn't mean eliminating the text. It means strategically placing more scannable, personalized, interactive, and emotionally engaging content within layered storytelling to generate attention momentum and encourage deeper exploration, *if* users have the time.

SPICE content variables do not just attract users' attention to content they might otherwise ignore/SPICE variables address incidental exposure (IE) on platforms such as social media. In that context, serendipity is possible. That means a user might unexpectedly encounter something they perceive as valuable [10–12]. To foster information environments in which users are more likely to experience serendipity, SPICE content is the key to interaction, attention momentum, and emotional resonance.

## 7.2 Situational Interest Is Not as Important to Engage a Target Audience

Most people tend to think of the term "interest" as binary, meaning you're either interested in something or you're not. Educational psychologists, however, argue that this view may be too simplistic. Since interest is a dynamic process, it's essential to distinguish between the individual interest we discussed in the previous chapter and this chapter's focus on situational interest generated by SPICE content.

As previously noted, scholars differentiate between *individual interest*—a person's long-term, internally driven affinity for a subject—and *situational interest*, which is sparked by features of the specific environment or content [13, 14].

Situational interest can emerge suddenly, triggered by novelty, surprise, personal relevance, or emotionally engaging material [15, 16]. It may be fleeting, or it can develop into sustained interest over time with appropriate support [17, 18]. Digital media has been shown to be particularly effective in facilitating situational interest through interactivity and immediate feedback [19], while adaptive learning systems excel at maintaining that interest [20].

Situational interest arises from cues from the content itself, such as novelty or surprise, charactering its spontaneous and short-lived nature. An individual with no previous experience or expertise in a topic who attends to content about that topic exempifies the effects of situational interest [21, 22]. This often occurs on social media platforms, where users scroll through unexpected content that captures their attention even without any prior connection to the topic [23]. The downside is that the effect of this content may be short-term, with only a marginal influence on individuals' knowledge and values.

Since readers who are disinterested in a news story are likely to stop reading it [24], so adjusting its structure can help to influence the way users process it [25, 26]. Several studies in psychology, communication, and media theory have suggested that media engagement is a multidimensional process influenced by an intricate interplay of situational factors [27–29]. Unlike users' established individual interest in specific topics specified in the digital DIET, situational interest, which is generated only by the content, does not exist prior to exposure to that content. In other words, situational interest is the product of a specific environment at a given point in time [30].

The key question, therefore, is whether your content can simultaneously address the individual interest of a target audience *and* generate situational interest for users who are exposed to it incidentally. The model suggests that it is possible when the content is structured with as many of the SPICE variables as possible.

## 7.3 Searching Is Not Required to Access Engaging Content

Content that appeals to users does not always require Google searches or specific websites [31]. At the same time, serendipity describes a positive, meaningful, and unexpected discovery, often made while searching for something else. A user might perceive relevance, leading to a positive response. One example is a marketer stumbling upon an article on psychology that unexpectedly reshapes their approach to content design. Serendipity isn't just a pleasant accident; it is a cognitive phenomenon with the potential to transform passive exposure into sustained engagement. In fragmented digital spaces where attention is fleeting, serendipity serves as a crucial pathway for content to create a lasting impact and connect with users.

Historically, research of serendipity has largely been conceptual and descriptive [32, 33], addressing how individuals notice or value unexpected information. Recently, however, interest in quantitative and experimental research on the concept has been increasing. (For a bibliometric review of 166 studies on serendipity, see Thakuria et al. [34].) André et al. [35] explored how content design can facilitate serendipitous discovery, while Kim et al. [36] developed a scale to measure individuals' tendencies toward information that is discovered, which represents serendipity during online browsing. The aim of these studies was to make serendipity more measurable and generalizable.

Drawing on a model proposed by Erdelez and Makri [37], a structured yet fluid process unfolds during the active online behaviors of browsing and searching. For instance, a user might unexpectedly encounter digital content they perceive as useful or meaningful. Unlike random or incidental exposure to content, this process is defined by a series of cognitive shifts that can lead to sustained user attention. The five core shifts include:

1. **Noticing**—the perception of promising or attention-worthy content
2. **Stopping**—the decision to pause the original task in response to the content
3. **Examining**—the exploration of new information to assess its relevance or usefulness
4. **Capturing**—the saving or bookmarking of the information for future use
5. **Returning**—the resumption of the original task after the diversion

These may not occur in every instance of browsing, but if one or more are present, the user's experience is more likely to result in what the researchers consider meaningful engagement. Building on this framework, we suggest that the depth and frequency of these dimensions can indicate a user's propensity to encounter information.

From a design perspective, Reviglio [11] argues that serendipity has the power to disrupt filter bubbles and weaken echo chambers in social media environments. Similarly, McCay-Peet et al. [38] identified several broad environmental factors that support serendipitous experiences, including the user's interest, their openness to exploration, and platforms that facilitate new connections. Although these factors do a good job of identifying various factors that can support serendipity (user interest, openness, and platform design), they may be too broad or complex to be easily applied in real-world designs.

The Digital Engagement Model takes a more focused approach. It views information encountering as a behavioral mode where incidental exposure and serendipity can overlap. In this way, we aim to understand how users discover relevance in unplanned moments, and how the ways content is presented can spark attention momentum, even for users who aren't actively searching for that content.

This propensity is not fixed. It is shaped first by the user's DIET variables, of demographics, individual interest, environment, and the time they have to engage. For example, a user with individual interest (I), in a low-distraction environment (E), with adequate time to engage (T), is more likely to respond to incidental content. This has practical implications for how content should be structured to engage users who are not explicitly searching for that content.

Considering incidental exposure as a form of serendipity enables clearer measurement and practical applications, particularly in digital environments where attention is fragmented and competition for users' attention is constant. Erdelez and Makri (2020) conceptualize information encounters as moments when users "find interesting, useful, or potentially useful information when looking for other different information, not looking for any information in particular, or not looking for any information at all" (p. 736). This highlights the flexible, often spontaneous nature of incidental exposure to unexpected content, emphasizing that perceived value can emerge in content even when intention is absent.

While a single encounter with content might not encompass every dimension of the incidental process, their combined presence and strength can suggest how likely a user is to engage serendipitously. Building on Erdelez's [32] foundational work, we view this propensity as a cognitive motivation with observable behavioral outcomes. For instance, users who are very curious are more likely to notice and explore unexpected content, thereby increasing the likelihood of meaningful interactions even in unplanned scenarios.

To translate these insights into practice, we propose integrating a new content framework with models of incidental exposure and serendipity. This approach combines the user's DIET variables with content designed for scannability, personalization, interactivity, curated curiosity, and emotional resonance. Together, the user and content variables jointly acknowledge the real difference between a target audience's interest in specific content and the engagement that follows unintentional exposure.

The key to this is that the attention momentum generated by content depends not on a user's prior knowledge or motivation, but on how effectively that content generates situational interest for them. Well-crafted multimedia can activate and sustain attention momentum by meeting users in the moment and turning incidental discovery into a more meaningful and engaging experience than reading text-heavy pages. In so doing, we move toward a more predictable and actionable understanding of digital engagement, one that is grounded in theory and built for content that can generate situational interest.

## 7.4 S: Scannable Content Serves Scanners and Readers

Content that is scannable doesn't just mean adding some bullet points and emboldened words. That content can help, but building in multiple scannable features throughout long-form content, especially, is the key to retaining users whose time and interest are limited following the first click.

To be clear, scanning is not the same as skimming. Skimming is the process of reading rapidly to obtain a general overview of content. Scanning, addressed by our model, describes reading rapidly to locate specific information [6]. In other words, skimming provides readers with a sense of the overall information, while scanning helps users to locate and focus on specific details.

Based on previous research, the Digital Engagement Model defines scannable content as text and media intentionally structured to support rapid, selective reading [39]. The Nielsen Norman Group tested five writing styles on websites and reported that one site scored 58% higher for usability when it was written concisely and 47% higher when the text was scannable. Usable content includes clear headings, bullet points, concise paragraphs, emboldened keywords, and elements often missing from current text-heavy content. This visual hierarchy guides a user's eyes and reduces cognitive load while they read. Scannable content thus accommodates users who browse or skim rather than read linearly, enabling efficient access to key points and improving engagement in information-dense environments.

More scannable content can also make news more navigable and digestible, helping readers to quickly identify and absorb key information. This is particularly true if time to read the news text is limited. To summarize, the benefits of scannable content include—but are not limited to:

**Reduced Cognitive Load**: By breaking information into more manageable chunks with clear headings, bullet points, visuals, user-controlled information, and concise paragraphs, scannable content reduces the cognitive effort required to process the information.

**Increased Accessibility**: Readers can quickly scan for relevant information, making it more likely that some of them will engage with content that aligns with their interests and needs.

A controlled eye-tracking study illustrated the benefits of scannable content by recording eye movements while participants read expository texts and answered questions about the texts [40]. The researchers hypothesized that participants would engage in strategic skimming under time constraints. This means reading just enough to feel confident in their understanding before moving on to subsequent content. Eyetracking data recording shorter eye fixation durations and increased eye movements, are behaviors consistent with scanning behaviors.

The results supported previous research, which found that instead of reading every word, readers allocated attention to content based on the perceived value of the information [40]. Users spent less time on content perceived as having low value, suggesting a possible unconscious trade-off between cognitive effort and the expected reward. Another finding was that participants exhibited shorter eye fixations and increased skipping when approaching the end of paragraphs or sections, indicating that the readers attempted to reduce cognitive load while maintaining adequate comprehension [40]. Another important finding is that reading is not always a linear process. The researcher found that behaviors adapt to the value readers perceive in the content within a given time constraint. This suggests that displaying the time required to read a text (e.g., three minutes) may discourage users with limited time, but structuring text with a host of scannable features would allow users to decide how much of the content they wish to consume.

Duggan and Payne's findings also help to dispel the myth that skim-reading reflects a user's failure to focus. Instead, results suggest skimming is often strategic, shaped by a user's current tasks, goals, and the structure of the content. These outcomes have significant implications for the design of content, which the Digital Engagement Model addresses explicitly. The way content is laid out and sectioned, as well as the density of the information, influences how thoroughly each user will consume it. As detailed in subsequent chapters, the DEM proposes more sectioning with user-selected content, among other strategies. Here, sectioning refers to dividing a long, scrollable page of text into separate, smaller, and cleaner sections that are labeled with informative subheadings, accompanied by blocks of text, bullet points, and thematic breaks, and complemented by visuals. This alone may sound obvious, but it is the addition of these techniques to several others proposed by the model that represents the most significant transformations.

Other studies have demonstrated the benefits of scanning, finding that it can significantly enhance comprehension [41–43]. Scanning can enhance comprehension by reducing the time required for consumption and improving speed reading [6, 44].

Many agree that long-form narratives and lengthy videos can lead to mental fatigue, making it more difficult for some users to stay focused [45, 46]. Employing a collection of scannable features within content can make information more accessible and easier to process [47]. For example, content about climate change with scannable sections on specific impacts, such as sea-level rise and extreme weather events, allows users to identify relevant points without feeling overwhelmed by a long form narrative.

## 7.5 P: Personalization Can Occur on Different Scales

Personalization is a powerful lever for capturing and sustaining user attention. It sparks a sense of relevance that pulls users into content they perceive as aligned with their interests and needs [48]. When done well, personalized content doesn't just inform—it connects. It makes users feel seen, and that drives deeper engagement. The benefits include:

**Enhanced Relevance**: Content tailored to specific interests and preferences is more likely to resonate and prompt interaction.

**Increased Loyalty**: When users consistently find content that matches what they care about, they're more likely to return.

Personalization can be applied across three levels: macro, meso, and micro. A news article reporting on citywide lead contamination offers *macro* personalization, appealing to a broad geographic audience. A follow-up story that focuses on the most affected neighborhoods reflects *meso*-personalization. *Micro* personalization zooms in further, guiding readers on how to test their own tap water, even if they're not in the affected area.

This layered approach helps content feel more personally relevant. Even when a topic seems distant or abstract, effective structuring and subtle personalization can bridge the psychological gap and enhance user engagement.

Still, personalization alone isn't a silver bullet. Like all SPICE variables, it works best in tandem. When combined with elements like surprise, proximity, or emotion, personalization becomes even more effective. In practice, personalization can be as simple as presenting clear, scannable content for users who have only seconds to decide whether to engage. Users often turn to personalized platforms to help navigate the overload of digital information. When faced with an overwhelming volume of content, personalization offers a filtering function that reduces cognitive load [49].

In fact, research shows that users form an opinion about a site in just 50 milliseconds [50]. Personalized platforms have a measurable advantage in this high-speed environment. Studies show that portals offering personalized content elicit more positive attitudes from users [51]. These positive attitudes stem from:

1. The user's ability to customize their experience
2. The content's perceived relevance
3. The novelty of what's being offered

Even users with little initial interest in a topic are more likely to engage when content is tailored more to their preferences or behaviors. This tailoring builds relevance, often using data such as users' demographics, browsing history, or declared interests [48].

Personalization also makes content feel more psychologically close. When content mirrors a user's values, experiences, or identity, it reduces the mental distance between the user and the information, increasing the likelihood of engagement [52]. It can also boost retention—people remember what feels meaningful. In essence, personalization is a tool for building social realities that users recognize and care about [53].

There are many ways to personalize content, ranging from algorithmic filtering to simple language cues. One primary method is algorithmic personalization, where systems analyze user behavior to curate content. These algorithms tailor exposure based on past interactions, time of day, location, or device type [54]. For example, news organizations might feed different headlines to students versus professionals, each reflecting unique habits and interests. Localized content also plays a role. News readers tend to prioritize content relevant to their area [55].

Social media platforms have become powerful personalization sources. Younger users, in particular, now expect personalized feeds, a trend supported by research of how personalization can shape engagement norms across generations [56]. Platforms such as *YouTube*, *Netflix*, and *Spotify* personalize recommendations based on user interaction history, a process known as interest matching [57]. Someone who frequently reads about sustainability, for example, can be served more content on climate policy or green technology. This reinforces relevance and builds platform loyalty [58].

Another effective technique is linguistic personalization. Even a simple shift in phrasing can drive higher engagement. Using second-person pronouns such as "you" or "your" makes content feel more direct and personal. For instance, "Your Sleep Habits Can Reveal a Lot About You" is more likely to draw clicks than the shorter title "The Science of Sleep Patterns." It's easy to find vague titles that merely introduce content when a personalized explanatory headline would be more effective in gaining attention. Studies confirm that second-person language triggers self-referencing, which can increase engagement [59, 60].

Demographic-based personalization is another layer worth exploring. Integrating the DEM model's DIET variable of demographics, with the SPICE framework can help producers to target content more effectively. Social media content, for example, can be tailored for users based on different age groups, languages, or educational levels. Over time, this targeting can be refined through the use of alerts, nudges, or suggestions. A political story might be framed one way for Gen Z and another for Boomers or localized for regional audiences instead of a generic national lens.

But personalization comes with responsibility. Done well, it enhances engagement without feeling invasive. Done poorly, it can feel manipulative or overly narrow. Studies emphasize the need for balance. Users respond positively when personalization feels helpful, not pushy [61]. The challenge for content creators is to make personalization feel like an invitation, not a limitation.

Ultimately, personalization is more than a marketing strategy. It's a structural requirement in the digital landscape. As content competes for attention in algorithm-driven feeds, producers must create content that is relevant across diverse user populations. This may involve intelligent algorithms, user-driven customization, or interfaces that allow readers to steer their own experience.

In a saturated digital environment, personalization isn't optional. It's how content breaks through the noise and stays with the user after the scroll. How much personalization does your content offer?

## 7.6 Interactivity Engages Unless It Overwhelms

Just as there are several definitions of interest, there is no universally adopted conceptualization of interactivity. One reason may be that the degree of online interactivity has evolved over time, from simple links on a webpage to user-generated social media interactions. Rafaeli and Ariel [62] noted that "a conceptual definition should be considered more broadly than just a single situation, determined by a specific environment and tools" (p. 73).

One of the reasons for the inconsistency may lie in the wide disparity in how interactivity has been operationalized, as evidenced by studies on perceived user interactivity [63, 64]. One experiment tracked "click streams" as users navigated websites to determine the level of interactivity [65]. Sundar [66] noted that, regardless of what mechanism generates interactivity, "greater interactivity breeds more involvement, focusing more user attention on content" (p. 96).

The DEM defines interactivity *as the degree to which digital content allows users to input choices, responses, or content.* This means an app or website with static content represents minimal interactivity. In contrast, content that offers active participation through choices, links, and visualizations can enhance attention, interactivity, and a user's overall experience, which makes the content more memorable.

Besides the ubiquitous likes and shares on social media, why aren't there more interactive features in digital content? It is interactivity that shapes a user's media experience, rather than passively consuming content. According to the DEM, interactivity generates situational interest and attention momentum. This is supported by the Theory of Interactive Media Effects [67], which predicts how interactivity can fulfill user motivations, including users' desire for customized content. Here, communication is not just about conveying information, but about users constructing meaning [68]. Users who feel a sense of agency are more likely to invest their attention in content, resulting in a deeper understanding and retention [69].

Engagement has consistently soared among users who are offered interactivity [70]. For example, interspersing content with quizzes and visualizations fosters curiosity, which builds attention momentum. Some researchers have taken it a step further to claim that interactivity fosters a user's sense of control [71]. The MAIN model, for example, argues that modality, agency, interactivity, and navigability can encourage deeper engagement with content. By engaging audiences as co-creators of knowledge, interactivity can help users to construct a personalized understanding through a participatory process (Sundar et al., 2012). Further benefits of interactive systems may lie in their ability to facilitate deep learning and problem-solving [72]. Similarly, another study found that interactivity leads to more information processing, higher favorability, and a more intense flow state [73].

At the same time, there are debates about whether interactivity facilitates or hinders the learning process. As examples, some claimed that providing a user with the freedom to control a message in a nonlinear way leads to better learning [74]. Others reported that interactivity can help to explain complex information more effectively, such as information about climate change [75]. Interactivity has also been shown to leverage active learning, where users process data in a self-guided way [76].

Conversely, interactivity can diminish users' memory of non-interactive content [77]. One reason may be that users tend to focus on interactive elements at the expense of non-interactive information. Another is that too much interactivity can overwhelm users' cognitive capacity. In the context of Immersive Virtual Reality (IVR), a 2024 study concentrated on the cognitive load of interactive learners. It found that while interactivity can enhance engagement, excessive interactivity increases cognitive load, potentially hindering learning [78]. Overall, these results suggest interactivity can enhance memory and information processing, but not without potential drawbacks.

In news, interactive visualizations and complex features are frequently provided to a general audience assumed to possess adequate knowledge. The question here is what constitutes too much interactivity? Although interactive news quizzes have the potential to increase users' knowledge [79], too much interactivity can still overload cognition. Early research, found that users who controlled their navigation learned more than those who did not [74]. Other research confirmed that excessive interactivity can inhibit comprehension by overwhelming one's cognitive resources [80, 81]. Even text with animation appeared to increase cognitive load by competing with the animation or demanding more of a user's cognitive resources [82]. With a proliferation of interactive elements, the potential for cognitive overload is greater than ever. The bottom line is to create interactive content that extends beyond common links, likes, and shares but is pre-tested in a pilot of users to ensure it doesn't overwhelm non-experts quickly.

In sum, the two benefits of ***managed*** interactive content are:

**Active Engagement**: Interactive elements that permit users to engage directly with the content without overwhelming them can increase their involvement in the content.

**Enhanced Learning**: Managing interactive content can make information understandable and more memorable.

Much like an enticing headline, new interactive features, such as visualizations, can generate a user's curiosity. The DEM, however, emphasizes the importance of cultivating ***continued*** curiosity after the initial exposure or click.

## 7.7 Curiosity Needs Curation After the First Click

In the digital world, curiosity is the desire to acquire new knowledge or information [83]. This approach is rooted in the Information-Gap Theory of Curiosity, which suggests that curiosity arises when there's a perceived gap between what one knows and what one wants to know [84]. The term "curiosity gap" was popularized by Upworthy co-founder Peter Koechley. It refers to the deliberate structuring of headlines to highlight what the reader does not yet know, prompting a click to resolve that gap. Effective curiosity-inducing content, therefore, leverages this gap to captivate and maintain user interest. Let's evaluate this in terms of the Digital Engagement Model:

- **Curated Curiosity** refers to content that continues to build attention momentum for users by generating situational interest that retains users who have the time to consume it.
- **Meaningful Engagement** occurs when curiosity-driven content structures build the attention momentum required for users to retain information.

Inducing curiosity in any digital content, whether it be breaking news or long-form storytelling, can involve a strategic and complex blend of engaging headlines, compelling introductions, mystery, suspense, interactive elements, surprising information, visual appeal, urgency, and personalization. While surprising content on social media can sometimes feel irritating or out of place, many younger users welcome unexpected news content on websites and apps [85, 86]. By leveraging these strategies for curated curiosity, creators can increase the likelihood that their content will sustain user interest, leading to deeper engagement and more interactions.

Curiosity is often sparked by unexpected or novel information, which motivates users to seek a deeper understanding [87]. Additionally, structural features such as bulleted or numbered lists can enhance scannability and encourage users to continue engaging with content, especially when these features highlight intriguing or incomplete information [39, 88]. For users who have the time to engage, presenting content in ways that hint at unanswered questions or unresolved issues, such as using ellipses, ambiguous phrases, or suggestive subheadings, can heighten curiosity and sustain attention [87]. Information about climate change that contrasts popular misconceptions with scientific realities, for example, has sparked curiosity [89]. Curiosity can also be sparked by content that is quick and easy to consume, rather than complex material that inflates engagement metrics because users need more time to understand its meaning [90]. Content that generates curiosity converts passive or disinterested users into active learners [84]. Conversely, curiosity and anticipation can be lost when a user is exposed to a series of similar or predictable content [13].

When you think about news that generates curiosity, you might think of clickbait, or vague content that seeks clicks from curious users. It is not quite as simple as that, however. Two studies investigated how curiosity evolves dynamically as individuals engage in ongoing information-gathering. The results revealed that curiosity is not static but fluctuates in relation to emotional and cognitive states, such as confidence and affect, throughout the information acquisition process [91]. Indeed, positive information can enhance both curiosity and long-term memory for information [92].

It helps to realize that curiosity is not only a fleeting opportunity. Unlike a single clickbait headline, movies and theatrical performances can curate curiosity for hours, demonstrating how curiosity can continue beyond the first seconds or moments. The challenge is to employ new content structures that build curiosity without overwhelming users with a collection of distracting content.

Many believe that simply teasing users with deliberately vague titles or questions that force them to devote their time and interest to the pursuit of key information is the best way to generate clicks [93, 94]. We know that clickbait will always generate some clicks. Yet one must ask whether clickbait always generates the most clicks? If so, how long does engagement last after the first click, and perhaps most importantly, what content structures sustain attention after the first click?

Experimental research has produced conflicting results. Testing different headline styles, including questions and listicles (e.g., "Five ways for content to generate interest"), found that headlines that asked users a question generated the fewest clicks compared with more detailed, informative headlines [95]. Researchers conducting two studies investigated how the presentation of either traditional news headlines, detailed summary headlines, or teasing clickbait headlines influenced news-seeking behavior [96]. In the first of two studies, researchers examined how different headline types, such as informative summary headlines versus clickbait-style curiosity headlines, affect users' perceptions of information adequacy. The findings indicated that summary headlines enhanced perceptions of adequacy, leading to increased expectations that the associated articles would provide clear information, which in turn heightened anticipated engagement with the content. The second field study analyzed user behavior on nine local newspaper websites to assess headline selections.

These results demonstrated that users were more inclined to select informative summary headlines over curiosity-driven ones.

While the results of studies on the effectiveness of curiosity gap headlines have been inconclusive, a meta-analysis of nearly 9000 headline experiments provides a more nuanced understanding [97]. The authors found that headlines that are too vague tend to reduce engagement by leaving users confused or skeptical, while headlines that are too informative offer little incentive to click. The optimal approach, therefore, lies in crafting headlines that strike a balance between conveying enough information to signal relevance while maintaining a sense of intrigue.

For journalists and news organizations, these findings offer a data-driven framework that suggests effective headline writing is not about choosing between summary and curiosity but about modulating the level of information. Researchers analyzing more than 100,000 WeChat headlines found that the most popular headlines also perceived as most important by users were surprising topics or sparked a question [98]. Testing headlines for only environmental news suggested that although a headline's format did not influence users' story selection or engagement, the headlines influenced participants' evaluations of credibility. Of all the categories, the clickbait-style question headlines were rated the least credible [99].

Similarly, a Dutch news service analyzed its headlines and found that clickbait question headlines reduced click-through rates on stories [100]. The researchers concluded that predicting the effectiveness of a headline based solely on its clickbait features was impossible, suggesting that a combination of variables is at play when associating curiosity with clickbait. In line with our understanding of *curated curiosity*, the empirical evidence suggests that curiosity in a headline might drive short-term consumption but not long-term engagement. Ultimately, any content must continue to curate curiosity and build the attention momentum needed for sustained user attention.

There is no question that curiosity can be a powerful motivator, driving users to seek new information and engage deeply with content. In the digital age, where information is continuous, attention spans are short, and competition for every user's attention is fierce, the goal is to produce content beyond a single title or headline. Content that will continue to generate users' curiosity, especially those with little to no interest in the topic. The Digital Engagement model responds with a "compound headline." A compound headline begins with a sentence that states useful information or a fact for all users, followed by a sentence that teases those users with time to pursue more information contained in the first sentence. What is the downside of serving both audiences with useful information, followed by the option to acquire more details?

Curating curiosity beyond a title or headline isn't easy, and this critical step in producing effective journalism is often overlooked. Yet the high number of users who leave after viewing just one page, a phenomenon known as the bounce rate, makes clear that sustaining curiosity with more effective structures should not be optional. It's essential if the goal is to keep users engaged, informed, and coming back for more.

However, like any strategy for producing engaging content, generating curiosity alone is still not enough. Even when users are intrigued, their decision to stay with content—or to care about it—often hinges on something more: emotion. Emotion plays a pivotal role in amplifying attention, deepening memory, and influencing how users interpret and respond to information.

The following section examines how emotional resonance can be intentionally incorporated into content to sustain engagement beyond the initial click.

## 7.8 Emotion Is a Cognitive Catalyst for Engagement

Media and communication scholars increasingly acknowledge the central role of emotion in shaping how audiences interact with and engage with content. Some argue that journalism research historically sidelined the emotional dimensions of news in favor of rationality and objectivity [101]. Yet in a media landscape saturated with emotionally charged stories, divisive user comments, and algorithmically curated content, this oversight is no longer sustainable. Wahl-Jorgensen calls for a renewed scholarly focus on emotion, framing it not as a distortion of truth but a key to understanding how media works and why it matters.

In the SPICE model for content, the final variable of emotion represents more than a design feature or a marketing hook. Foundational work on the cognitive-mediational theory of emotion argued that emotions arise from how individuals appraise their interactions with the environment, particularly in terms of personal relevance and available coping resources [102]. This appraisal-driven perspective helps explain why emotional responses may influence which content users attend to, how deeply they process it, and what they remember afterward.

Rather than researching the concept of emotion as a result of content, producers should consider how emotion can be generated by their content, when appropriate, to enhance attention, memory, and even sharing behavior. Emotionally arousing content, whether positive or negative, is more likely to be shared online [103]. Within the DEM framework, emotion interacts dynamically with the other SPICE variables, making it a crucial factor in designing content that will resonate with today's users of digital media. One of the most frequently asked questions by news consumers is, "Why does there have to be so much negative news?"

The answer is that a robust body of research confirms that negative content consistently attracts more attention than positive content. A large-scale study published in *Nature Human Behaviour* analyzed approximately 105,000 headline variations from the website *Upworthy*, encompassing more than 5.7 million clicks across 370 million impressions. Through randomized controlled trials with more than 22,000 participants, researchers found that each additional negative word in a headline increased the click-through rate by 2.3% [104]. In contrast, positive words slightly reduced user engagement. This compelling evidence suggests that negativity isn't only more prevalent but also more effective at capturing attention in online environments.

The reasons why negative content appeals to us lie in our evolutionary wiring. Humans are biologically predisposed to prioritize negative stimuli because they often signal threat or danger. This deeply ingrained **negativity bias** is thought to have conferred survival advantages. Our ancestors who paid more attention to dangerous cues were more likely to survive. Modern cognitive psychology supports this perspective. Rozin and Royzman [105] describe four cognitive mechanisms explaining the disproportionate influence of negative stimuli. They include negative potency (bad events are more impactful), steeper negative gradients (they escalate more quickly), negative dominance (bad overrides good), and negative differentiation (bad is processed with more nuance). This bias is not confined to adulthood. One study found that even infants as young as six months showed stronger responses to negative emotional signals, suggesting that the bias is present early in development [106].

Neuroscience and psychological research further reinforce the idea that negative content engages human cognition more deeply than positive content. A key electrophysiological study used event-related potentials (ERPs) to examine brain responses to emotionally valanced stimuli. The researchers found that negative stimuli elicited significantly larger P3 components, which are neural signals associated with attentional and cognitive processing, compared to positive or neutral stimuli [107]. This provided direct evidence that the brain allocates greater neural resources to the processing of negative information, supporting a neural basis for the negativity bias.

Complementing these neural findings, a subsequent behavioral study by Ito and Cacioppo [108] investigated how individuals vary in their evaluative responses to emotional content. Rather than using physiological measures, this research examined the stability and predictive validity of individual differences in the positivity offset (a tendency to respond more positively to neutral stimuli) and negativity bias (a tendency to react more negatively to aversive information). They found that individuals with stronger negativity biases were more likely to form disproportionately negative impressions in response to mildly negative or ambiguous descriptions. This suggests that while negativity bias may have evolutionary and neurological roots, it also operates at the level of stable psychological traits that vary across individuals.

Additional psychophysiological studies further support these findings by demonstrating that negative content elicits stronger autonomic responses. One large cross-national experiment measured skin conductance and heart rate while participants viewed televised news stories [109]. They found that negative news consistently produced greater physiological arousal than neutral or positive news, across all cultural contexts studied.

Taken together, these findings suggest that our preference for negative content is not merely a media-driven phenomenon, but rather a reflection of human psychology and neurobiology. Understanding this bias is essential for both media producers and consumers alike. While it may enhance engagement, persistent exposure to negative content has been linked to heightened anxiety, stress, and diminished well-being. The challenge lies in balancing truthful reporting with content strategies that do not exploit this bias to the detriment of public mental health.

In an information landscape flooded with video and content competing for attention, content of an emotional nature helps users to decide what deserves their limited time and cognitive resources. Emotional cues can even interrupt scrolling on a mobile device and flag content as not just more interesting but more important. Research into negative news videos conducted well before the advent of YouTube found that the downbeat content increased users' attention, their mental capacity to process the video, and their later recall of the story, while inhibiting their recognition of the information presented before the negative video [110].

Emotion should not simply be inserted into media whenever possible, but woven into the structure of content as a functional variable when appropriate. Emotionally resonant content can also encourage users to connect more deeply with social issues [101].

Emotion can also infuse the language used to influence attention and digital engagement. A study by Baylor University found that language that elicited high arousal and uncertainty, such as excitement, hope, anxiety, and anger, sustained readers' attention more effectively than language associated with sadness or contentment [111]. The results also confirmed that pairing simpler language structures with emotional content enhanced cognitive processing and sustained engagement.

Emotion also builds shared meaning and social connection. Content that evokes emotion becomes more than information. It can become an experience. Audiences often gravitate toward narratives that guide them through desired emotional shifts—particularly ones that resolve tension or elevate mood [112]. This may help explain broader patterns of emotional self-regulation in media use, including on social platforms.

When participants were intentionally made to feel happy or upset, they were less likely to feel the urge to visit social media [113]. At the same time, using social media boosted their positive feelings more than browsing a neutral website, suggesting that social platforms can help lift one's mood in the short term. Similarly, positively framed content increased sharing intentions, indicating that having emotional heft can also affect the distribution of content [114].

One study examined emotional expression in live digital environments, such as in YouTube chat interactions, finding that positive emotions were more readily transmitted and shared live, whereas negative emotions were retained longer in memory [115]. It was peer interactions, rather than just exposure to content, that played a significant role in emotional expression. These findings confirm that emotional engagement arises from both individual cognitive responses and social interactions.

Not only do emotionally charged stories sustain our attention, but they are also more likely to go viral [103]. This is not because articles are manipulative, but because they provide psychological and social value. Intense emotional narratives have been shown to lead to higher engagement, particularly in news stories [116]. Framing content in a hopeful, optimistic way has shown promise in promoting proactive information-seeking. This approach was described as creating an "experience of involvement" that fosters users' investment in messages and their meaning [117].

This is true even for really gloomy subjects. Emotional content that emphasizes joy and optimism is most effective in increasing engagement with climate change information, for example [118]. While fear plays a role, joy emerged as a more consistent and constructive motivator. In tourism marketing, a similar effect was measured. Emotional engagement was a stronger predictor of intent to visit a place than cognitive engagement, reinforcing the persuasive power of emotional resonance in consumer behavior [119].

Other research emphasizes that emotional engagement extends beyond immediate reactions and can have long-term effects on well-being, identity formation, and the ethical dimensions of our digital experiences [120]. Specifically, emotional responses to content can influence how individuals perceive themselves and their communities, guide future content choices, and shape their emotional resilience or vulnerability in online environments. This underscores the responsibility of digital designers and platforms to consider not just what will capture attention, but also how content can emotionally condition user behaviors over time.

We have shown that emotional narratives in digital learning and advertising environments can deepen retention and motivate behavior change. Emotion plays a critical role in memory because emotions activate cognitive resources that aid in the storage and retrieval of information [121]. This means that content that is emotionally resonant is more likely to be encoded deeply and recalled accurately [122]. Verma et al. [123] went further by proposing empathic content recommendation systems that would regulate user emotions through tailored digital content, illustrating the growing role of affective computing in education and engagement.

Successfully producing emotionally charged content can turn abstract concepts into *felt experiences*, which can ultimately enhance user comprehension and longer-term retention [124].

### *Emotion Is a Powerful SPICE Variable*

Emotion is central to SPICE because content that evokes emotion in ways that align with a message can make digital content more engaging, memorable, and socially meaningful. The implications are clear:

- Emotion can signal relevance and capture attention.
- Emotion can create resonant experiences that match user goals.
- Emotional narratives can facilitate learning.
- Emotional tone and framing can enhance the user connection.
- Emotions such as joy, hope, and empathy can promote more clicks and meaningful action.

Emotion can enhance the cognitive and social aspects of any digital content while amplifying the effectiveness of the other SPICE variables in the Digital Engagement Model. Content that reflects or triggers a user's concerns, values, or emotional states is more likely to be remembered, but this must be applied judiciously because emotion is most effective when contextually appropriate and aligned with a message's core purpose [117]. Conversely, overuse or manipulation of emotional cues can backfire, undermining trust or provoking disengagement.

To realize the full potential for emotion in SPICE content, we must understand the importance of combining these variables, not only in text but also in visual media. This includes the strategic use of photographs, graphics, and charts, all of which play a critical role in capturing users' attention, shaping perception, and sustaining engagement in digital content. Chap. 8 examines how explanatory visual elements can serve as integral components in the engagement equation, efficiently conveying important information to busy, distracted users who are often overwhelmed by the volume and pace of digital content.

## References

1. Green, J., and H. Jenkins. 2011. How audiences create value and meaning in a networked economy. In *The handbook of media audiences*, ed. V. Nightingale, 109. Blackwell.
2. Wu, S., M.-A. Rizoiu, and L. Xie. 2018. Beyond views: Measuring and predicting engagement in online videos. In *Proceedings of the international AAAI conference on web and social media.*
3. Nixon, L. J. 2020. Predicting your future audience: Experiments in picking the best topic for future content. In *Proceedings of the 2020 ACM international conference on interactive media experiences.* Cornella, Barcelona: Association for Computing Machinery.
4. Shao, Y. 2024. Research on prediction model of audience viewing behavior of new media driven by big data. In *2024 IEEE 2nd international conference on image processing and computer applications (ICIPCA).* Shenyang, China: IEEE.
5. Lu, Y., et al. 2014. Integrating predictive analytics and social media. In *2014 IEEE conference on visual analytics science and technology (VAST).* IEEE.
6. Fatmawan, A. R., N. P. A. Dewi, and I. P. A. D. Hita. 2023. Skimming and scanning technique: Is it effective for improving Indonesian students' reading and comprehension. *Edusaintek: Jurnal Pendidikan, Sains dan Teknologi* **10** (3): 1,181–1,198.
7. Ahmadi, M., and D. Y. Wohn. 2018. The antecedents of incidental news exposure on social media. *Social Media+ Society* 4 (2): 1–8.
8. Boczkowski, P., E. Mitchelstein, and M. Matassi. 2017. Incidental news: How young people consume news on social media. In *Proceedings of the 50th Hawaii international conference on system sciences.*
9. Takano, M., et al. 2021. Effects of incidental brief exposure to news on news knowledge while scrolling through videos. *IEEE Access* **9**:37,772–37,783.
10. Makri, S., et al. 2015. Observing serendipity in digital information environments. *Proceedings of the Association for Information Science and Technology* **52** (1): 1–10.
11. Reviglio, U. 2019. Serendipity as an emerging design principle of the infosphere: Challenges and opportunities. *Ethics and Information Technology* **21** (2): 151–166.

12. Rohlf, R., and A. Walters. 2015. Developing a predictive media model for measuring userengagement with web-based hyperlocal news services. In *EdMedia + Innovate Learning*. Montreal, Quebec, Canada: Association for the Advancement of Computing in Education (AACE).
13. Hidi, S. E., and K. A. Renninger. 2019. Interest development and its relation to curiosity: Needed neuroscientific research. *Educational Psychology Review* **31** (4): 833–852.
14. Renninger, K. A., and S. Hidi. 2011. Revisiting the conceptualization, measurement, and generation of interest. *Educational Psychologist* **46** (3): 168–184.
15. Mitchell, M. 1993. Situational interest: Its multifaceted structure in the secondary school mathematics classroom. *Journal of Educational Psychology* **85** (3): 424.
16. Ainley, M., S. Hidi, and D. Berndorff. 2002. Interest, learning, and the psychological processes that mediate their relationship. *Journal of Educational Psychology* **94** (3): 545–561.
17. Renninger, K. A., and S. E. Hidi. 2022. Interest development, self-related information processing, and practice. *Theory Into Practice* **61** (1): 23–34.
18. Renninger, K. A., and S. Hidi. 2015. *The power of interest for motivation and engagement*. 1st ed. New York: Routledge.
19. D'Mello, S., E. Dieterle, and A. Duckworth. 2017. Advanced, analytic, automated (AAA) measurement of engagement during learning. *Educational Psychologist* **52** (2): 104–123.
20. Walkington, C., and M. L. Bernacki. 2020. *Appraising research on personalized learning: Definitions, theoretical alignment, advancements, and future directions*, 235–252. Taylor & Francis.
21. Krapp, A. 1988. Interest, learning and academic achievement. In *Third European conference of learning and instruction (EARLI)*, P. Nenniger (chair). Madrid.
22. Krapp, A., and M. Prenzel. 2011. Research on interest in science: Theories, methods, and findings. *International Journal of Science Education* **33** (1): 27–50.
23. Schraw, G., and S. Lehman. 2001. Situational interest: A review of the literature and directions for future research. *Educational Psychology Review* **13**:23–52.
24. Eveland, W. P., and S. Dunwoody. 2001. User control and structural isomorphism or disorientation and cognitive load? Learning from the web versus print. *Communication Research* **28**:48–78.
25. Schiefele, U. 1991. Interest, learning, and motivation. *Educational Psychologist* **26** (3 & 4): 299–323.
26. Hidi, S., and W. Baird. 1986. Interestingness—A neglected variable in discourse processing. *Cognitive Science* **10**:179–194.

27. Petty, R. E., and J. T. Cacioppo. 1984. Source factors and the elaboration likelihood model of persuasion. *Advances in Consumer Research* **11**:668–672.
28. Katz, E., J. G. Blumler, and M. Gurevitch. 1973. Uses and gratifications research. *The Public Opinion Quarterly* **37** (4): 509–523.
29. Csikszentmihalyi, M. 1990. The domain of creativity. In *Theories of creativity*, ed. M. A. Runco and R. S. Albert, 190–212. Newbury Park, CA: Sage.
30. Hidi, S., and J. McLaren. 1990. The effect of topic and theme interestingness on the production of school expositions. In *Learning and instruction: European research in an international context*, ed. H. Mandl et al., 295–308. Oxford: Pergamon.
31. Levine, T. R., and D. M. Markowitz. 2024. The role of theory in researching and understanding human communication. *Human Communication Research* **50** (2): 154–161.
32. Erdelez, S. 1997. Information encountering: A conceptual framework for accidental information discovery. In *Proceedings of an international conference on information seeking in context.*
33. Foster, A., and N. Ford. 2003. Serendipity and information seeking: An empirical study. *Journal of Documentation* **59** (3): 321–340.
34. Thakuria, A., I. Chakraborty, and D. Deka. 2024. A bibliometric review on serendipity literature available in Web of Science database using HistCite and Biblioshiny. *Information Discovery and Delivery* **52** (2): 227–242.
35. André, P., et al. 2009. Discovery is never by chance: designing for (un) serendipity. In *Proceedings of the seventh ACM conference on creativity and cognition.*
36. Kim, H., et al. 2023. Dispositional and contextual correlates of in-play sports betting and related harms: A 2-week ecological momentary assessment study. *Psychology of Addictive Behaviors: Journal of the Society of Psychologists in Addictive Behaviors* **37** (8): 1,066–1,079.
37. Erdelez, S., and S. Makri. 2020. Information encountering re-encountered. *Journal of Documentation* **76** (3): 731–751. https://doi.org/10.1108/jd-08-2019-0151.
38. McCay-Peet, L., E. G. Toms, and E. K. Kelloway. 2015. Examination of relationships among serendipity, the environment, and individual differences. *Information Processing & Management* **51** (4): 391–412.
39. Nielsen, J. 1997. *How users read on the web* [cited 2005 April 14, 2005]. https://www.nngroup.com/articles/how-users-read-on-the-web/.
40. Duggan, G. B., and S. J. Payne. 2011. Skim reading by satisficing: Evidence from eye tracking. In *CHI'11: Proceedings of the SIGCHI conference on human factors in computing systems.*
41. Abidin, A. Z. 2020. Students reading comprehension through scanning technique. *Journal of Asian Multicultural Research for Educational Study* **1** (1): 28–35.

42. Edvieanto, E., R. Munandar, and A. Munandar. 2018. Improving students' reading comprehension using scanning techniques. *PROJECT (Professional Journal of English Education)* **1** (2): 157–164.
43. Thamrin, N. S. 2014. Scanning technique in developing students reading comprehension. *Kreatif* **15** (1): 31–35.
44. Darmawan, S. L. 2017. The implementation of skimming technique towards students' reading comprehension. premise. *Journal of English Education and Applied Linguistics* **5** (2): 1–10.
45. Latini, N., I. Bråten, and L. Salmerón. 2020. Does reading medium affect processing and integration of textual and pictorial information? A multimedia eye-tracking study. *Contemporary Educational Psychology* **62**:101870.
46. Luo, W. 2019. User choice of interactive data visualization format: The effects of cognitive style and spatial ability. *Decision Support Systems* **122**:113061.
47. Bergstrom, J., and A. Schall. 2014. *Eye tracking in user experience design*. Elsevier.
48. Arora, N., et al. 2008. Putting one-to-one marketing to work: Personalization, customization, and choice. *Marketing Letters* **19**:305–321.
49. Eppler, M. J., and J. Mengis. 2004. The concept of information overload: A review of literature from organization, science, accounting, marketing, MIS, and related disciplines. *The Information Society* **20**:325–344.
50. Lindgaard, G., et al. 2006. Attention web designers: You have 50 milliseconds to make a good first impression! *Behaviour & Information Technology* **25** (2): 115–126.
51. Kalyanaraman, S., and S. S. Sundar. 2006. The psychological appeal of personalized online content in web portals: Does customization affect attitudes and behaviors? *Journal of Communication* **56**:110–132.
52. Petty, R. E., and J. T. Cacioppo. 1986. The elaboration likelihood model of persuasion. In *Advances in Experimental Social Psychology*, ed. L. Berkowitz, 123–205. New York.: Academic.
53. Sundar, S. S., and S. Marathe. 2010. Personalization versus customization: The importance of agency, privacy, and power usage. *Human Communication Research* **36** (3): 298–322.
54. Shen, H., et al. 2021. Everyday algorithm auditing: Understanding the power of everyday users in surfacing harmful algorithmic behaviors. *Proceedings of the ACM on Human-Computer Interaction* **5** (CSCW2): 1–29.
55. Kliman-Silver, C., et al. 2015. Location, location, location: The impact of geolocation on web search personalization. In *IMC'15: Proceedings of the 2015 Internet measurement Conference.*
56. Thorson, K., et al. 2021. Algorithmic inference, political interest, and exposure to news and politics on Facebook. *Information, Communication & Society* **24** (2): 183–200.

57. Andry, J. F., et al. 2021. Algorithm of trending videos on YouTube analysis using classification, association and clustering. In *2021 International conference on data and software engineering (ICoDSE)*. IEEE.
58. Obiegbu, C., and G. Larsen. 2024. Algorithmic personalization and brand loyalty: An experiential perspective. *Marketing Theory*. https://doi.org/10.1177/14705931241230041.
59. Packard, G., and J. Berger. 2021. How concrete language shapes customer satisfaction. *Journal of Consumer Research* **47** (5): 787–806.
60. Chakraborty, A., et al. 2016. Stop clickbait: Detecting and preventing clickbaits in online news media. In *ASONAM '16 Proceedings of the 2016 EEE/ACM international conference on advances in social networks analysis and mining*. IEEE.
61. Tam, K. Y., and S. Y. Ho. 2006. Understanding the impact of web personalization on user information processing and decision outcomes. *MIS Quarterly* **30** (4): 865–890. https://doi.org/10.2307/25148757.
62. Rafaeli, S., and Y. Ariel. 2007. Assessing interactivity in computer-mediated research. In *The Oxford handbook of internet psychology*, ed. A. Joinson et al., 71–88. Oxford, UK: Oxford University Press.
63. Cho, C.-H., and J. D. Leckenby. 1999. Interactivity as a measure of advertising effectiveness. In *Proceedings of the American academy of advertising*, ed. M. S. Roberts, vol. 1(21), 33–50. University of Florida.
64. Wu, G. 1999. Perceived interactivity and attitude toward websites. In *American Academy of Advertising, Albuquerque, NM*.
65. Coyle, J. R., and S. J. Gould. 2002. How consumers generate clickstreams through web sites: An empirical investigation of hypertext, scema and mapping theoretical explanations. *Journal of Interactive Advertising* **2** (2): 55–73.
66. Sundar, S. S. 2008. The MAIN model: A heuristic approach to understanding technology effects on credibility. In *Digital Media, Youth, and Credibility*, eds. M. J. Metzger and A. J. Flanagin, 73–100. MIT Press.
67. Sundar, S. S., et al. 2015. Toward a theory of interactive media effects (TIME) four models for explaining how interface features affect user psychology. In *The handbook of the psychology of communication technology*, 47–86. Wiley.
68. Qian, X., and S. S. Sundar. 2016. Interactivity and memory: Information processing of interactive versus non-interactive content. *Computers in Human Behavior* **63**:620–629.
69. Boczkowski, P. J., and E. Mitchelstein. 2012. How users take advantage of different forms of interactivity on online news sites: Clicking, e-mailing, and commenting. *Human Communication Research* **38** (1): 1–22.
70. Kinzie, M. B. 1990. Requirements and benefits of effective interactive instruction: Learner control, self-regulation, and continuing motivation. *Educational Technology Research & Development* **38** (1): 5–21.

71. Sundar, S. S., S. Bellur, J. Oh, H. Jia, and H.-S. Kim. 2016. Theoretical importance of contingency in human-computer interaction: Effects of message interactivity on user engagement. *Communication Research* **43** (5): 595–625. https://doi.org/10.1177/0093650214534962.
72. Evans, C., et al. 2004. Virtual learning in the biological sciences: Pitfalls of simply "putting notes on the web". *Computers & Education* **43** (1–2): 49–61.
73. Sicilia, M., S. Ruiz, and J. L. Munuera. 2005. Effects of interactivity in a web site: The moderating effect of need for cognition. *Journal of Advertising* **34** (3): 31–44.
74. Young, J. D. 1996. The effect of self-regulated learning strategies on performance in learner controlled computer-based instruction. *Educational Technology Research & Development* **44**:17–27.
75. Terrado, M., et al. 2018. Climate change communication and user engagement: A tool to anticipate climate change. In *Handbook of climate change communication: Vol. 3: Case studies in climate change communication*, 285–302.
76. Fiorella, L., and R. Mayer. 2015. *Learning as a generative activity*. Cambridge University Press.
77. Xu, Q., and S. S. Sundar. 2016. Interactivity and memory: Information processing of interactive versus non-interactive content. *Computers in Human Behavior* **63**:620–629.
78. Lehikko, A., et al. 2024. Exploring interactivity effects on learners' sense of agency, cognitive load, and learning outcomes in immersive virtual reality: A mixed methods study. *Computers & Education: X Reality* **4**:100066.
79. Scacco, J. M., A. Muddiman, and N. J. Stroud. 2016. The influence of online quizzes on the acquisition of public affairs knowledge. *Journal of Information Technology & Politics* **13** (4): 311–325.
80. McDonald, S., and R. J. Stevenson. 1996. Disorientation in hypertext: The effects of three text structures on navigation performance. *Applied Ergonomics* **27**:61–68.
81. Darken, R. P., and J. L. Sibert. 1996. Navigating large virtual spaces. *International Journal of Human-Computer Interaction* **8** (1): 49–71.
82. Mayer, R. E., J. Heiser, and S. Lonn. 2001. Cognitive constraints on multimedia learning: When presenting more material results in less understanding. *Journal of Educational Psychology* **93** (1): 187.
83. Jach, H. K., C. G. DeYoung, and L. D. Smillie. 2022. Why do people seek information? The role of personality traits and situation perception. *Journal of Experimental Psychology: General* **151** (4): 934–959.
84. Loewenstein, G. 1994. The psychology of curiosity: A review and reinterpretation. *Psychological Bulletin* **116** (1): 75–98.
85. Fletcher, R., and R. K. Nielsen. 2019. Generalised scepticism: How people navigate news on social media. *Information, Communication & Society* **22** (12): 1,751–1,769.

86. Thurman, N., et al. 2019. My friends, editors, algorithms, and I: Examining audience attitudes to news selection. *Digital Journalism* 7 (4): 447–469.
87. Wilson, T. D. 2024. Curiosity and information-seeking behaviour: A review of psychological research and a comparison with the information science literature. *Journal of Documentation* **80** (7): 43–59.
88. Nielsen, J., and K. Pernice. 2009. *Eyetracking web usability.* New Riders Press.
89. Litman, J. 2005. Curiosity and the pleasures of learning: Wanting and liking new information. *Cognition and Emotion* **19** (6): 793–814.
90. Yaros, R., and A. Cook. 2013. Attention versus learning of online content: Preliminary findings from an eye-tracking study. In *Evolving psychological and educational perspectives on cyber behavior*, ed. R. Z. Zheng, 132–154. Hershey, PA: IGI Global.
91. Hsiung, A., et al. 2023. Curiosity evolves as information unfolds. *Proceedings of the National Academy of Sciences* **120** (43): e2301974120.
92. Marvin, C. B., and D. Shohamy. 2016. Curiosity and reward: Valence predicts choice and information prediction errors enhance learning. *Journal of Experimental Psychology: General* **145** (3): 266–272.
93. Blom, J. N., and K. R. Hansen. 2015. Click bait: Forward-reference as lure in online news headlines. *Journal of Pragmatics* **76**:87–100.
94. Kilgo, D. K., and V. Sinta. 2016. Six things you didn't know about headline writing: Sensationalistic form in viral news content from traditional and digitally native news organizations. *Research Journal of the International Symposium on Online Journalism* 6 (1): 111–130. https://isoj.org/research/six-things-you-didnt-know-about-headline-writing-sensationalistic-form-in-viral-news-content-from-traditional-and-digitally-native-news-organizations/.
95. Yaros, R. A., et al. 2020. Varying amounts of information in health news headlines can affect user selection and interactivity. In *ASSN for Educatoin in Journalsim & Mass Communications.* Virtual.
96. Scacco, J. M., and A. Muddiman. 2020. The curiosity effect: Information seeking in the contemporary news environment. *New Media & Society* **22** (3): 429–448.
97. Aubin Le Quéré, M., and J. N. Matias. 2025. When curiosity gaps backfire: effects of headline concreteness on information selection decisions. *Scientific Reports* **15** (1): 994.
98. Qiu, J., and R. Golman. 2024. Curiosity in news consumption. *Applied Cognitive Psychology* **38** (2): e4195.
99. Janét, K., O. Richards, and A. R. Landrum. 2022. Headline format influences evaluation of, but not engagement with, environmental news. *Journalism Practice* **16** (1): 35–55.
100. Kuiken, J., et al. 2017. Effective headlines of newspaper articles in a digital environment. *Digital Journalism* **5** (10): 1,300–1,314.

101. Wahl-Korgensen, K. 2020. An emotional turn in journalism studies? *Digital Journalism* **8**:175–194. https://doi.org/10.1080/21670811.2019.1697626.
102. Lazarus, R. S. 1968. Emotions and adaptation: Conceptual and empirical relations. In *Nebraska Symposium on Motivation*. University of Nebraska Press.
103. Berger, J., and K. L. Milkman. 2012. What makes online content viral? *Journal of Marketing Research* **49** (2): 192–205.
104. Robertson, C. E., et al. 2023. Negativity drives online news consumption. *Nature Human Behaviour* 7 (5): 812–822.
105. Rozin, P., and E. B. Royzman. 2001. Negativity bias, negativity dominance, and contagion. *Personality and Social Psychology Review* **5** (4): 296–320.
106. Vaish, A., T. Grossmann, and A. Woodward. 2008. Not all emotions are created equal: The negativity bias in social-emotional development. *Psychological Bulletin* **134** (3): 383.
107. Ito, T. A., et al. 1998. Negative information weighs more heavily on the brain: The negativity bias in evaluative categorizations. *Journal of Personality and Social Psychology* **75** (4): 887.
108. Ito, T., and J. Cacioppo. 2005. Variations on a human universal: Individual differences in positivity offset and negativity bias. *Cognition & Emotion* **19** (1): 1–26.
109. Soroka, S., P. Fournier, and L. Nir. 2019. Cross-national evidence of a negativity bias in psychophysiological reactions to news. *Proceedings of the National Academy of Sciences* **116** (38): 18888–18892.
110. Lang, A., J. E. Newhagen, and B. Reeves. 1996. Negative video as structure: Emotion, attention, capacity, and memory. *Journal of Broadcasting & Electronic Media* **40**:460–477.
111. Berger, J., W. W. Moe, and D. A. Schweidel. 2023. What holds attention? Linguistic drivers of engagement. *Journal of Marketing* **87** (5): 793–809.
112. Nabi, R., and M. Green. 2015. The role of a narrative's emotional flow in promoting persuasive outcomes. *Media Psychology* **18** (2): 137–162.
113. Drach, R. D., N. C. Orloff, and J. M. Hormes. 2021. The emotion regulatory function of online social networking: Preliminary experimental evidence. *Addictive Behaviors* **112**:106559.
114. Alhabash, S., et al. 2013. Between likes and shares: Effects of emotional appeal and virality on the persuasiveness of anticyberbullying messages on Facebook. *Cyberpsychology, Behavior, and Social Networking* **16** (3): 175–182.
115. Luo, Y., D. Sornette, and S. C. Lera. 2024. *Quantification of the self-excited emotion dynamics in online interactions.* arXiv preprint arXiv:2408.05700.
116. Choi, J., S. Y. Lee, and S. W. Ji. 2021. Engagement in emotional news on social media: Intensity and type of emotions. *Journalism and Mass Communication Quarterly* **98** (4): 1017–1040.

117. Peters, C. 2011. Emotion aside or emotional side? Crafting an ‘experience of involvement’ in the news. *Journalism* **12** (3): 297–316.
118. McCormick, S., A. Aldous, and L. Yarbrough. 2024. Joy: The key to using media to move the needle on climate change. *Frontiers in Communication* **9**:1410775.
119. Khairani, A., and I. Fachira. 2022. The influence of cognitive and emotional engagement on digital content marketing in the tourism industry. *Journal of Tourism Leisure and Hospitality* **4** (1): 14–29.
120. Steinert, S., and M. J. Dennis. 2022. Emotions and digital well-being: On social media’s emotional affordances. *Philosophy and Technology* **35** (2): 36.
121. Lazarus, R. S. 1991. Cognition and motivation in emotion. *American Psychologist* **46** (4): 352–367.
122. Wijekumar, K. 2021. Influence of emotions on digital learning. *Educational Technology Research and Development* **69** (1): 55–57.
123. Verma, A., S. Islam, V. Moghaddam, A. Anwar, and S. Horwood. 2025. Empathic responding for digital interpersonal emotion regulation via content recommendation. *International Journal of Human–Computer Interaction* **41**:9978–9993. https://doi.org/10.1080/10447318.2024.2430428.
124. Smith, C., and R. Lazarus. 1990. Emotion and adaptation. In *Handbook of personality: Theory and research*, vol. 21, 609–637. The Guilford Press.

CHAPTER 8

# Photos, Charts and Video Must Explain Quickly

- Explanatory visuals enhance context and support deeper user engagement.
- Explanatory charts function like visual bullet points, aiding rapid comprehension.
- Visually rich content that overloads cognitive capacity can reduce retention.
- AI-generated visuals raise concerns about authenticity and engagement.



R. Yaros, *The Digital Engagement Model*, Palgrave Practical Guides in Communication,
https://doi.org/10.1007/978-3-032-03822-7_8

The latest research examines how visual elements, including photos, charts, and data visualizations, can effectively capture attention and convey key information quickly. Rather than providing a technical guide for professional graphic design, this chapter focuses on how and why visuals shape meaning, guide attention, influence understanding, and ultimately enhance user engagement in a digital environment. The creation of effective visuals is no longer confined to graphic designers and data programmers. Although virtually every smartphone owner can now create and interpret visuals, including photos and charts, this chapter introduces a series of relatively easy practices that can facilitate quick interpretation and understanding of visuals. A compelling visual must quickly capture and retain attention to effectively convey a message.

Social media platforms such as Facebook and Instagram thrive on video content. There, infographics take the place of long-form reports. And in professional settings, data dashboards often replace written summaries. Visuals are often the first and most important contact between users and a message.

A social media image can become a powerful message if it is framed as explanatory, not just decorative. Similarly, charts can do more than display data. They can engage more users if designed with clarity and purpose. The first seconds a user is exposed to any content are critical, which is why our Digital Engagement Model emphasizes the instant when users decide whether a graphic is salient. The most engaging visuals quickly capture attention, convey information efficiently, and spark cognitive curiosity. We'll see what cognitive connections are necessary for engagement and offer some practical guidelines for enhancing attention with even basic visuals. Whether they are shot on a phone or generated in a spreadsheet, visuals are now central to digital content consumption. To overlook their role would be to miss a crucial aspect of the user experience. This chapter ensures that we won't.

Photography has transformed from a supplemental illustration to a central narrative device in journalism, fundamentally altering how news is consumed and remembered. Yet the integration of visuals is no recent enhancement, but a longstanding evolution in how information is communicated to the public [1]. Photojournalism has evolved to shape not only how events are perceived but also how they are emotionally processed, foreshadowing the more recent cognitive theories that describe the picture superiority effect and dual-coding. Dual-coding theory posits that the human brain processes visual and verbal information through separate channels, enhancing memory retention when both are engaged [2]. This theory supports the picture superiority effect, which predicts that images are more likely to be remembered than words [3]. It is not a great leap to argue, therefore, that images do more than decorate. They can actively structure understanding and retention, reinforcing the need for digital content producers to treat visual elements as core components of narrative design, not mere afterthoughts.

But while visuals align naturally with the goals of the Digital Engagement Model (DEM), they also introduce new demands. They must be as clear, intentional, and strategic as written content. A photo can be simple or cluttered, purposeful or generic. A chart can be insightful or too complex, depending on its design. Video can still fail to connect with a user if it lacks cultural or emotional context or doesn't convey its message in the time it takes most users to view it. In other words, visuals should be designed with the same precision and awareness as other digital content.

The good news is that explanatory photos, charts, visualizations, and video maximize a message, as long as you apply the same rigor to them as your writing. As digital audiences become increasingly visually literate and more discerning about what content they view, the pressure to create visuals that instantly attract and engage users has never been greater. From the moment we unlock our phones in the morning to the time we scroll our feeds before bed, images dominate the information we see.

Photos, videos, and graphics are not simply accessories; they are often the only message. Whether visual content refers to a compelling photograph, a short-form video, or an infographic, it can capture attention and make the message more memorable for a wider audience. For some practitioners, therefore, the ability to communicate visually isn't optional. It is essential and must be efficient.

Research has found that people can begin to extract the meaning of an image in as little as 13 milliseconds, highlighting how quickly the brain processes visual information [4]. This rapid recognition suggests that visuals can be more immediately accessible than text, particularly in fast-paced digital environments. Users often spend only a few seconds deciding whether to engage with content that includes photographs [5]. In a landscape saturated with competing stimuli, those seconds are critical. Images can act as cognitive shortcuts that quickly convey meaning and reduce the mental effort required to interpret other content.

Including images also facilitates subsequent recall of information, which is helpful if we want our content to make an impact. A study in the *Journal of Education and Practice* highlighted that using visual aids in teaching increased retention rates by as much as 80% [6]. It also found that combining visual and audio stimuli engages multiple senses, thus supporting more effective learning.

Similar to the previous chapters focusing on text, the DEM emphasizes that visuals must also quickly capture users' interest and convey meaning with precision. However, visuals can vary in their effectiveness. For example, some photos and charts contain contextual elements, such as secondary features, that provide clues to help users understand the information as quickly as possible. The value of any visual is not only to capture attention. Its real power lies in what the visual communicates.

## 8.1 Photos with Context Explain

> *Graphics must not quote data out of context.*
>
> *- Edward Tufte*

Photos carry narrative potential. From war photos to family albums, images hold time still while hinting at what came before and what might come next. We know that "visual grammar" allows images to express action, causality, and relationships through composition, gesture, and framing [7]. Building on this capacity for visual content to explain a message, the Digital Engagement Model differentiates between common *point-and-shoot* photos from more informative or compelling *explanatory* photos that add elements to provide context [8]. In the digital environment where competition for attention is fierce, producers of visual content must work harder and smarter. Whether you're telling a story, selling a product, explaining an idea, or inspiring action, the time to produce more explanatory visuals is worth the effort.

The process of inferring a story through visual cues is a form of nonlinguistic representation that begins in early childhood education and continues through cross-cultural communication. In contexts where language is a barrier, an explanatory photo is a more accessible, inclusive, and educational medium. Research assessing how well text-to-image generation models performed in producing and testing visuals found they made easy-to-read texts more comprehensible [9]. An explanatory photo without text can empower marginalized voices, allowing viewers to interpret and emotionally engage with the content [10]. This is because thoughtfully composed and presented images, particularly within specific social or cultural contexts, can serve as powerful tools for expression. They can convey meaning beyond language, offering alternative modes of interpretation and emotional resonance, and allowing viewers to engage on their terms [10].

Award-winning photos go beyond a quick, so-called point-and-shoot image that displays a primary person or scene without context. A point-and-shoot photo could show a building, a selfie, a pet, or a family portrait, as shown in Fig. 8.1. By comparison, the explanatory example places the

**Fig. 8.1** Comparing a "point and shoot" versus an explanatory photo

family in a specific room (a kitchen) with an activity (preparing food) and a specific task (cutting a pepper).

By placing a primary feature (the family) in context with a secondary feature (cooking in a kitchen), we create a layered message that viewers can instantly decode, often without even needing a caption or text.

Good visual composition isn't just about aesthetic balance, but also narrative clarity. Including a contextual secondary element with the primary element in a photo adds depth and meaning by communicating a broader story. A portrait of a physician gains greater relevance when framed with hospital signage and patients in the periphery. A photo of an angry citizen tells a much bigger story if that person is a protester with placards, surrounded by police lines, and reacting to the crowd.

This layering aligns with the semiotic principle of *anchorage*, which means that visual elements provide interpretive anchors that guide users toward a preferred meaning [11]. In other words, contextual elements in a photo can shape how the viewer interprets its subject. But for a photograph to be truly explanatory, visual features such as contrast, composition, and directional cues must also guide the eye and reduce ambiguity [7, 12]. Engagement is most likely to be sustained when these design choices are not merely aesthetic but function as communicative elements. Although technology has evolved rapidly, the theoretical principles of how the brain responds to photos remain applicable [13].

There are other benefits of explanatory photos. One is that people interpret and engage with images more deeply when they feel a sense of realism or authenticity. By including unposed background elements, such as a location or action, greater trust and emotional responses can develop.

This is particularly critical in journalism, nonprofit work, and brand storytelling.

Secondly, from a digital engagement perspective, providing context can reduce cognitive load for busy mobile users. When users do not have to piece meaning together from disjointed cues, they can comprehend an image more rapidly. This is reinforced by multimedia learning theory, which suggests that combining images with clear context enhances knowledge transfer and memory. It should be no surprise, therefore, that photos that accurately situate their primary subject outperform text in comprehension tests [14]. Mayer's theory suggests that images facilitate the organization of mental models, resulting in more effective knowledge transfer and enhanced memory.

Thirdly, images readily ignite learning. In classrooms, teachers utilize photographic storytelling to foster visual literacy, creativity, and critical thinking. Students can combine analytical and technical skills when asked to organize elements in photos, consider framing, and plan a visual sequence to create a story that is instantly coherent. A team of researchers synthesizing findings from a wide range of empirical studies on visual storytelling found that multimedia tools consistently improved learner performance [15]. Their review highlights that multimedia not only enhances visual appeal but also helps to scaffold understanding, particularly for complex or abstract topics.

Finally, images can have direct emotive power. Based on qualitative research, visual storytelling techniques such as photo elicitation or photo voice provide a means to share personal insights that text may be unable to express. For example, researchers working with youth in conflict zones or patients in health studies have used photo stories to access nuanced emotional realities, social structures, and unspoken experiences [16, 17]. These efforts leveraged the storytelling capacity of photos to generate knowledge and, in turn, produce more authentic or unfiltered responses than text, as long as the photographer has taken the time to assemble suitably explanatory images.

However, not all photos and photo sequences communicate effectively. Visual elements are not neutral, as they convey specific relationships, processes, and intentions. Explanatory visuals often function through what some researchers call "conceptual representations" that illustrate how things work or relate [7]. They do this by relying on compositional features such as framing, salience, and vectors to guide viewers' attention and suggest meaning. Kress and van Leeuwen argue that we must understand these visual grammars to decode how images explain ideas, reinforce ideologies, and influence interpretation, especially in educational and media contexts where explanatory graphics often support textual content.

All of this suggests that content producers and visual communicators should treat photography not just as filler but as a potentially powerful tool that facilitates engagement. Its appeal justifies the investment in sourcing or producing images with a narrative context. Metrics such as time spent on content, the number of social media shares, and click-through rates consistently favor rich, authentic visuals, particularly those with emotional value [5, 18].

## 8.2 Visuals Can Convey Attention-Getting Emotion Instantly

An explanatory image can instantly tell a story that would take paragraphs to explain. Compelling photos are symbols etched into our collective memory. Visual journalists argue that this is because photographs can create an emotional immediacy that words can rarely replicate, connecting viewers to events and issues in a visceral way [19]. That emotional connection boosts engagement and motivates people to take action. In social media, powerful imagery can turn a news story into a social movement [20, 21].

In the best journalism, photos have evolved from iconic stills to immersive narratives. *The New York Times*, *National Geographic*, and *Magnum Photos* have all published silent photo essays that rely solely on the strength of the images to evoke empathy and understanding. While language might polarize or politicize content, a carefully framed explanatory photo or curated visual sequence can bypass verbal defenses and speak directly to human emotion.

Explanatory photo stories are more than aesthetic exercises. They are cognitive powerhouses. By eliminating language and carefully placing the best possible photographic moment into context, photos challenge us to engage with the moment actively. Whether in the classroom, a newsroom, in the workplace, or on social media, explanatory photos can distill the complexity of life into something instantly seen and deeply felt.

On social media, images serve as a form of currency, so users must internalize their meaning and develop visual literacy on platforms such as Instagram, TikTok, and Facebook. It is this literacy that enables many users to recognize when an image lacks depth or appears staged. Therefore, contextual photography not only aids in information delivery but also fosters authenticity.

Since social media users often mute sound or truncate captions, the image becomes the dominant and sometimes sole carrier of a message. When it encompasses both subject and context sufficiently, it can function independently and reliably across various channels and audiences. According to the Reuters Institute for the Study of Journalism, articles with compelling visuals are more likely to be clicked, shared, and read to completion [22]. This report, based on a YouGov survey of more than 92,000 online news consumers across 46 markets, provides insights into digital news consumption trends. Social media often features a "hero" image that serves as the primary visual element for a story. This suggests that a striking photograph doesn't just represent the story—it *sells* it.

A study analyzing 100 million articles published in 2017 found that Facebook posts with images received 2.3 times more interactive likes, comments, and shares than those without [23] images. Apps such as Instagram and YouTube have built their business models on the power of visuals to engage. However, even on platforms like X or Facebook, where more text is typically used, posts with images consistently outperform those without images. Part of this success is driven by how users interact with social media quickly, emotionally, and visually.

A study by the University of Pennsylvania analyzed nearly 7000 *New York Times* articles during a three-month period to investigate whether sharing patterns correlate with emotional content [24]. Sharing increased, both for more positive high-arousal emotions, such as awe, and negative high-arousal emotions, including anger or anxiety. By contrast, the low-arousal emotions, such as sadness, did not drive sharing. Indeed, these effects were independent of article topic or author.

Brands and influencers have long understood the power of visuals. Specifically, they know that the quality, composition, and relevance of photos primarily drive engagement on platforms such as Instagram. When Instagram photos have been subjected to both quantitative and qualitative analysis, it has been possible to identify eight of the most popular categories: selfies, friends, activities, fashion, food, pets, gadgets, and captioned photos [25].

The engagement boost from visuals represents more than simply vanity metrics. For media companies and content creators, photo-driven engagement yields measurable outcomes, including higher dwell times (the length of time users pause on visuals) and stronger brand recognition. Spending more time on content can also increase impressions of the ads that accompany it. More shares mean more eyes on your content. More engagement leads to better algorithmic placement, which in turn increases visibility.

Studies also highlight the powerful role that human faces play in shaping engagement and perception. In news and social media, users tend to engage more with content that features people and faces. A study by Georgia Tech and Yahoo Labs in 2014 found that Instagram photos featuring human faces were 38% more likely to receive likes and 32% more likely to receive comments than those without faces [26]. Others found that the presence of faces in user-generated videos boosts viewer engagement, especially for influencers with fewer than 100,000 followers. Another multi-method study, which included an extensive dataset analysis, controlled experiments, and eye-tracking, found that early face presence in content is particularly effective in capturing attention [27]. At the same time, others reported a troubling trend. AI-generated faces are increasingly being used in fake social media profiles to spread scams, spam, and coordinated disinformation [28]. An analysis of more than 1400 X accounts revealed the deceptive use of synthetic images designed to appear trustworthy.

Together, these findings suggest that human faces, whether authentic or manufactured, carry powerful psychological weight. A well-chosen image can set the emotional tone, establish perceived credibility, and drive interaction before a single word is read.

There's also a cultural factor. We're living in what one media theorist has called a "pictorial turn," or in other words, a shift in how societies process meaning, now that images are taking more plentiful [29]. In a time where attention to digital content is currency, a strong photo, or better yet, explanatory photo essays, aren't just worth a thousand words; they are worth the enhanced engagement that follows.

## 8.3 Photo Essays Can Be the Entire Story

While news stories have traditionally been dominated by headlines and a single photo, followed by scrollable text, a series of photos or a photo essay can tell a compelling story with only minimal text. This form of visual storytelling, where a sequence of images conveys meaning, narrative, and emotion without relying on text, is not just an artistic endeavor; it is a cognitive form of cultural communication and a strategic journalistic method.

Explanatory visual narratives are structured to tell a coherent story on their own. Whether composed by professional photojournalists, students, or a team within an organization, photo essays are powerful because they activate the viewer's ability to interpret visual cues, infer meaning, and construct narratives. An essay can narrate any topic or event, ranging from a local protest to a personal journey, and when done correctly, without a single word or caption.

Photo essays encourage viewers to interpret, contextualize, and sequence meaning visually rather than linguistically [30]. This fosters not just engagement but higher-order thinking. When people "read" images, they apply similar cognitive strategies as when reading text [7]. Making sense of narrative in images involves drawing inferences, predicting outcomes, and identifying patterns [31].

Examples of how visual essays can contribute to academic discourse are plentiful, including in the context of urban health, where a series of images and text can offer nuanced insights into complex social issues [32]. Similarly, a visual essay that focused on the role of photography in housing activism explored how critical image-making practices highlighted the experiences of those affected by gentrification-induced displacement, demonstrating the power of visual narratives in social activism [33]. And these instances can inform the collection of story-driven training data, such as the anthology of 100 visual stories created when image sequences were used to identify themes in improvised story-building [34]. And images have been shown to foster cross-cultural understanding. In one study, students were asked to write visual essays mediated by social networks. The researchers found the essays to enhance learning in intercultural communication [35].

Interactive slideshows of photos can also offer more than aesthetic appeal. They invite users into a more cognitively engaging relationship with visual content. When users can control the pace, order, or focus of a photo essay, they are not passively viewing the information; they are interpreting and constructing their own narrative paths. This pedagogical strategy is grounded in empirical evidence and has been shown to go far beyond simple design preferences [36].

Of course, the rise of visual media isn't without challenges. Images can be misleading, and research has highlighted the powerful, yet problematic role they can play in shaping public perception and trust. Deepfakes, for example, have emerged as a significant concern. One study found that although only 8% of individuals had created deepfakes, 90% were concerned about their potential for misuse [37]. US government reports echo these concerns, noting that deepfakes can erode trust in elections, media, and public institutions [38]. Similarly, infographics, often assumed to clarify data, can distort it. Nearly one-third of infographics in medical research were found to "spin" non-significant findings, misleading viewers about study results [39].

Beyond deception, the emotional power of visuals can manipulate attitudes and decisions. Emotional imagery in social media and agent-based communications can affect relative bias, trustworthiness, and empathy. For instance, in charitable giving contexts, visuals have been found to affect decision-making, sometimes decreasing trust while increasing emotional impact [40]. Another study demonstrated that emotionally charged images of faces in news content significantly influenced perceived credibility and bias [41]. Two separate studies reported that the presence of angry facial emotions lead to elevated perceptions of bias, and consistent negative portrayals of some politicians, reducing their perceived credibility. These findings underscore the importance of designers and communicators prioritizing ethical visual communication, as well as the need for media consumers to critically evaluate visual content. As one media scholar reflected, we need to learn not just how to look, but how to *see* [29]. It goes without saying that this includes other visuals that affect engagement, such as charts and graphs.

## 8.4 Explanatory Charts Engage More Users

We are all familiar with standard bar, pie, and line charts. In an age of information overload, the ability to translate raw data into clear, visual explanations has never been more important. While complex data visualizations garner attention, it's the simple, explanatory charts that remain among the most trusted and widely used tools in everyday communication. From newspapers to boardrooms and classrooms, charts help audiences to quickly understand patterns, relationships, and comparisons in a way that words and statistics alone can't. The effectiveness of these charts lies not in flashy design or data complexity, but in simplicity. When done well, simple charts don't just describe data—they tell stories quickly. They reveal what matters and can drive understanding. But this doesn't mean they always explain.

One study challenged the assumption that visuals always enhance comprehension. Tracking users' eye movements revealed the nuanced interactions between graphics and textual structure in online health news, which can be cognitively complex and information-dense for the average user [42]. Participants were exposed to two linear text structures: one presented information in a logically progressive sequence with graphics, while the other utilized the standard "inverted pyramid" structure with the same graphics. In the linear text, graphics improved participants' comprehension and reduced cognitive load, as indicated by shorter viewing times and fewer eye fixations. In the inverted pyramid text, which can disrupt the linear flow of information, graphics hindered comprehension, possibly by introducing cognitive dissonance or redundancy. Consistent with earlier research, increased eye fixations and longer viewing times were associated with greater processing difficulty. This contradicts the common belief that visuals always support understanding.

The study also highlighted the importance of context and message structure. Graphics must be cognitively aligned with the flow of information to enhance engagement and learning. When visuals are not adjacent to the corresponding text, the misalignment may increase cognitive load for users rather than reduce it. This suggests that visual design for digital news must also consider narrative coherence and reader expectations to avoid counterproductive outcomes [43]. These findings demonstrate that multimedia elements can either facilitate or hinder comprehension, depending on the semantic structure of the accompanying text. Linear formats may be more suitable for conveying complex scientific or health information when paired with explanatory graphics.

## 8.5 Simple Charts Simply Work

The strength of simple explanatory charts lies in how the human brain processes visual information. Our cognitive system is designed to quickly detect patterns, edges, and proportions, far more efficiently than it processes long blocks of news text or spreadsheets of numbers. Explanatory charts take advantage of this, using visual encoding to offload cognitive effort.

Research on chart literacy shows that users often rely on visual heuristics, such as comparing the lengths of bars or the direction of slopes, rather than interpreting exact numerical values. Well-designed charts with clear labels and minimal clutter can be understood almost instantly [44]. In science communication, visuals can produce effects beyond comprehension. Researchers found that the mere presence of a simple graph in a science news article increased readers' belief in the scientific credibility of the information, even when the chart did not improve understanding or recall. This suggests that visuals can act as persuasive cues, not just explanatory tools [45].

While infographics and data visualizations can be powerful, it's the simple graphics, such as basic charts and illustrations with more explanatory elements, that can consistently increase engagement. Regardless of the type of data, bar charts are one of the most popular, and for good reason. They are ideal for comparing quantities across categories, such as sales by region, votes by candidate, or budgets by department. Bar charts make it easy to compare items side by side. Research shows that bar charts tend to be faster when it comes to value comparison and ranking, but there is debate as to whether bar or pie charts are more accurate [46, 47]. From social media feeds to news articles, a clearly presented explanatory chart can increase attention, interaction, and retention, without overwhelming users. Explanatory charts work not because they show everything, but because they show *just enough.*

Based on research in cognitive psychology, the Digital Engagement Model proposes that four relatively simple, yet essential guidelines can speed the comprehension of bar chart data for a general population of users. Compare the "standard" bar chart in Fig. 8.2 with the "explanatory" chart in Fig. 8.3. Although most charts display a summarizing title, much like a news headline, it takes time for users to determine what the measure in the chart represents and what the values on the scales signify. The "standard" chart in Fig. 8.2 is titled "Engagement Rates Across Social Media Platforms." Users can see differences in engagement rates but what is the measure? Users must examine the chart to determine how engagement is measured, then estimate the approximate values for each social network, which are not ranked in any order.

Consider the "explanatory chart" with a title that begins with the unit of measure to immediately tell the user what the bars represent, and replaces the less approximate y scale with precise values on each bar. What's the downside of presenting users with exact numbers instead of estimates? The bars are also ranked from highest to lowest, allowing users to compare networks instantly and identify the one with the most and least interactions.

Generally speaking, people learn more effectively from a combination of words and visuals than from words alone. The Cognitive Theory of Multimedia Learning predicts that simple graphics with precise values can

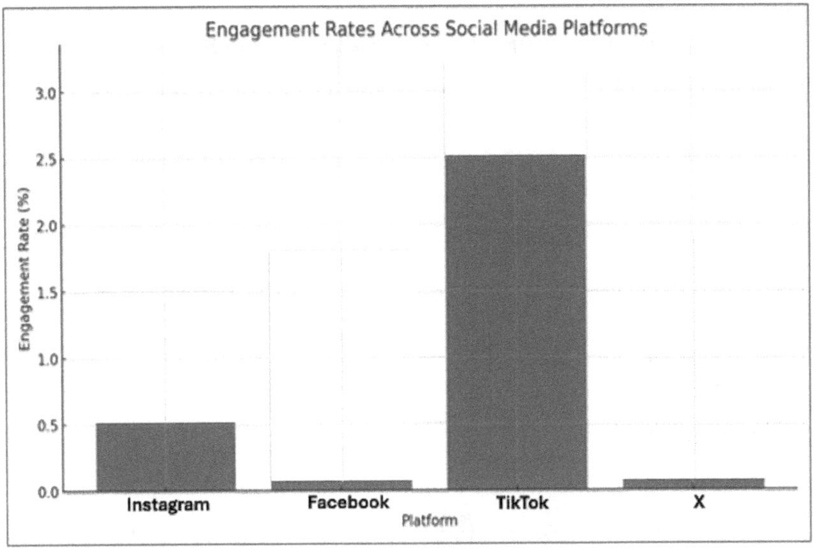


**Fig. 8.2** A typical bar chart with a summarizing title and scales

make abstract or technical ideas far more digestible [48]. A bar chart showing the engagement rate on social networks as a percentage, ranked from highest to lowest, is more effective than a paragraph of text that describes it. Here, users don't just see data. They interpret it quickly.

Given that simple graphics thrive on clarity for engagement, it is perplexing why so many traditional chart formats are still used. Many of today's users don't have time—or don't wish to devote the time—to decode titles, guess measures, or estimate scales, and values. Mobile users are more likely to stay with content if simple visual elements can quickly indicate the content's value to the user [49].

Simple graphics also align with the principles of **visual hierarchy**, which help users process content more easily. People naturally group and prioritize information based on proximity, size, color, and contrast [50]. Visual elements are either perceived as cohesive (unification) or distinct parts (differentiation), depending on their properties. This aligns with Gestalt principles, which assert that people tend to organize visual elements into groups or unified wholes when certain principles are applied. For instance, elements that are close together (proximity), similar in appearance (similarity), or share common attributes like color and size are more likely to be perceived as part of the same group.

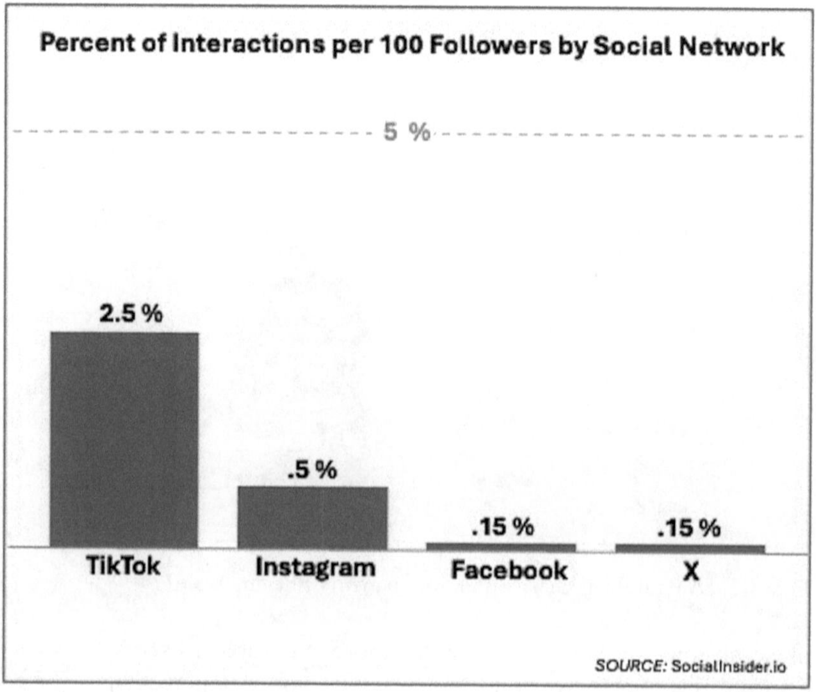


**Fig. 8.3** An *explanatory* bar chart

In the context of mobile user interfaces, users are therefore likely to interpret information based on how visual elements in content are grouped and contrasted. Designers can leverage these insights to create interfaces that align with natural perceptual tendencies. Visualizations take time, data, and design skill. But a content team—or a single creator—can produce simple graphics quickly using tools like Canva or Adobe Express. This matters because news cycles move fast and trends shift daily. The ability to create and publish clean, engaging graphics on the fly is undoubtedly a competitive advantage. This may also help to increase the use of more situationally interesting and educational charts in news still dominated by text.

At the same time, not all graphics are created equal. A poorly designed graphic is still a poor graphic, even if it's meant to be basic. The simplest visuals intentionally use whitespace to limit clutter and focus on a single idea. Conversely, the clumsy use of a bar graph can exaggerate effects, contributing to data misinterpretation in scientific communication [51]. Analyzing bar graphs published across 3,387 articles in 15 journals, researchers reported that the data were consistently distorted. These findings highlight the importance of carefully designing data graphs to ensure accurate representation in scientific publications.

The trend is clear. In all types of news, marketing, education, and social media, visual literacy is on the rise, but visual patience is dwindling. Many expect content to look good, be easy to process, and deliver value fast. Simple and effective graphics meet all three requirements. They respect the audience's variations in time to consume content and help messages cut through the noise. The strategic use of simple visuals is crucial for effective digital engagement.

### *Pie Charts Quickly Visualize Proportions*

Pie charts, first published in 1801 by William Playfair, still get a bad rap in some parts of the data community, but when used to show parts of a whole, they do exactly what they're supposed to do. Each slice can represent a percentage, making a pie chart particularly helpful for showing proportions of a whole. They are best used when there are ideally five or fewer categories and when the focus is on proportions rather than comparisons. When used for their intended purpose, they are nearly as effective as bar charts in terms of user accuracy.

In their study titled *Task-Based Effectiveness of Basic Visualizations*, researchers conducted a crowdsourced experiment to evaluate the effectiveness of five visualization types, including pie charts and bar charts, across ten everyday data analysis tasks [52]. They found that while bar charts generally outperformed pie charts in precise comparisons of value, pie charts were nearly as effective when it came to estimating proportion.

Another study examined how well subjects could estimate the relative size of segments in charts [53]. The results indicated that participants could estimate proportions with similar accuracy using both pie and bar charts, supporting the argument that pie charts can be nearly as effective as bar charts for visualizing proportions.

Finally, a third study examined whether the use of pie charts negatively impacts high-level decision-making compared with bar charts [54]. The findings revealed no significant differences in the quality of decisions made using pie charts versus bar charts, again suggesting pie charts are nearly as effective as bar charts in conveying proportional information.

So, there you have it. Pie charts may have been the butt of data jokes for years, but research consistently suggests they deserve a seat at the visualization table. They might not always be the fastest or most precise, but when it comes to conveying proportions, they hold their own. While pie charts effectively illustrate proportions at a glance, line charts excel in depicting trends over time, offering clarity and simplicity in visualizing the progression of data.

### *Line Charts Map Trends with Clarity*

Line charts are essential for visualizing trends, growth, and movement across time. Whether tracking stock prices, weather changes, or web traffic, line charts help audiences see direction and momentum in the data. That's why they are preferred for time-series data and trend analysis. Research confirms that line charts support long-term thinking by showing how something has evolved, not just where it stands today. In a crowdsourced experiment to evaluate how visualizations performed across ten everyday data analysis tasks, researchers found that line charts were particularly effective for trend analyses and time-series data [52]. Line charts are invaluable for their ability to illustrate changes over time (once users figure out what the measure is, what the lines represent, and what the values are), making line charts the preferred choice [55]. Others note that line charts are ideal for tracking progress, engagement, and the long-term impact of learning initiatives [56]. The Digital Engagement Model prompts the question, what can transform a standard line chart that takes a user several seconds to interpret into an explanatory line chart that immediately orients the user to clear, more specific data? The answer is to apply at least four relatively simple rules.

To illustrate, the "standard" line chart in Fig. 8.4 displays data courtesy of *Exploding Topics and DataReportal (2024)*. It displays a summarizing title, horizontal grid lines to represent the values at which the two lines intersect, a legend revealing what the lines and colors represent, and, at best, estimates the values of each line according to the traditional y-axis of minutes per day.

By contrast, four simple rules to communicate easy-to-understand information quickly (Fig. 8.5) include:

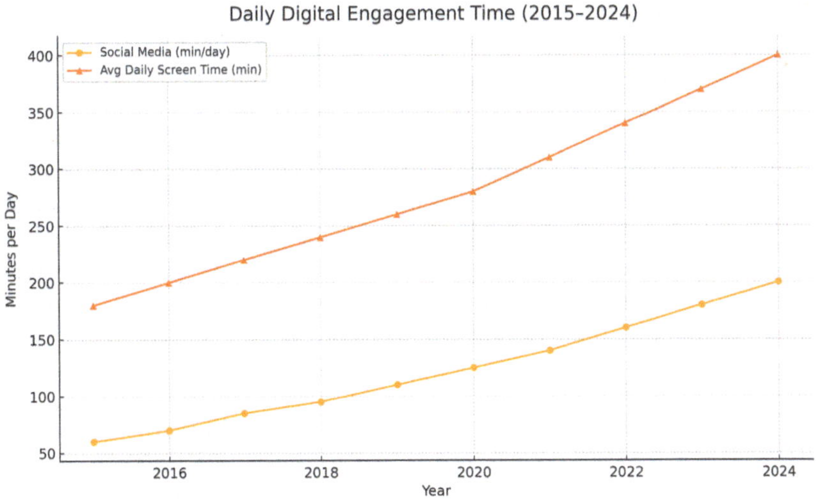


Fig. 8.4 Standard line chart

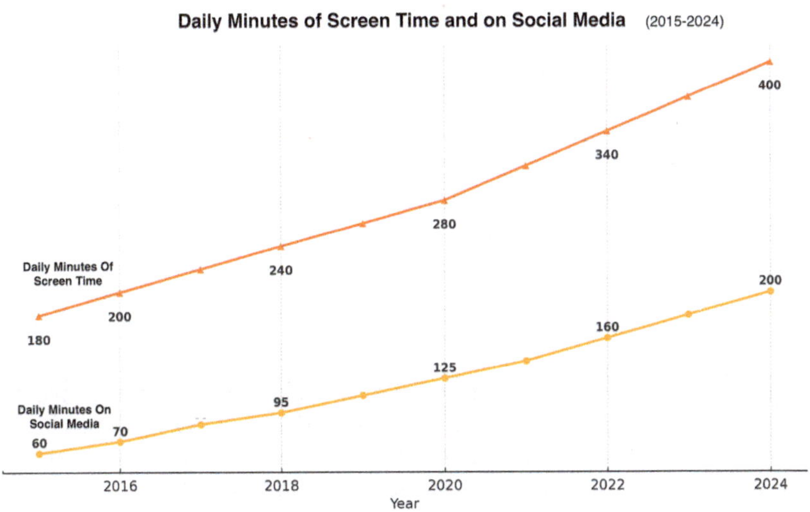


Fig. 8.5 Explanatory line chart

1. The chart title starts with the measure (e.g., Daily minutes….).
2. The legend is replaced with a title placed on each line.
3. The y-axis which provides only estimated values, is removed.
4. Exact values are placed on each line.

These recommendations for explanatory data are the results of our research on ease of comprehension and recall of information. Context matters. A chart should reflect its purpose—be it comparison, trend spotting, or part-to-whole relationships. No chart type is universal because clear interpretation depends on the data and the audience. At the same time, even simple charts can be misleading when used improperly. Common pitfalls include:

- Bar charts with broken axes, exaggerating differences.
- Line charts without clear time intervals cause confusion.
- Pie charts with too many slices making interpretation difficult.
- Over-cluttered visuals, where too many elements compete for attention.

To avoid these traps, many data platforms now incorporate automated chart selection tools. Design choices, such as using familiar chart types, limiting jargon, and avoiding overly complex visuals, ensure that the visualization enhances comprehension rather than causing confusion. Familiar formats, like bar, pie, and line charts, are approachable and understandable, especially for non-expert audiences.

Additionally, color schemes should be accessible to all users, including those with color vision deficiencies, which affect approximately 8% of men and 0.5% of women globally [57]. It's best to use colors only if they enhance the visualization, for example, by emphasizing important categories.

As emphasized above, choosing the wrong chart type can distort the message or lead to misinterpretation. 3D effects and decorative charts, such as radial graphs or pictograms, should generally be avoided unless the intent supports more time to engage and understanding, as they can obscure proportional differences or exaggerate visual effects [58]. Even when the differences in accuracy between chart types are minor, perceived clarity often drive user engagement. That's one argument for designers to prioritize user familiarity and task relevance to support engagement over novelty or complexity. This can be particularly challenging when the visuals have numerous moving parts. A lot of interactive data in visualizations can be attractive and initially interesting, but can also become cognitively overwhelming.

## 8.6 Striking Visualizations Can Still Overwhelm the Brain

Interactive data visualizations grab attention. Can they keep it? Traditional text-based journalism is no longer sufficient to capture the attention of all users, particularly given the complexity of data and the global news it describes. Users crave clarity, context, and control, which they are increasingly finding in interactive data visualizations. From animated graphs that track the spread of a pandemic to maps that chart election results by county or region as they happen, dynamic tools help users connect, explore, and understand the stories behind the numbers.

This transformation is not just cosmetic. Interactive visualizations have transformed the way news is produced, consumed, and remembered. They enable users to navigate large datasets, identify patterns, and personalize their news content journeys.

Interactive news visualizations can take many forms. Some are purely data-driven, while others are structured narratives designed to unfold as digital storytelling. There are those that operate like tools, allowing users to filter their data, search for specific trends, or simulate outcomes. At the core of each, however, is a shared goal by the producers of visualizations. Namely, to make complex data more comprehensible to non-expert users.

Data visualizations are perhaps the most familiar, and include interactive bar charts, animated line graphs, and responsive infographics that update as users manipulate filters and sliders, or roll the cursor over datapoints. These tools can enhance user engagement and comprehension, particularly in scientific or data-intensive stories. In one study, participants interacting with animated scientific news graphics demonstrated better recall and understanding than those exposed to static visuals [59]. However, this outcome hinges on careful design. Without clear guidance provided within a visualization, users may become fixated on flashy visuals and overlook crucial textual context.

Narrative visualizations, such as *NewsLines* or *TimeSets*, go beyond static timelines. The *NewsLines* prototype was tested through a user study involving journalists and an online survey with 178 participants. The findings indicate that such narrative visualizations empower readers to navigate stories at their own pace, enhancing engagement and comprehension [60]. This process will be one of several incorporated into the new engagement interface we introduce in the next chapter. Research into another visualization tool, *TimeSets*, enabled users to explore temporal data with set relations [61]. The study demonstrated that the interactive features of such tools support users in comprehending complex narratives by enabling them to explore relationships between events, people, and institutions over time.

Visualizations also enabled users to trace evolving stories, track events across time, and explore relationships between people, institutions, or themes. By featuring easy-to-use control panels that allow readers to delve deeper into subplots or related events, users can navigate stories at their own pace, thereby deepening engagement while supporting their comprehension of multifaceted issues. But there are other types of visualizations.

For stories with clear spatial or chronological elements, geospatial and temporal visualizations are especially useful. For instance, interactive 3D globes and timeline-based area charts allow users to navigate news information based on geography and time [62]. These visuals do more than decorate. Instead, such visualizations could uncover where and when information is being reported, enabling users to discover blind spots in coverage or overemphasized regions in news.

Similarly, network and sentiment visualizations can reveal hidden structures in the news. These tools visualize the relationships between entities, including political figures, corporations, or countries, or apply sentiment analysis to headlines or quotes. By constructing co-occurrence networks or emotional heatmaps, users can see which figures appear together, what issues are emotionally charged, or how narratives evolve. In this way, bias, polarization, or the narrative framing of an event can be laid bare.

When conversations on Twitter (now X) were analyzed, distinct network structures, such as polarized crowds and community clusters, could be identified [63]. Visualizing these networks highlighted how social media discussions can reflect and reinforce societal divisions that perpetuate bias and polarization. Another study examined how news outlets handle controversial topics by analyzing sentiment and emotional expression in articles [64]. The findings revealed that controversial issues are often associated with negative sentiment and biased language, uncovering the emotional framing and potential bias in news reporting. Semantic differences in the language used by broadcast media outlets, such as CNN and Fox News, have been shown to contribute to polarization on social media platforms, including X [65]. By analyzing linguistic patterns, the research demonstrated that variations in word usage and narrative framing can lead audiences to form divergent interpretations and engage in discussions surrounding events.

User interaction with visualizations offers numerous additional benefits. Visualizations offer novelty, facilitate exploration, and aid in the formation of memory. According to cognitive frameworks of information visualization, tools that allow users to manipulate views, filter results, or hover over components help direct both exogenous (stimulus-driven) and endogenous (goal-driven) attention [66].

When designed effectively, visualizations support a cognitive phenomenon known as chunking. In cognitive psychology, chunking refers to the process by which individuals organize individual pieces of information into larger, more meaningful units or "chunks." This reduces cognitive load, allowing more information to be stored in working memory, which has a limited capacity [67]. As demonstrated in the next chapter, chunking information for diverse audiences is the newly proposed format for presenting digital content that would otherwise be presented as longer linear narratives that many users will ignore. Miller demonstrated that a typical user could retain about seven items (plus or minus two) in working memory. However, when those items are grouped or "chunked" into meaningful units such as words, phrases, or familiar patterns, the number of "chunks" remains constant as the amount of information per chunk can increase. For example, a user wanting to remember a string of eight digits, such as 1-9-4-5-1-7-7-6, could instead make chunks of the years "1945" and "1776" instead of trying to recall eight separate digits.

The cognitive process of chunking explains why experts can remember more information that relates to their specific interests, such as when chess players recall board positions. Phone numbers represent chunks of numbers, and teachers convey complex material or processes into conceptual "chunks." In my teaching, I have found that most students struggle to quickly recall the four variables of demographics, interests, environment, and time that all users bring to any content, that is, until the variables were chunked into the acronym "DIET." The "Smart Story" interface described in the next chapter is informed, in part, by Miller's (1956) seminal work. This principle also represents a key aspect of visualization design by addressing users' memory and learning. Grouping-related data visually reduces the cognitive load on users, thereby enhancing pattern recognition.

### *Powerful Visualizations Must Be User-Friendly*

Interactive visualizations are powerful, not just for audiences but also for journalists and researchers. In journalism, interactive data visualizations are no longer a novelty but a necessity for stories that require critical information to be communicated effectively. These tools can help reporters sift through vast archives of text, video, or metadata, revealing connections and trends that might otherwise be invisible in large amounts of raw data. For users of digital media, interactivity also fosters a sense of agency. Users aren't just fed information. They can engage with it to ask their own questions and discover patterns in the data.

As the volume and complexity of information expand, well-designed interactive visuals not only make complex information readable but also support exploration, enhance memory, and sustain engagement across diverse user populations, especially when designed with the DIET variables of users' environments and time to engage in mind.

In the case of online science news, users were more likely to remember key facts and report deeper understanding when interacting with animated infographics [68]. By employing a multimethod approach that included eye tracking, cued retrospective reporting, and memory tests, researchers examined how individuals engage with static, interactive, and interactive-animated data visualizations embedded in the content. Their findings suggest that interactivity and animation resulted in longer eye fixation times on certain parts of the articles, which can translate into higher learning outcomes.

Note that excessive complexity in visualizations can be counterproductive. Studies testing general news audiences revealed a consistent preference for simpler visualizations that "chunk" key events or terms, avoid excessive hierarchy in data, and highlight key people or places. Compared with traditional search engines that rely on textual input and output, interactive visualizations offer potential benefits by providing multiple representations of large and complex datasets while allowing users to engage with data more intuitively. One framework proposes embedding interactive visualizations into web-based information retrieval systems [69]. This model addresses the challenges posed by the heterogeneous nature of web information and the limitations of traditional search interfaces, and it comprises five key components:

1. The **information layer** recognizes the heterogeneity of web information, encompassing various formats (e.g., text, images, videos) and structures (e.g., databases, documents).
2. The **information structure layer** maps heterogeneous information onto basic structures that are suitable for visualization, thereby facilitating the representation of complex data.
3. The **visualization layer** utilizes coordinated views to represent various information structures, allowing users to interact with multiple visualizations simultaneously.
4. **Interaction techniques** incorporate methods such as filtering, zooming, and linking within and across visualizations to support user exploration and analysis.
5. Finally, **search integration** seamlessly integrates visualizations into the broader search process, allowing users to initiate searches directly from visual elements (glyphs) and navigate between related information with ease.

The model was evaluated using four methods. The first was user testing, which demonstrated that participants could successfully create visualizations and establish links between heterogeneous information types, validating the model's usability and effectiveness. Secondly, statistical data integration combined data with related information, such as historical events, to demonstrate the model's capacity to handle diverse data sources. Thirdly, new visualizations were integrated into existing systems, enhancing users' ability to discover and connect related information efficiently. Finally, the model was applied to stock market data, allowing users to link, analyze, and interactively explore stock data, news, and related articles.

The results suggest that Hienert's visualization model provides a structured approach to integrating interactive visualizations into web-based information search and linking processes. By addressing the challenges of information heterogeneity and enhancing user interaction, the model paves the way for more effective and intuitive information retrieval systems.

Despite the communicative potential of interactive visualizations, they are not always easy to produce quickly. The traditional tenets of journalistic accuracy and clarity must coexist with newer design considerations, such as the usability of a visualization and whether users possess sufficient visual literacy to quickly interpret the data.

Creating compelling visualizations often requires collaboration across disciplines. When journalists partner with developers, designers, and data analysts, they can create tools that are both informative and accessible to users without expert knowledge. However, specific challenges can limit the effectiveness of visualizations. Cognitive and information processing constraints, along with real-world pressures such as tight deadlines and limited budgets, often hinder innovation. Additionally, not every story is suited for interactive formats.

Language and accessibility also pose challenges. Most current systems are built around English-language content, which can limit their relevance and usability in other languages and multilingual contexts. While prototype tools have emerged to address this gap, inclusive design remains a priority and a work in progress [69].

Tools such as EventRiver were developed to help both professionals and lay users analyze large-scale datasets, including video footage, social media posts, or news text. These systems integrate timeline filtering, semantic search, and entity tracking to support discovery and make sense of raw data [70]. Looking ahead, researchers emphasize the need for ongoing refinement, particularly the improvement of data extraction automation, the development of more responsive user interfaces, and the incorporation of broader accessibility features that have been empirically tested to demonstrate effectiveness. Evaluating a visualization solely based on its visual appeal overlooks its capacity to communicate complex data efficiently, especially given the limited time users often devote to interacting with digital content. These additional processes are key to ensuring that interactive visualizations continue to serve a wide range of users across languages, cultures, and literacy levels.

## 8.7 Best Practices for Visualizations Extend Beyond Color and Interactivity

Whether through simple bar charts or detailed infographics, visual representations of data are central to digital communication. However, designing effective visuals involves more than choosing a chart type. It requires strategic thinking grounded in communication principles and design. *The New York Times* and *Reuters* are among the leaders in this practice, integrating dynamic charts with explanatory notes and journalistic voiceovers that guide interpretation.

The primary goal is to simplify information with less clutter and greater clarity. At the same time, however, one of the most common mistakes in data visualization is over-design. Overuse of colors, grids, labels, and unnecessary decorations distracts from the story the data is meant to tell. Edward Tufte, a pioneer in data visualization, advocates for what he calls "data-ink ratio." In other words, maximize the ink that communicates data and minimize everything else [71].

Tufte's revised 2001 edition of his 1983 classic text remains a cornerstone in the field. Tufte's critique of visual clutter, which he calls "chart junk," underscores the importance of design that prioritizes information over embellishment, a principle just as relevant in screen-based visualizations now as it was in print. Using restraint in design means removing redundant labels, using muted background colors, maintaining a clear visual hierarchy, and focusing users' attention on one or two key takeaways, rather than every datapoint. This principle is particularly important for mobile consumption, where limited screen real estate demands streamlined visuals.

Data very rarely speaks for itself. The role of the visual communicator is to provide digital content that enables users to understand not only what the data says, but also what it means. This might include descriptive headlines and subheads. You be the judge if a user's ability to instantly identify their location on a rather cluttered US map by NOAA (Fig. 8.6) outweighs the simplicity of zooming in and rolling the cursor over their city to acquire localized data.

Visual storytelling means guiding the viewer through a sequence of steps or emphasizing a narrative insight. This may involve highlighting key values or anomalies, using animation or annotations to illustrate change over time, or presenting multiple visuals as a cohesive sequence.

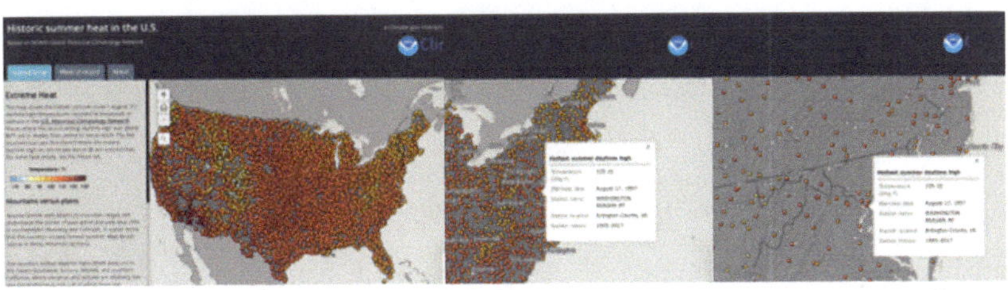


**Fig. 8.6** A US map visualization

Data visualizations that tell a story can outperform those that present only facts [72]. This is especially true in long-form journalism or explanatory pieces, where a visual narrative can deepen emotional and cognitive engagement, as defined by the Digital Engagement Model. Data storytelling empowers users to make informed decisions based on data they can understand. It can also help users receive just the right amount of data, preventing confusion or the perception that the data is misleading.

There is also noteworthy early research that sheds light on the effects of animation versus static text. Lang et al. [73] conducted an experiment to examine how animation and pacing (user-controlled vs. computer-controlled content) affected users' memory for online banner ads. Using physiological measures to detect orienting responses, which signal a user's attentional engagement, the study tested whether animation improved recall. Surprisingly, animated ads did not significantly enhance recall compared to static ads. Users recalled 29% of the content in animated banners, compared to 30% in non-animated banners (Fig. 8.7).

Users who did not exhibit an orienting response showed significantly better recall (36%) with computer-paced, non-animated ads than with

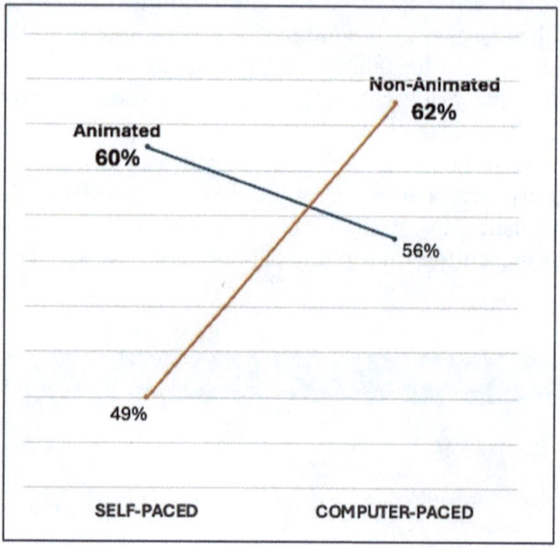


**Fig. 8.7** Percent of recall of banner ad information by pacing and animation

user-paced versions (24%). These findings suggest that while animation can attract attention by triggering an orienting response in users, it does not necessarily enhance memory for the content. In fact, overly dynamic or user-controlled elements can disrupt processing, potentially leading to reduced recall. For designers, this implies that subtle, strategically paced static visualizations may outperform more animated or interactive ones in promoting long-term information retention, particularly when users are not already deeply engaged.

Formal training in the production of visualizations extends beyond the scope of this chapter. Still, we have presented some important guidelines for creating or recognizing clear, accurate, and engaging data visualizations. Compelling visualizations begin with empathy for the viewer. By synthesizing communication and psychology, research has identified several standard rhetorical techniques in narrative visualizations. These include:

- *Emphasis framing* highlights specific data or trends to steer interpretation.
- *Ordering and sequencing* guides users in a set order to shape a narrative.
- *Visual contrast* uses size, color, and position to draw attention to certain elements.
- *Annotation*, including labels and captions, steers interpretation.
- *Metaphoric representations* are visual forms (e.g., tree maps suggesting hierarchy) that carry implicit meaning.

Producers must consider the audience's familiarity with the subject and the level of statistical literacy required to understand the data. For example, financial charts in a business publication frequently assume all readers understand percentage changes and compound interest, whereas a general news outlet may need to explain these concepts visually first. Accessible designs also ensure that the largest possible audience can benefit from the information, an ethical and legal imperative for public-serving media organizations.

Accessibility needs must also be addressed, even though many sites currently do not. Accessibility should be baked into every stage of the design process. In addition to choosing fonts that are legible on all screen sizes and using sufficient contrast between the text and the background, visualizations still need alt-text descriptions for screen readers. They should avoid relying on colors, shapes, or patterns to distinguish between categories. The organization "Web Accessibility in Mind" (WebAIM) conducts an annual analysis of accessibility for the top one million homepages. The 2025 report found that the majority of sites failed to meet basic accessibility standards, highlighting the challenges in creating an inclusive web environment [74]. Accessibilitychecker.org's 2024 report evaluated more than 63,000 websites globally and found that 88% of the sites were not compliant with accessibility standards [75]. The average website earned an accessibility score of about 60 out of 100 points. E-commerce websites averaged 64 points, and sites with an accessibility score of 75 or higher were associated with higher revenue levels.

Before publishing, most professionals, but fewer students, know the value of testing their visualizations with sample users to determine whether the key takeaway is immediately clear. Is the data interpreted as intended? Are all the visualization labels readable on all devices? Even small refinements can improve comprehension.

As producers of digital content strive to meet the demands of a fast-moving, information-rich world, the skills needed to visualize data clearly and ethically extend beyond just creativity. The four variables in the model's "digital DIET" provides new guidance for how the best visualizations also respect a user's time, intelligence, and diversity, thereby engaging and informing them while earning their trust. By reviewing the research in this chapter and following the design principles that emphasize clarity, context, accessibility, narrative structure, and visual integrity, producers can make data speak in ways that are both powerful and responsible. Arguably, the visual medium that is just as powerful—if not more powerful than charts and visualizations—is video.

## 8.8 There's a Reason Why Video Is the Dominant Visual Medium

Video is dominant not because it's trendy, but because it's effective. The proliferation of high-speed Internet and mobile devices has enabled the widespread consumption of video across various platforms, making it a preferred medium for storytelling, education, and marketing. As the demand for immediate content increases, understanding the nuances of video, particularly the distinctions between long-form and short-form video, is crucial for engaging the largest populations of users. As with clickbait, there will always be an audience that clicks a teasing headline and an audience that will always watch longer videos. The question is: do you want to reach the *largest* possible audience?

According to a report on video marketing in 2024, 89% of businesses used video as a marketing tool, a slight reduction from previous years [76]. LinkedIn, originally a text-heavy platform, reports that video is now 20 times more likely to be shared than any other type of content [77]. At the same time, marketers cite barriers to adopting video, including not knowing where to start (37%) and not having enough time to watch the video (approximately 25%).

In education, too, video remains a vital tool. Compared with students who watched long videos, research has shown significantly longer engagement by students who watched short videos (six minutes or less). In fact, their overall viewing time increased by 24.7% and final exam scores by 9% [78]. In addition to being effective, videos should be concise, focused, and integrated with interactive elements to promote active learning [79]. If these criteria are met, videos enable students to learn at their own pace and revisit complex topics as needed. Finally, a study that tested 7,776 students found that videos of traditional lecture teaching methods led to only minor improvements in student learning, whereas adding other video to the recorded lecture led to significant learning benefits [80].

When comparing video, photo, and text, researchers sought to determine which content components, interactivity cues, and media richness are most effective in inducing clicking, liking, commenting, and sharing behaviors [81]. An analysis of 757 Facebook posts showed that the relative media richness of photos and videos influenced all four interactivity behaviors. Although the study focused on only one social network (Facebook), the practical implications are that media richness and interactivity are correlated. In terms of sharing, the study showed that photo-based posts were more effective than video-based posts.

Other research investigated how well a short video engages viewers on social media before user interactions, such as likes, views, or comments, are counted [82]. Surprisingly, the quality scores of short videos on Snapchat did not predict how engaging a video would be. In other words, a video that looks good didn't necessarily get watched or liked more than other videos.

The researchers then collected a new dataset of 90,000 short Snapchat videos, using two new measures of engagement:

(1) The average percentage of the video that users watched, adjusted for video length (or *Normalized Average Watch Percentage,* NAWP)
(2) How likely users were to keep watching more videos afterward (*Engagement Continuation Rate* or ECR)

Then, instead of counting likes or views, the researchers trained a model to predict engagement based only on a video's visual features, audio, including music, and the text of overlays and captions on the video.

The new metrics outperformed the previous measures, exhibiting a higher correlation between media richness features and engagement. Previous measures had tended to favor longer videos or shorter ones. These results suggested the new measures could be more reliable indicators of viewer engagement across different video lengths.

The predicted video engagement that was based on content such as visuals, music, and text, rather than likes or shares, more closely matched the observed engagement behavior, including how long people watched and whether they continued to watch additional videos.

The video platform YouTube needs little introduction as a primary exponent of the medium. While much research has focused on YouTube's uses in formal education, a substantial body of literature also describes the platform's broader social function for communities, emotional connections, and participatory cultures. YouTube's vast ecosystem of creators and viewers fosters the co-construction of shared values, norms, and identities. Through mechanisms such as comments, algorithmic content, and creator-audience interactions, in this digital environment, communities can be shaped and sustained.

YouTube's experimental "Hype" feature, launched in 2024, reveals how platform affordances can empower user agency and redefine community influence [83]. Hype enables viewers to "boost" videos from creators who have fewer than 500,000 subscribers, adding them to a visible leaderboard that prioritizes smaller channels. Unlike traditional recommendation algorithms, which often replicate existing popularity hierarchies, YouTube's Hype feature imbues users with promotional power, giving fans a measurable role in a creator's visibility. YouTube's official announcement stated that its intention is to give fans a stake in promoting their favorite emerging creators [83]. This reconfigured the YouTube viewer from a passive user to an active curator and gatekeeper.

Unfortunately, research found that not all community activity on YouTube fosters positive engagement. One study analyzed more than

290,000 commenters across thousands of videos to identify patterns of coordinated commenting [84]. These "commenter mobs" often appeared in politically charged or ideologically motivated videos, where groups of users deployed synchronized comments to amplify messages or challenge alternative narratives. Using network analysis and algorithms, the study found that these groups can be organized and strategic, raising ongoing concerns about the dissemination of misinformation. This aspect of YouTube illustrates its dual nature. While some users can contribute constructively to discourse, YouTube is equally vulnerable to coordinated campaigns that can undermine more genuine community dialogue.

We surmise that YouTube is not merely a video-sharing platform, but a complex system that can influence how people of all ages and cultures connect, organize, and interact. Whether they involve users' emotional bonds with their favorite creators, the promotion of emerging talent, resistance movements, or do-it-yourself guidance, YouTube videos enable various forms of digital community building. The platform's design, ranging from simple hearts to algorithmic tweaks like Hype, can play a powerful role in creating opportunities for greater engagement. Understanding the multidisciplinary benefits video offers is therefore critical for media scholars, practitioners, educators, public officials, and journalists.

### *Like Text, User Interest and Time Determine Video Engagement*

In a blog post titled *Long-form vs. Short-form videos: which one is best for you?* the benefits and drawbacks of long-form video content are considered, particularly for niche audiences [85]. It states that while long-form videos can enhance brand authority and promote significant engagement, their effectiveness depends on maintaining viewer interest throughout the video's duration. If only viewer interest were the single determinant for video engagement. The Digital Engagement Model predicts that the rest of a user's digital DIET plays a significant role.

Consider an alternative explanation for the observed variations in video engagement. Independent research by the global agency Billion Dollar Boy reported that long-form video, podcasts, live streaming, and even text were experiencing a resurgence [86]. The agency found that more than two-thirds of the surveyed marketers (68%) had increased production of long-form creator content. At the same time, a significant proportion cited longer-form video as a priority for the future. In such cases, they should consider the findings of the *2025 State of Video Report* by the marketing platform Wistia, which analyzed more than 100 million videos and webinars totaling 2.7 million hours of content [87].

Wistia found that as video length increased, average viewer engagement decreased. Specifically, videos of one minute or shorter recorded an average engagement rate of 50%, which dropped to 38% for videos between five and 30 minutes, and further to 15% for videos longer than 60 minutes [87].

Academic research provides nuance to this trend [88]. Evaluating instructional videos in a controlled setting, three- to five-minute videos achieved engagement rates as high as 74%, suggesting longer videos can hold attention when users perceive the content as useful. Still, it's important to remember that digital and social media analytics, like Wistia's, are drawn from existing videos with varied content, audiences, and distribution strategies. They do not offer the controlled comparisons necessary to predict optimal strategies across diverse user groups and digital environments, particularly in relation to user-specific DIET variables.

In terms of video interactions, YouTube introduced its Shorts format in 2020, allowing users to prominently upload and showcase their short videos on the platform's website and app [89]. Subsequently, a study analyzed nearly 17 million YouTube videos to compare approximately 10 million Shorts with seven million longer videos across various content categories [90]. It found that Shorts were primarily used in entertainment categories, while regular videos covered a broader range of topics. Although Shorts received more views and likes per view, they generated fewer comments per view compared with regular-length videos.

Some have claimed that the reason short videos (defined as five to 90 seconds in length) are so popular is because they provide "a quick-fix of content wherever you are—in the dentist's waiting room, on your lunch break at work, standing in line at the store, or relaxing on your sofa in the evening" [91]. That claim refers to the collection of additional variables in the model's digital DIET, which predicts why users watch videos in different ways. It depends on who the viewers are (demographics), what they're interested in (individual interests), where they are, and on what device they're using (environment), and how much time they have. An effective digital engagement strategy leverages both short and long-form formats to guide different users through the engagement funnel.

Short-form videos can serve as entry points for scanning viewers, sparking interest, and directing some viewers to longer, more detailed content. Longer-form videos support users with individual interest in specific content and the time to engage. Don't forget that even users with an interest in digital content may not be in an environment or have the time to view it. Incorporating both long- and short-form videos into engagement strategies enables a more comprehensive approach to engaging more users and fostering interaction. A deeper understanding of how video formats cater to the diverse needs of video viewers can help producers and marketers craft compelling content that captures attention, delivers value, and fosters lasting connections.

Of the content that is frequently shared, high-arousal emotions, such as awe, anger, and amusement, increase the likelihood of content going viral [24]. Conversely, content that elicits low-arousal emotions, such as sadness, was less likely to be shared. Emotional arousal is clearly a significant factor in the social transmission of content.

It is also important to note the well-documented psychological reasons behind video engagement. We are wired to respond to motion and sound. The combination of visuals, spoken words, music, and movement activates more parts of the brain than static content, leading to deeper cognitive processing and stronger emotional reactions. Video content stimulates both the auditory and visual cortices, helping viewers better understand and remember the information being presented [92].

Despite the debates about the ideal length of videos or the variables that determine video engagement, video uniquely drives cross-platform engagement. For example, a clip shared on Instagram can drive traffic to a full article on a news site. A video teaser posted on Facebook can funnel viewers to a YouTube documentary or a newsletter subscription. Video can serve as a quick gateway to capture viewers' attention and guide them toward more in-depth forms of content. That explains why some publishers use videos not just to entertain but to *convert* viewers to a view, read, follow, share, or purchase. This chapter concludes with the most recent development in—and threat to—visual content, artificial intelligence.

## 8.9 Deceptive AI-Generated Visuals Can Do More Harm Than Good

It's impossible to ignore how AI-generated deepfakes that convincingly mimic natural environments and real people have proliferated across digital platforms, blurring the lines between reality and deception. From fabricated photos of public figures to manipulated videos that spread misinformation, the digital landscape is increasingly rife with content designed to mislead.

For example, AI-generated images of celebrities, such as Billie Eilish, seeming to appear at events they never attended, went viral, confusing viewers [93]. Nor are these deepfakes limited to entertainment. They also pose serious threats to political discourse, public trust, and societal cohesion [94]. Synthetic content raises pressing questions about the reliability of visual content and the tools at our disposal to interpret and present it.

The role of authentic visuals will become increasingly important because AI's ability to fabricate content that contains realistic images instantly and video is challenging our ability to discern truth from fiction. A large-scale study analyzing 15.2 million posts on Pixiv, a central online platform for artists, included 2.4 million AI-generated submissions [95]. The research aimed to track how AI-generated visuals influence content creation, community engagement, and user behavior. With the site drawing over a billion page views per month, the findings revealed that AI-generated content is reshaping platform dynamics in specific ways. First, the influx of AI art led to a measurable decline in content diversity, with a rise in repetitive themes, particularly adult content and depictions of female characters. Second, while AI submissions increased the overall volume of artwork, they attracted fewer comments and lower engagement, suggesting that users were less inclined to interact with AI-generated content. Third, AI creators tended to be less communicative and more commercially focused, often posting without engaging in meaningful community participation. In effect, AI-generated content shifted how users engage, reducing interactivity, narrowing content themes, and altering the platform's social fabric. The question is whether this shift will persist as AI technology continues to evolve.

Another study by Utah Valley University's Center for National Security Studies and the SMART Lab examined the psychological and biometric effects of AI-generated deepfake media on viewers [96]. Researchers tested the impact of both real and deepfake video and audio content on 244 participants, 40 of whom were monitored using biometric tools, including eye tracking and facial coding. The study assessed the credibility, trustworthiness, and persuasiveness of the content and found that deepfake content was rated as equally or more credible and trustworthy than authentic media. More than 50% of the participants believed the deepfakes were real, even after being told that "some content may have been AI-generated." Biometric data indicated that deepfakes elicited higher unconscious engagement and confusion, even though participants did not consciously report these reactions. The study highlights the difficulty individuals face in detecting deepfakes and the potential impact on trust and decision-making, particularly in political contexts.

Beyond photos and videos, AI can also generate data visualizations that appear professional and trustworthy yet are based on flawed or fabricated data. These "visualization mirages" can skew interpretation by emphasizing or de-emphasizing particular narratives, whether intentionally or not [97]. The danger is compounded by the fact that charts and infographics often carry a veneer of objectivity, which may lead users to trust misleading information without sufficient scrutiny. A study published in the *Journal of Research in Social Science and Humanities* has emphasized that transparency in AI use and an awareness of the limitations of machine-generated content are essential to rebuilding trust in AI-powered journalism [98].

The paper argues that media outlets must strike a delicate balance between automation and ethical journalism to maintain public trust. While AI tools can improve the speed and accuracy of reporting, especially in data-intensive fields like finance and sports, they also raise concerns about bias, lack of human judgment, and the opacity of machine-generated content. Using case studies and credibility analyses, the study finds that maintaining public trust in AI-powered journalism depends heavily on transparency about AI use and a clear understanding of its limitations.

Journalists and fact-checkers often struggle to quickly verify photos and videos because the process is complex and requires specialized skills that most newsroom tools don't fully support. One study explored how social media, while essential for news circulation, makes it easier to disseminate false or misleading visual content [99]. Verifying user-generated visual content typically involves five key steps:

1. Identifying the original source
2. Confirming the date
3. Verifying the location
4. Checking for manipulation
5. Corroborating the content with other evidence

However, researchers claim these steps may still fall short when confronting more advanced or subtle forms of visual misinformation. To strengthen the process, the study proposes an additional sixth step of multimedia forensics. This step would use computational techniques to analyze digital images and videos for signs of tampering invisible to the human eye, such as inconsistent lighting, unnatural shadows, or irregularities in image compression and noise patterns. The researchers reviewed several categories of visual forgeries, including splicing, retouching, and deepfakes, and outlined the detection methods the computer science community has developed to uncover them. The study also mapped the current tools used by journalists, highlighted their limitations, and argued that integrating multimedia forensics into daily newsroom practices could significantly enhance the credibility and efficiency of visual verification.

On the other hand, while AI contributes to the spread of misinformation, it also offers tools to detect and verify it. Advanced algorithms, such as those used in tools such as *TruthLens*, can identify deepfakes by analyzing visual-textual inconsistencies and providing justifications for their assessments [100]. However, the rapid evolution of generative AI often outpaces the detection tools, creating a constant game of catch-up. In evaluating 16 leading models across a range of attack scenarios, including black-box, white-box, and gray-box settings, one study revealed critical limitations in the current detection tools, underscoring the need for more robust, generalizable defenses [101].

The success of these detection systems hinges on widespread adoption and public awareness. Without clear guidance and education, even the most advanced detection tools may fail to mitigate the harm caused by false visual content. In the article *AI Misinformation: Challenges and Solutions for Businesses*, Gita Johar of the Columbia Business School discusses the role of public awareness and education in combating AI-generated misinformation [89]. Johar emphasizes that even the most advanced detection tools may fall short without widespread adoption and clear guidance for users. She notes that the rapid spread of AI-generated content, coupled with a lack of cues prompting individuals to fact-check, can significantly hinder efforts to mitigate the harm of false visual content. Organizations need not only to develop sophisticated detection technologies but also to invest in educating the public about their use and the importance of critically evaluating digital content. Pertinent to this book, the new interface proposes to instantly make fact-checking easy for users.

Consequently, boosting AI media literacy is more pressing than ever. Users of digital technologies must know how and when to question the authenticity of not only images and videos but also charts, diagrams, and infographics. Transparency from content creators and platforms, mainly when AI is used in content production, could also play a crucial role in rebuilding public trust.

This chapter explains why photos, charts, videos, and data visualizations are the most structured and effective ways to engage with digital users. Visuals are not, however, immune to distortion. As AI technologies evolve, so must our strategies for identifying truth, whether through improved technological detection, regulatory oversight, or comprehensive media literacy education. Without these tools, even the most persuasive visual could lead users further from understanding, rather than toward it.

The next and final chapter brings together the core insights presented throughout this book, synthesizing the user and content variables proposed by the new Digital Engagement Model. By drawing on key literature from journalism, cognitive psychology, neuroscience, human-computer interaction, education, and visual communication, the previous chapters have laid a multidisciplinary foundation for rethinking how digital content can be structured to facilitate engagement. This synthesis leads to a central argument. If the goal is to engage more users with more content for longer periods, then new, evidence-based content structures must be developed.

While there is no expectation that all elements of the model will be universally adopted, this book argues that the intensifying competition for users' attention stems in part from the limitations of traditional, linear storytelling formats. These once-reliable structures no longer align with all the evolving needs, behaviors, and expectations of today's—and especially tomorrow's—digital users. There is little doubt that keeping some text and video shorter and incorporating compelling visualizations, can boost engagement. However, without fundamentally rethinking how digital content is structured and presented for the human brain that can access information at any time, even the most valuable content risks being overlooked. Not because it lacks importance, but because it fails to resonate with the moment. Let the next chapter show how it can.

## References


1. Gervais, T., and G. Morel. 2020. *The making of visual news: A history of photography in the press*, 248. Taylor & Francis.
2. Paivio, A. 1991. Dual coding theory: Retrospect and current status. *Canadian Journal of Psychology/Revue canadienne de psychologie* **45** (3): 255.

3. Whitehouse, A. J., M. T. Maybery, and K. Durkin. 2006. The development of the picture-superiority effect. *British Journal of Developmental Psychology* **24** (4): 767–773.
4. Potter, M. C., et al. 2014. Detecting meaning in RSVP at 13 ms per picture. *Attention, Perception, & Psychophysics* **76**:270–279.
5. Kaur, H., and K. R. Kaur. 2021. Investigating the effects of consistent visual identity on social media. *Journal of Indian Business Research* **13** (2): 236–252.
6. Shabiralyani, G., et al. 2015. Impact of visual aids in enhancing the learning process case research: District Dera Ghazi Khan. *Journal of education and practice* **6** (19): 226–233.
7. Kress, G., and T. Van Leeuwen. 2020. *Reading images: The grammar of visual design*, 310. Routledge.
8. Yaros, R. 2009. Producing citizen journalism or producing journalism for citizens: A new multimedia model to enhance understanding of complex news. In *Journalism and citizenship: New agendas*, ed. Z. Papacharissi, 71–90. New York, NY: Routledge.
9. Anschütz, M., T. Sylaj, and G. Groh. 2024. Images speak volumes: User-centric assessment of image generation for accessible communication. In *Proceedings of the third workshop on text simplification, accessibility and readability (TSAR 2024).* Miami, Florida, USA: Association for Computational Linguistics. arXiv preprint arXiv:2410.03430.
10. Rose, G. 2023. *Visual methodologies: An introduction to researching with visual materials*, 100. Sage Publications.
11. Barthes, R. 1977. *Image-music-text.* Vol. 220. Hill and Wang/Farrar, Straus and Giroux.
12. Mather, G. 2013. *The psychology of visual art: Eye, brain and art.* Cambridge University Press.
13. Barry, A. M. 1997. *Visual intelligence: Perception, image, and manipulation in visual communication*, 425. State University of New York Press.
14. Mayer, R. E. 2014. Introduction to multimedia learning. In *The Cambridge handbook of multimedia learning*, ed. R. E. Mayer, 1–24. Cambridge University Press.
15. Abdulrahaman, M. D., et al. 2020. Multimedia tools in the teaching and learning processes: A systematic review. *Heliyon* **6** (11): e05312.
16. Naqshbandi, M. M., and W. Amin. 2013. Conflict zone and developmental issues faced by youth: "A study from Kashmir". *International Journal of Peace and Development Studies* **4** (1): 8–15.
17. Plunkett, R., B. D. Leipert, and S. L. Ray. 2013. Unspoken phenomena: Using the photovoice method to enrich phenomenological inquiry. *Nursing Inquiry* **20** (2): 156–164.
18. Krause, R. 2023. Using imagery in visual design. 2025.

19. Ritchin, F. 2013. *Bending the frame: Photojournalism, documentary, and the citizen*. Aperture.
20. Neumayer, C., and L. Rossi. 2018. Images of protest in social media: Struggle over visibility and visual narratives. *New Media & Society* **20** (11): 4,293–4,310.
21. Bestvater, S., et al. 2023. *BlackLivesMatter turns 10: Social media, online activism and 10 years of# BlackLivesMatter*. Pew Research Center. pewresearch.org.
22. Newman, N., et al. 2021. *Reuters institute digital news report 2021* [cited 2024 October 15, 2024]. https://reutersinstitute.politics.ox.ac.uk/digital-news-report/2021.
23. Rayson, S. 2018. *Content trends report 2018*, 35.
24. Berger, J., and K. L. Milkman. 2012. What makes online content viral? *Journal of Marketing Research* **49** (2): 192–205.
25. Hu, Y., L. Manikonda, and S. Kambhampati. 2014. What we Instagram: A first analysis of Instagram photo content and user types. In *Proceedings of the international AAAI conference on web and social media*.
26. Bakhshi, S., D. A. Shamma, and E. Gilbert. 2014. Faces engage us: Photos with faces attract more likes and comments on Instagram. In *Proceedings of the SIGCHI conference on human factors in computing systems*.
27. Wang, X., Y. Ding, and Y. Hu. 2025. The impact of face presence in user-generated videos on consumer engagement: Insights into how, when, and who. *International Journal of Research in Marketing* **42**(4B). https://doi.org/10.1016/j.ijresmar.2025.02.003.
28. Yang, K.-C., D. Singh, and F. Menczer. 2024. Characteristics and prevalence of fake social media profiles with AI-generated faces. *Journal of Online Trust & Safety* **2** (4): 18.
29. Mitchell, W. T. 2005. *What do pictures want?: The lives and loves of images*, 408. University of Chicago Press.
30. Barrett, T. 2020. *Criticizing photographs: An introduction to understanding images*, 228. Routledge.
31. Messaris, P. 1994. *Visual "literacy": Image, mind, and reality*, 224. Westview Press.
32. Davey, G., and M. Grant. 2024. The visual essay and knowledge production: Towards a visually informed understanding of urban health. *Cities & Health* **8** (1): 1–7.
33. Strasser, A. 2024. Visibilising gentrification-induced displacement: A visual essay on the role of a socially and politically engaged photographic practice in housing activism. *Visual Studies* **39** (1–2): 118–126.
34. Halperin, B. A., and S. M. Lukin. 2023. Envisioning narrative intelligence: A creative visual storytelling anthology. In *Proceedings of the 2023 CHI conference on human factors in computing systems*.

35. Tambunan, A. R. S., and S. Ferdiansyah. 2024. Engaging students in SNS-mediated visual essay-writing tasks to develop intercultural communication skills. *Communication Teacher* 39:1–9.
36. Mayer, R. E., and R. Moreno. 2003. Nine ways to reduce cognitive load in multimedia learning. *Educational Psychologist* **38** (1): 43–52.
37. Sippy, T., et al. 2024. *Behind the deepfake: 8% create; 90% concerned. Surveying public exposure to and perceptions of deepfakes in the UK*. arXiv preprint arXiv:2407.05529.
38. Gao, G. 2024. *Science & tech spotlight: Combating deepfakes* [cited 2024 November 6, 2024]. https://www.gao.gov/products/gao-24-107292.
39. Muller, R., et al. 2025. Do infographics 'spin' the findings of health and medical research? *BMJ Evidence-Based Medicine* **30** (2): 84–90.
40. Genç, H. U., et al. 2025. Persuasion in pixels and prose: The effects of emotional language and visuals in agent conversations on decision-making. In *CHI conference on human factors in computing systems (Yokohama, Japan) (CHI'25)*. New York, NY, USA: Association for Computing Machinery.
41. Karduni, A., et al. 2023. Images, emotions, and credibility: Effect of emotional facial expressions on perceptions of news content bias and source credibility in social media. In *Proceedings of the international AAAI conference on web and social media*.
42. Yaros, R., and A. Cook. 2013. Attention versus learning of online content: Preliminary findings from an eye-tracking study. In *Evolving psychological and educational perspectives on cyber behavior*, ed. R. Z. Zheng, 132–154. Hershey, PA: IGI Global.
43. Makransky, G., T. S. Terkildsen, and R. E. Mayer. 2019. Role of subjective and objective measures of cognitive processing during learning in explaining the spatial contiguity effect. *Learning and Instruction* **61**:23–34.
44. Cleveland, W. S., and R. McGill. 1984. Graphical perception: Theory, experimentation, and application to the development of graphical methods. *Journal of the American Statistical Association* **79** (387): 531–554.
45. Tal, A., and B. Wansink. 2016. Blinded with science: Trivial graphs and formulas increase ad persuasiveness and belief in product efficacy. *Public Understanding of Science* **25** (1): 117–125.
46. Bertini, E., N. Elmqvist, and T. Wischgoll. 2016. Judgment error in pie chart variations. In *Proceedings of the eurographics/IEEE VGTC conference on visualization: Short papers*, 91–95.
47. Spence, I., and S. Lewandowsky. 1991. Displaying proportions and percentages. *Applied Cognitive Psychology* **5** (1): 61–77.
48. Mayer, R. E. 2024. The past, present, and future of the cognitive theory of multimedia learning. *Educational Psychology Review* **36** (1): 8.
49. Newman, N., et al. 2019. *Digital news report 2019*, 54–59. Reuters Institute.

50. Pinna, B., and D. Porcheddu. 2023. Visual information beyond gestalt principles: Unification vs. differentiation, similarity vs. dissimilarity. *Arkete–Rivista di Filosofia* **6**:77–104.
51. Lin, T.-J., and M. P. Landry. 2024. *Quantifying data distortion in bar graphs in biological research.* bioRxiv. https://doi.org/10.1101/2024.09.20.609464.
52. Saket, B., A. Endert, and Ç. Demiralp. 2018. Task-based effectiveness of basic visualizations. *IEEE transactions on visualization and computer graphics* **25** (7): 2505–2512.
53. Redmond, S. 2019. Visual cues in estimation of part-to-whole comparisons.
54. Li, Y., et al. 2025. *Does the infamous pie chart really hurt decision-making in the real world? Assessing the role of visualization in high-level academic decisions.* arXiv preprint arXiv:2410.04686. https://arxiv.org/abs/2410.04686.
55. Smiljanić, D. 2023. *The line chart: An indispensable tool in data visualization* [cited 2024]. https://www.binfire.com/blog/line-chart-indispensable-tool-data-visualization/.
56. Smith, A. 2025. *Line charts: Tracking L & D data and trends in precision* [cited 2025 April 14, 2025]. https://www.watershedlrs.com/blog/business-and-data-alignment/line-charts-tracking-l-and-d-data-trends-precision/.
57. van Dijk, D. 2022. *A guide to effective data visualization* [cited 2024 March 8, 2024]. https://www.datylon.com/blog/guide-to-effective-data-visualization.
58. Kraemer, S. 2023. *How to spot misleading charts, a checklist* [cited 2024 June 5, 2024]. https://www.tableau.com/blog/spot-misleading-charts-checklist.
59. Ploetzner, R., S. Berney, and M. Bétrancourt. 2021. When learning from animations is more successful than learning from static pictures: Learning the specifics of change. *Instructional Science* **49** (4): 497–514.
60. Costa, M., and S. Nunes. 2023. NewsLines: Narrative visualization of news stories. In *Text2story '23 workshop.*
61. Nguyen, P. H., et al. 2016. TimeSets: Timeline visualization with set relations. *Information Visualization* **15** (3): 253–269.
62. Fillis, V. and S. Tselova. 2023. *Explore the world in data: Introducing the 3D Globe. Data visualization and storytelling* [cited 2025 August 8, 2024]. https://flourish.studio/blog/interactive-3d-globe/?utm_source=chatgpt.com.
63. Smith, M. A., et al. 2014. Mapping Twitter topic networks: From polarized crowds to community clusters.
64. Mejova, Y., et al. 2014. Controversy and sentiment in online news. In *Computation + Journalism symposium 2014.* New York: Columbia University.

65. Ding, X., M. Horning, and E. H. Rho. 2023. Same words, different meanings: Semantic polarization in broadcast media language forecasts polarity in online public discourse. In *Proceedings of the international AAAI conference on web and social media.*
66. Patterson, R. E., et al. 2014. A human cognition framework for information visualization. *Computers & Graphics* **42**:42–58.
67. Miller, G. A. 1956. The magical number seven, plus or minus two: Some limits on our capacity for processing information. *Psychological Review* **63** (2): 81–97.
68. Greussing, E., S. H. Kessler, and H. G. Boomgaarden. 2020. Learning from science news via interactive and animated data visualizations: An investigation combining eye tracking, online survey, and cued retrospective reporting. *Science Communication* **42** (6): 803–828.
69. Hienert, D. 2014. A model for the integration of interactive visualizations into the process of information searching and linking on the Web. *Historical Social Research/Historische Sozialforschung* 39:179–192.
70. Luo, D., et al. 2010. Eventriver: Visually exploring text collections with temporal references. *IEEE Transactions on Visualization and Computer Graphics* **18** (1): 93–105.
71. Tufte, E. R. 2001. *The visual display of quantitative information.* 2nd ed, 197. Graphics Press.
72. Czaban, T. 2023. Top 10 proven data visualization best practices. 2025.
73. Lang, A., J. Borse, K. Wise, and P. David. 2002. Captured by the world wide web: Orienting to structural and content features of computer-presented information. *Communication Research* **29** (3): 215–245. https://doi.org/10.1177/009365020202900300 1.
74. WebAIM.org. 2025. *We have web accessibility in mind* [cited 2025 January 9, 2025; Expanding the potential of the web for people with disabilities by empowering individuals and organizations to create accessible content]. https://webaim.org.
75. Visser, C., Y. Flohr, and D. Trichter. 2024. *The state of web accessibility in 2024 (research report)* [cited 2025 September 12, 2024]. https://www.accessibilitychecker.org/research-papers/the-state-of-web-accessibility-in-2024-research-report/?utm_source=chatgpt.com.
76. Wyzowl. 2025. *Video marketing statistics 2025* [cited 2025 March 14, 2025]. https://www.wyzowl.com/video-marketing-statistics/#:~:text=Section%202:%20Types%20of%20video,for%20video%20marketing%20in%202025.
77. Chaves, L. 2025. *20+ Interesting short form video trends & statistics (2025)* [cited 2025 April 10, 2025]. https://vidico.com/news/short-form-video-statistics/?utm_source=chatgpt.com.
78. Zhu, J., et al. 2022. The impact of short videos on student performance in an online-flipped college engineering course. *Humanities and Social Sciences Communications* **9** (1): 1–10.

79. Smith, D. P., and N. J. Francis. 2022. Engagement with video content in the blended classroom. *Essays in Biochemistry* **66** (1): 5–13.
80. Noetel, M., et al. 2021. Video improves learning in higher education: A systematic review. *Review of Educational Research* **91** (2): 204–236.
81. Moran, G., L. Muzellec, and D. Johnson. 2020. Message content features and social media engagement: Evidence from the media industry. *Journal of Product & Brand Management* **29** (5): 533–545.
82. Li, D., et al. 2025. Delving deep into engagement prediction of short videos. In *Computer vision-ECCV 2024*, 289–306. Springer.
83. Locke, J. 2024. *Hype: Giving fans a stake in the success of their favorite emerging creators* [cited 2025 November 10, 2024]. https://blog.youtube/news-and-events/youtube-hype/?utm_source=chatgpt.com.
84. Shajari, S., N. Agarwal, and M. Alassad. 2023. *Commenter behavior characterization on YouTube channels.* arXiv preprint arXiv:2304.07681.
85. HostArmada. 2024. *Long-form vs. short-form videos: Which one is best for you?* [cited 2024 November 28, 2024]. https://www.hostarmada.com/blog/long-form-vs-short-form-videos-which-one-is-best-for-you/.
86. Billion Dollar Boy. 2024. *Long-form content is surging: Two thirds of marketers and creators have boosted production* [cited 2024 October 18, 2024]. https://www.billiondollarboy.com/news/long-form-content-is-surging/?utm_source=chatgpt.com.
87. Wistia. 2025. *2025 State of video report* [cited 2025]. https://wistia.com/learn/marketing/video-marketing-statistics.
88. Guo, P. J., J. Kim, and R. Rubin. 2014. How video production affects student engagement: An empirical study of MOOC videos. In *Proceedings of the first ACM conference on Learning@ scale conference.*
89. Sherman, T. 2021. One year of YouTube Shorts—What we've learned so far. In *YouTube Official Blog*. YouTube: blog.youtube.
90. Violot, C., et al. 2024. Shorts vs. regular videos on YouTube: A comparative analysis of user engagement and content creation trends. In *Proceedings of the 16th ACM web science conference.*
91. Lascar, M. 2015. *Short-form video: The ultimate guide 2025* [cited 2025 May 5, 2025]. https://www.outbrain.com/blog/short-form-video/?utm_source=chatgpt.com.
92. Shams, L., and A. R. Seitz. 2008. Benefits of multisensory learning. *Trends in Cognitive Sciences* **12** (11): 411–417.
93. Kim, A. 2025. Billie Eilish reacts to 'trash; comments on her 2025 met gala look—But she wasn't even there.
94. Walsh, M. 2024. Deepfake creator Maria Walsh says punishment needed as AI 'poses huge threat to society.
95. Wei, Y., and G. Tyson. 2024. Understanding the impact of AI-generated content on social media: The Pixiv case. In *Proceedings of the 32nd ACM international conference on multimedia.*

96. Utah Valley University. 2024. *Research summary: Impact of AI-generated media* [cited 2025 November 7, 2024]. https://www.uvu.edu/news/2024/10/ai-deepfake-media-event-recap.html.
97. Sooriyapatabandige, P. 2025. AI-generated data visualizations: Opportunities and challenges.
98. Sinclair, V. L. 2025. The influence of AI-generated news on public trust in journalism: Evidence from the UK. *Journal of Research in Social Science and Humanities* **4** (2): 1–6.
99. Khan, S. A., et al. 2023. Visual user-generated content verification in journalism: An overview. *IEEE Access* **11**:6,748–6,769.
100. Kundu, R., A. Balachandran, and A.K. Roy-Chowdhury. 2025. *TruthLens: Explainable DeepFake detection for face manipulated and fully synthetic data.* arXiv preprint arXiv:2503.15867.
101. Le, B., et al. 2025. SoK: Systematization and benchmarking of Deepfake detectors in a unified framework. In *EEE European symposium on security and privacy 2025.*

CHAPTER 9

# The Smart Story Suite Offers a New Approach: Not a Single Template

- *The Smart Story Suite* applies the previous chapters for continuous user interaction to instantly inform users who need either short OR long-form versions of content.
- *Progressive disclosure* helps content build ***attention momentum*** so users with varying demographics, interests, environments, and time remain interested and engaged.
- This new structure outperformed traditional linear formats in an experiment with a diverse sample of more than 1500 participants.

My earliest research examined how complex scientific information can be structured so that general audiences can understand it. Explanatory features played a decisive role in addressing the different ways content is consumed. Subsequent research on younger users distinguished between attention and learning and showed why exposure or interaction alone does not ensure comprehension [1, 2]. My focus on micro-level cognitive variables was carried into later work, which examined personalization, interest, and user choice through an early "PICK" framework [3], and my study of young mobile users showed how demographics and devices can significantly reshape engagement [4, 5]. My health communication research extended these principles, showing how interest and interactivity also influence engagement and perceived credibility [6–8]. A review of this body of research shows that these investigations are not unrelated but



R. Yaros, *The Digital Engagement Model*, Palgrave Practical Guides in Communication,
https://doi.org/10.1007/978-3-032-03822-7_9

cumulative tests of the variables that eventually built this model of variables that regulate engagement across contexts, populations, and content types. The interface described in this final chapter is not the only way to operationalize the Digital Engagement Model. It is just one innovative option that demonstrates how multimedia can accommodate the needs of today's information consumers, their motivations, environments, and available time. The interface challenges the popular assumption that well-written or well-reported information alone—supplemented by photos, videos, or visualizations—is sufficient to engage the largest possible audience. We'll demonstrate and compare the *Smart Story Structure's* "adaptive content flow" with a standard news story to see how users respond to a progressive disclosure of information they can select. The structure is designed to satisfy both scanners and readers simultaneously, providing content that is most interesting to them while reducing cognitive overload in the process. When these principles are applied, the structure can build attention momentum to inform a broader range of users (Fig. 9.1).

## 9.1 It's Time to Implement Supporting Research for a *Smart Story*

The book *Designing for User Engagement* lays a theoretical and empirical foundation for understanding engagement in digital systems. Grounded in cognitive science, software engineering, and human-computer interaction, Sutcliffe models engagement as a multi-layered process progressing through attention, interest, affective investment, immersion, and flow. This sequenceh is shaped by four variables, including user traits and goals, task complexity and novelty, system responsiveness, and the user's context of use (device type and environment).

Sutcliffe [9] built on the earlier framework, shifting toward emotional design, user disposition, and contextual awareness. The point was that engagement doesn't happen in a vacuum. It is shaped by when, where, and why the user engages. The framework draws attention to temporal factors (such as time-on-task), physical settings (like mobile versus desktop use), and social contexts (solo or collaborative interaction). The design space for engagement is defined along the dimensions of:

- Challenge versus skill balance (to induce flow)
- Information scent and affordances
- Aesthetic stimulation

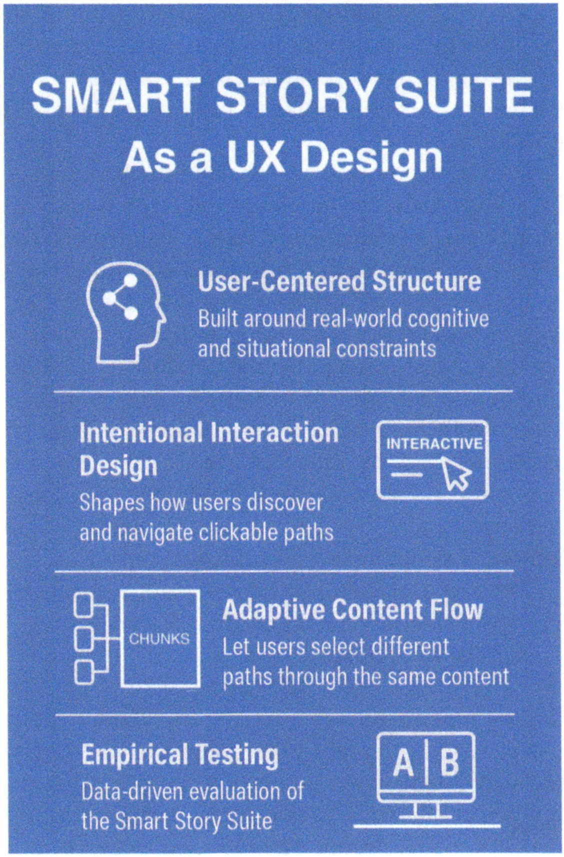


**Fig. 9.1** Smart Story Suite as UX design

- Feedback immediacy
- User control and agency

These dimensions influence the likelihood of sustained or broken engagement. Sutcliffe also proposes a triangulated method for evaluating engagement: behavioral metrics (e.g., dwell time), subjective reporting (e.g., surveys), task performance, and—when feasible—physiological measures. This multi-method approach is critical, particularly for systems aiming to integrate emotional and cognitive engagement.

The concept of engagement profiles or patterns of how different users engage (e.g., immersive, analytical, playful) and engagement trajectories describe how engagement evolves. These concepts offer an understanding not only of whether users are engaged but also of how and when their engagement shifts.

As the field matured, emotion moved from the background to the center. Sutcliffe's framework treats an emotional response not as a byproduct of engagement but as a primary driver [9]. Positive emotions reinforce continued use, while negative emotions, such as confusion or friction, may either disrupt a user's flow or, when managed well, foster productive tension. Rather than presenting predictable and rigid models, the interface distills theory into the actionable heuristics of novelty, clarity, challenge, aesthetic richness, and narrative coherence.

This previous work, in part, informs the development of the Digital Engagement Model and its interface, the *Smart Story Suite*. Where Sutcliffe's work offers a cognitive-emotional framework, the next step is to operationalize engagement through interactive design. Another applied engagement model provides a valuable bridge.

Originally developed through empirical studies with children, a six-factor model identifies concrete interaction design features that sustain engagement: simulation, construct interaction, immediacy, feedback, goals, and prior experience [10]. Although this research focused on children, the factors remain relevant across age groups. When reframed through the lens of adult digital engagement, each element offers design strategies for Smart Story Suite's adaptive storytelling system.

Similar to when children are drawn to role-play and simulation, adults engage more deeply with content when given agency, the power to make decisions, and the opportunity to adopt alternate perspectives. In the Smart Story Suite, this means offering branching narratives, multimedia choices, and identity-driven paths.

Constructing environments captured children's attention. For general users, this means the ability to customize narratives, select explanatory data, or skip known information to focus on new information. Modular components of content can support user co-authorship and more coherence.

While children require obvious cause-and-effect feedback, adult users respond to subtler cues. The Smart Story Suite integrates text, audio, visual, data, and fact-checking, along with pacing tailored to a user's available time. Immediacy becomes fluid responsiveness, where the content feels attuned to the user.

Fixed goals support young users; adults prefer open-ended exploration. The Smart Story Suite supports both short-form and long-form consumption of useful information. This flexibility accommodates varied motivations (skimming, scanning, reading).

The Smart Story Suite supports the "learning by doing" approach and progressive disclosure, or the ability for users to pursue choices of the information they prefer, starting with intuitive controls and gradually revealing complexity as users become more interested.

These design principles make the Smart Story Suite a platform not just informed by theory but tested by real-world interaction patterns. Its design is guided by research questions derived from both models:

- Does narrative customization (construct interaction) increase session duration more for adults than for children?
- Does immediate emotional feedback enhance retention more in older users?
- Does goal ambiguity discourage young users but increase exploration in older ones?

Structured experimental testing—across age groups, content variations, and engagement levels—will help validate and refine the system. Measuring engagement through time-on-task, self-reports, and emotional responses aligns directly with Sutcliffe's triangulated evaluation framework.

By aligning Sutcliffe's cognitive-emotional engagement model with design-centered interaction features, the Smart Story Suite provides a robust and adaptable platform. It merges theory and practice, supporting users across age groups with tailored experiences that are emotionally resonant, cognitively stimulating, and narratively rich. Rather than treating engagement as a fixed outcome, the suite supports a dynamic, adaptive process supported by theory, shaped by design, and refined through evidence.

Pages filled with text and media assume and require that users consume most or all of the content, which is of not the goal of users with limited time. Should we ignore the needs of those users, or should we consider new structures that engage more users, even if they don't consume all the information? Relying solely on a headline or title, a photo, and a narrative to engage the maximum number of users can lead many users to skipping the information.

A simple example of a design meeting a user's needs is the affordances of a doorknob that is grasped and turned. Its size permits a human hand to wrap around and rotate it. The knob's signifier is a visual cue that suggests it should be turned. Its round shape and central placement on the door signal, "Grab me and twist." An arrow or label indicating the direction of the turn can serve as another signifier. The feedback from the knob is that the door opens. Feedback appears in multiple forms, including auditory (hearing a click of the latch releasing), tactile (feeling the resistance drop as the latch disengages), and visual (the door opening). If the door doesn't open, or there's no sound or movement, that's the cue that it is probably locked.

To date, linear textual narratives confined to a predictable format can't adapt to the varying needs of a user's digital diet. What is the length of most stories being presented? To obtain the answer, our lab continuously recorded the number of daily articles and their word length of the two news organizations, CNN.com and FOXnews.com. Data was collected during a 60-day period ending in February 2025. This data provided a snapshot of the length of textual content exposed to users. Figure 9.2 presents a computer generated chart and a corresponding table for comparing the content.

The software recorded the number of words in 879 articles, including 357 articles from CNN and 522 from FOXnews.com. The largest number of FOX News articles ($n = 151$) contained less than 500 words (322 to 468 words). At the same time, the largest number of CNN articles ($n = 63$ articles) contained more words, ranging from 469 to 615. Comparing short-form content (less than 615 words), CNN posted 141 compared to more than double that amount for FOX News (340 or 66% of all FOX News articles). CNN posted longer form texts (more than 615 words) in 61% of its articles ($n = 216$ articles) versus 182 FOX News stories or 35% of its stories. Based on this sample, FOX posted more stories and shorter stories than CNN. What would happen if both of these organizations divided their stories into easy-to-read and view sections? To review the six propositions from the theory in Chap. 3.

*Proposition 1* Every user brings four core variables to digital content that shape engagement decisions: demographics, long-term interests, environment (physical and technological), and available time.

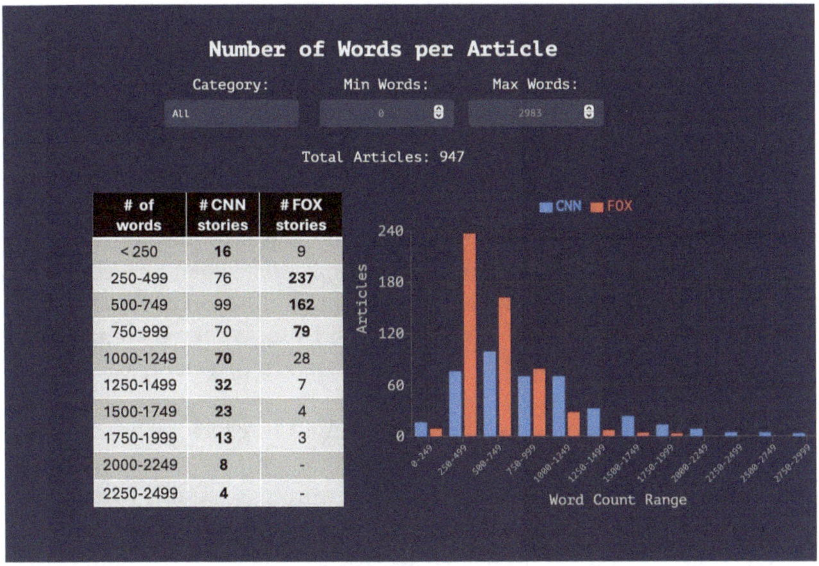


**Fig. 9.2** Article counts by number of words, CNN.com versus FOX.com

*Proposition 2* A user's motivation is reflected in behaviors such as searching, scanning, reading, interacting, and passively viewing or skipping content.

*Proposition 3* Users with a prior interest in a topic are more likely to engage with content about that topic (i.e., sports). For users without such interest, content must generate situational interest through content that offers scannability, personalization, interactivity, curated curiosity, and emotional appeal.

*Proposition 4* A user's environment can influence whether users engage with it and, if so, how—including distractions and technological factors like interface design, device, and algorithmic delivery.

*Proposition 5* A user's time availability affects the duration of engagement. Even highly interested users may disengage if they lack sufficient time.

*Proposition 6* Users disengage when content is too long, complex, irrelevant, or poorly structured.

The **Smart Story Suite** introduced in this chapter is a user interface that illustrates how longer-form content can also be managed for short-form consumption without overwhelming users. Individual and situational interests are addressed through labeled buttons that users select based on their needs, environment, and time to consume different sections. The Smart Story Suite builds on Norman's work by specifying how and why new structures of content can be as important as the content itself. Innovative designs can enhance functionality and prevent ineffective layouts that generate little to no engagement, even when the content is essential for users to know. By integrating the production of text and multimedia with concepts from psychology and user-centered thinking, we apply and empirically test Smart Story elements that cater to the next generation of digital consumers.

Previous chapters presented multiple studies to explain why, how, and when users engage with different forms of content. One study identified six prototypical modes of reading, ranging from scanning to extensive reading [11]. A range of approaches has been proposed for news summarization, each with its strengths. Others focused on extractive summarization of text [12], and studies presented systems for multimedia summarization [13]. Initial efforts to summarize multiple news articles [14] led to the development of a Newsblaster system that clusters, categorizes, and summarizes content [15].

## 9.2 The "Smart Story" Structure Requires a New Mindset

The structure of content is a foundational element in human-computer interaction (HCI). It acts as the framework that shapes how users perceive, interpret, and engage with digital information. HCI isn't just about designing computer interfaces; it's also about understanding the user's experience. It's also about crafting user experiences that are intuitive, meaningful, and cognitively effective. Fundamental aspects of achieving this include organizing, presenting, and prioritizing information.

> *Design is not just what it looks like and feels like. Design is how it works.*
>
> *-Steve Jobs*

Interfaces can significantly impact how users allocate their attention, maintain engagement, and learn from the information presented in an interface. Whether designing interactive websites or mobile apps, O'Brien and Toms [16] support the Smart Story's structuring of content that aligns with users' cognitive limits to guide attention, deepen engagement, and support meaningful communication. Their study of users searching, shopping, and gaming online suggests that the four stages of point of engagement, period of sustained engagement, disengagement, and reengagement all reflect attributes defined by the user, the system, and human-computer interaction. All of this still involves cognitive psychology, which describes every user's attention as a limited mental resource.

Here, the previously discussed cognitive load theory applies directly to interface design. When content is disorganized or overwhelming, users experience extraneous cognitive load, which reduces their ability to focus on what matters. Structuring digital media in a new interface that differs from the traditional text-only content structure can be a game-changer. Strategically including clear and informative headings, scannable bullet points, hierarchical layouts, explanatory photos and short videos, selectable sections of interest, easy-to-understand data charts, and ways to quickly confirm the credibility of content can affect attention more than just a headline, photo, and blocks of text. But that's still not all of the elements of the structure. Placement is yet another variable that, when combined with the other components, improves the user experience. Researching the effects of where content is positioned on a screen, for example, revealed an F reading pattern. When eye movements during exposure to text resemble the letter "F," content near the top left is the primary region of interest. The F pattern then describes how fewer words are read as a user's eyes move down the page [17]. The "F" pattern doesn't describe all reading but this result suggests content structures can continue to generate interest as eyes move across digestible chunks of information, minimize cognitive overload, and enhance a user's attentional control.

Would such behaviors support a new structure? The book *Rebuilding the News* discusses how digital technologies have reshaped the routines, structures, and cultures of newsrooms [18]. Based on ethnographic research, the author illustrates how journalists navigate the tension between long-standing professional norms and emerging digital practices. The challenges outlined in Anderson's book mirror those in this text and still address the institutional inertia that characterizes most traditional organizations. Despite having access to new storytelling tools, such as data visualizations and interactive graphics, many content producers remain risk-averse. This caution stems from established organizational routines, constrained resources, and a deep-seated preference for formats with predictable outcomes.

There's a reason for that caution. Jakob's Law states that users expect digital experiences to follow familiar patterns [19]. Consequently, most producers hesitate to experiment with new formats unless there is a clear, immediate benefit, such as increased traffic or engagement. Anderson suggested that this hesitancy arises not only from logistical limitations such as budgets, staffing, and time but also from uncertainty about how users will react to unfamiliar presentation forms. This debate highlights the complex interplay between innovation and institutional conservatism that this chapter's Smart Story structure may face, suggesting that transformation in digital communication requires not only new tools but a shift in professional culture.

The solution relates to what we know about the need for structure and consistency. It requires navigation paths to be sensible, related elements to be grouped, and interactive elements to be easily identifiable. One solution is progressive disclosure of content, which evolved from the broader principles of minimalism in interface design. This solution was initially conceived to address information overload. Progressive disclosure offers a layered user experience, presenting key concepts first and revealing more details only when a user requests [20]. Presenting a news story in this way, for example, supports cognitive theories that recognize the limits of our working memory. Progressive disclosure also enables users to filter information that's easy to consume initially and scaffolds their experience based on their immediate needs.

This new approach replaces current practices that quickly overwhelm users with excessive content, choices, pop-up windows, etc., making online engagement notably different from engagement with a book. In the context of human-computer interaction, this process translates into the benefits of progressive disclosure, where content is presented to all users in a core format, followed by options for various additional information. For users not typically drawn to the content, this is when individual interest becomes less critical than the situational interest generated by the content if engagement is to continue. This approach also respects users' attention limits. It is the sole reason why explanatory headlines, bullet points, and detailed subheads can instantly inform scanners with meaningful information, even though, for a host of reasons, some users may not be able to consume more of the content. In summary, progressive disclosure exposes all users, including scanners, to chunks of information. At the same time, the more extended version is always just a click or more away for users who want more.

## 9.3 Progressive Disclosure Replaces Perpetual Scrolling

Progressive disclosure is implemented in a Smart Story Suite with:

- A textual and visual interface that minimizes cognitive load to inform users instantly and generate situational interest with options for subsequent user-selected content.
- Explanatory links or buttons that enable users to explore subsequent content of interest in either a linear path (step-by-step) or a nonlinear way (based on interest).
- Conditional branching that adapts content to user preferences.

Offering progressive disclosure in the Smart Story Suite means users are not overwhelmed by all the available content at once. This structure mirrors instructional scaffolding, where related content is introduced incrementally. The structure also addresses two pervasive barriers to engagement. (1) Too much content on a page or subsequent page is information users can't consume without devoting several more seconds or minutes to comprehend the content, links, videos, etc. (2) When a related headline or title is clicked, the typical structure of pages dominated by text is replaced by additional progressive disclosure of content that respects user autonomy with "just-in-time" access to more information of interest to a user, which may be of little to no interest to another user. The Smart Story Suite caters to users' diverse motivations and self-efficacy, which are crucial for effective comprehension and learning [21]. Multimedia learning theory posits that learning is more effective when extraneous content is minimized, and instructional elements are presented in a coherent, *phased* manner. Some refer to this as a *segmenting principle* that separates information into smaller, manageable segments, allowing learners to control the pace of information delivery.

Accordingly, the best practices for implementing progressive disclosure in the Smart Story Suite include:

- Prioritize the most important information and reveal details only as they become relevant to the user. In other words, let users construct their sequence of details.
- Ensure consistency in the placement and presentation of subsequent views or pages.
- Enable users to control the pace of content exploration.
- Avoid excessive nesting or hidden layers, as they can create confusion.

Well-structured content minimizes cognitive friction by enabling users to quickly find what they need, thereby enhancing their satisfaction and motivation. For instance, card sorting studies, a standard method in user experience research, can help researchers identify how users expect information to be organized, guiding the arrangement of content in a manner that aligns with user expectations [22].

The value of progressive disclosure becomes even more evident when viewed through the lens of the book *Eight Golden Rules of Interface Design* [23]. The book offers four heuristics that align with the benefits of progressive disclosure in the Smart Story Suite.

1. Strive for consistency: Progressive disclosure is most effective when the method of revealing content remains consistent across the interface.
2. Reduce short-term memory load: Progressive interaction closure reduces mental effort by concealing non-essential information until necessary, an approach supported by cognitive load theorists.
3. Offer informative feedback: When learners engage with disclosed content, the system should respond clearly and allow them to reverse or skip steps, reinforcing a sense of control and responsiveness.
4. In addition to these rules, the book's concept of direct manipulation interfaces supports the type of interaction encouraged by progressive disclosure. By allowing users to reveal content through intentional actions such as clicking, designers employing a Smart Story structure can create immediate, reversible, and visually engaging experiences. This kind of interface strengthens learner agency and encourages exploration.

Shneiderman's *Visual Information-Seeking Mantra*, "Overview first, zoom and filter, then details on demand," echoes the logic of the Smart Story Suite [24]. This framework is highly adaptable to digital content.

For example, Smart story structures ensure that users are neither overwhelmed nor restricted. They provide a structured yet flexible pathway through content, striking a balance between clarity and autonomy, making it an ideal match for modern digital environments. In essence, Shneiderman's work not only supports the cognitive and experiential logic of progressive disclosure but also enriches it by grounding it in a broader framework of usability, interaction, and user empowerment.

User accessibility also improves with simplicity. Clean visuals with high contrast, large type, and alt text are easier for users to read, especially those with visual impairments or cognitive challenges. This enhancement improves the user experience across the board. It aligns with the *Web Content Accessibility Guidelines (WCAG) 2.1*, as researched in the context of new digital technologies [25]. The extensive collection of elements, placement, and best practices for a Smart Story structure is not equivalent to a few individual features inserted into content, including photos, videos, or bullet points. The multifaceted interface combines and presents all of the information to suit today's users. In the following sample and experimental study, an original story composed by the lab was based on the climate information addressing melting Arctic ice (Fig. 9.3). The article was structured according to news information on mainstream news sites (excluding advertisements), including the headline, photo, and text.

## 9.4 Users Compose Their Narratives Based on Their Interests and Needs

The eight screens that follow describe the Smart Story Suite interface for the same story presented in Fig. 9.2. The suite's home page (Fig. 9.4) represents a visual format for all pages. All pages begin with an informative, explanatory headline or subhead, followed by three bullet-point highlights (typically 15 words or less in length). Users can click any related buttons of interest, representing story sections, data, the latest developments, instant fact-checking of the information, or the original linear format if preferred. Perhaps only one angle of the story interests the user. Conversely, maybe a section or two can be skipped because the user has already acquired that information from a previous story.

When a section's button is clicked, the interface provides feedback through a consistent multimedia structure that always features easy-to-read subtitles and summaries, a related photo or video, and a manageable "chunk" of text. Successfully presenting the selected content rewards the

**Climate Change Is Quietly Reshaping Our Planet**

Credit: karenfoleyphotography

When people think about climate change, they often picture stronger storms, hotter summers, and rising sea levels. But climate change is also producing less visible—yet profound—shifts that are altering how the planet itself functions.

One of the most surprising discoveries of the past few decades is that Earth's axis is shifting. Scientists have confirmed that the geographic poles are drifting because of glacial melt. As massive ice sheets in Greenland and Antarctica disappear, the redistribution of weight across the planet is literally changing how it spins. This polar drift, while slow, is measurable—and increasingly influenced by human-driven warming.

At the same time, ecosystems are experiencing a breakdown in timing. Many species depend on precise seasonal rhythms to survive. Birds like the red knot, which rely on mid-Atlantic crab eggs during migration, are now arriving too late due to shifting climate patterns. Insects and pollinators are emerging at different times than the plants they feed on, causing mismatches that threaten reproduction and biodiversity. These unsynchronized life cycles have serious ripple effects on crops and food chains.

Meanwhile, climate change is already taking a toll on human health. Extreme heat is increasing cases of heatstroke, especially among vulnerable populations. Poor air quality from wildfires and rising ozone levels is worsening asthma and other respiratory conditions. Mental health is also suffering—climate-related disasters and long-term anxiety are linked to depression, PTSD, and emotional strain. Low-income and marginalized communities often face the highest risk.

Some of these effects may not be reversible. Even if emissions were drastically reduced today, the consequences of past decades may continue unfolding. Arctic ice, once lost, takes centuries to return. Animal population declines and habitat disruptions can trigger chain reactions that are hard to undo. Scientists warn that delaying climate action raises the risk of tipping points—thresholds beyond which changes accelerate irreversibly.

The data behind these trends is sobering. Global average temperatures have risen dramatically since the industrial era, and current emissions paths suggest further warming without major intervention. Sea levels are rising faster than at any point in recorded history. Charts and climate models from NASA and the Intergovernmental Panel on Climate Change (IPCC) all point in the same direction: continued warming unless global emissions are curbed.

Importantly, there is broad scientific consensus on these issues. Thousands of climate scientists across dozens of nations agree that recent warming is primarily caused by human activities. Claims to the contrary often stem from misinformation or misinterpreted science. Understanding what is real—and what is not—is essential to navigating the road ahead.

Climate change is not just about extreme weather. It's a long-term transformation that affects the systems we depend on: our bodies, our food, our environment, and the physical balance of the planet itself.

**Fig. 9.3** Original inverted pyramid climate change story

user with the information they seek. This feedback loop can enhance engagement by demonstrating to users that their interactions lead to meaningful outcomes. Clear affordances, intuitive signifiers, and purposeful feedback combine to create a user experience that feels responsive, empowering, and educational rather than merely functional. Each page marries brief text with an explanatory photo.

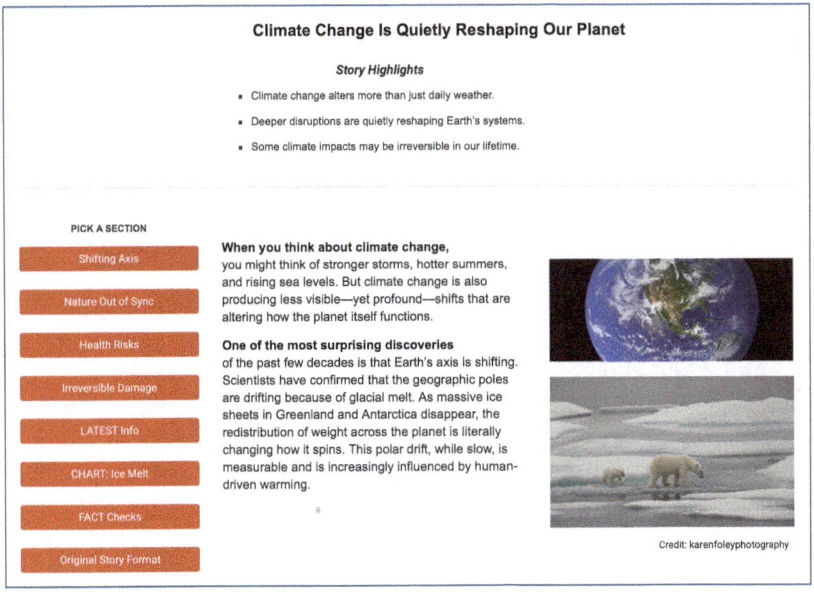


**Fig. 9.4** The Smart Story Suite *Home Page*

There is no need to tease users with clickbait, as they have already chosen the story. The goal is to inform a diverse population of users with options tailored to their interests, environment, and time. The first of three bullet highlights, specified to be 15 words or fewer, is to ensure all users understand the difference between short-term "weather" and long-term "climate." Failing to establish that basic definition could make the rest of the content meaningless or confusing. Based on years of research into the DEM, all headlines, subheads, and highlights on every page are explanatory declarative sentences that do not exceed 15 words. The highlight closest to "teasing" users is the one reading, "Some climate impacts may be irreversible in our lifetime." Yet, it still presents a fact to scanning readers.

Along with this same format for all pages, about 125 words of the story's text cater to users who have time to read it, accompanied by a related photo. This format allows users with limited time to gather helpful information before leaving. In contrast, those with interest and time can delve deeper into other pages, which also contain content supporting the SPICE variables. A teasing headline that reads "How climate change threatens our future" offers little meaningful information to scanners with limited time. An explanatory headline immediately informs all users and may even "convert" some scanners to readers.

(If desired an *Original Story* button could appear at the bottom of the menu for users who would prefer to view the story as the traditional full page of text.)

**Button One**

If the top "Home" button is clicked, after viewing any of the pages the user is exposed to the explanatory headline, three short bullet point highlights, plus approximately 125 words of details below, accompanied by a photo or graphic (Fig. 9.5). Note the lack of scrollable content. This is in response to research suggesting that to maximize reach, but not necessarily time on content, place your content in first screen of view [26, 27]. The second of the five buttons (Fig. 9.6) is a bit more descriptive. It reads "Nature out of Sync" to curate curiosity with a focus on observed climate effects on nature.

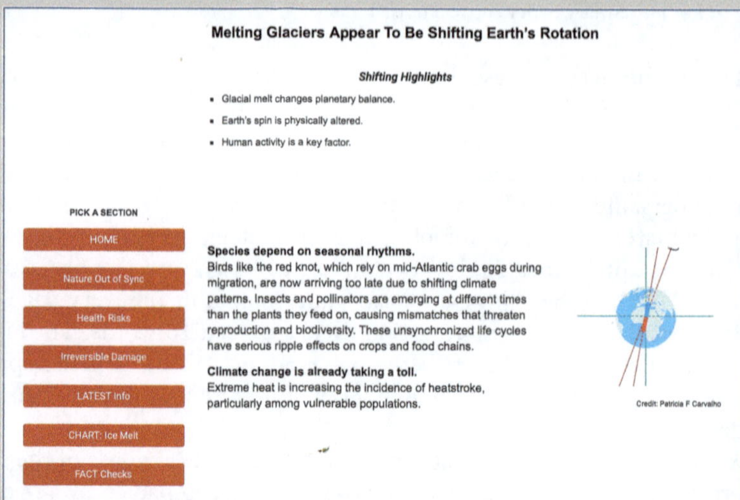


**Fig. 9.5** Button one: *Shifting Axis*

(continued)

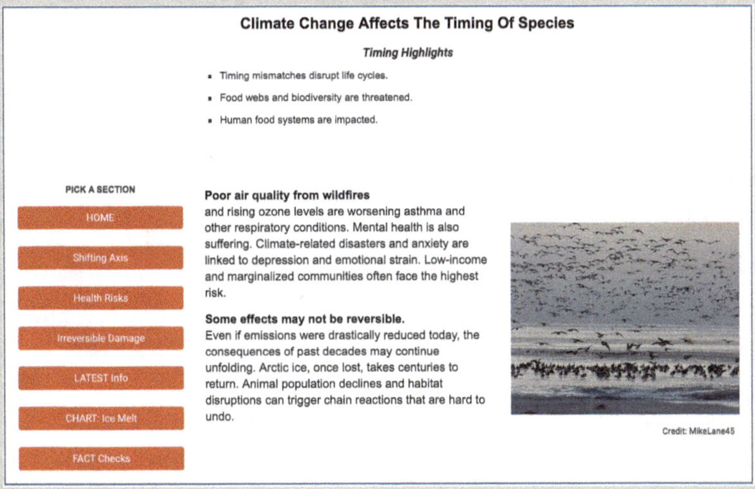


**Fig. 9.6** Button two: *Nature Out of Sync*

**Button Two**

These bullet-point sentences are shorter than those on the home page. The first reads, "Glacier melt changes planetary balance." The next reads, "Earth's spin is physically altered" (results of a changing balance). The final bullet is, "Human activity is a key factor." Unlike a page of just text, every section provides a photo or graphic.

By this point (probably while viewing the home page), users will have read all of the button labels that provide options for more information within the same story. Figure 9.7 displays the page for button 3.

**Button Three**

The third button of the four main story sections is labeled *Health Risks.*

The goal is still to provide short but informative highlights; however, three brief subheads below in bold reveal observable climate change effects. Unlike a textual news story, a user without interest in climate health news is not forced to read the text and leave the story.

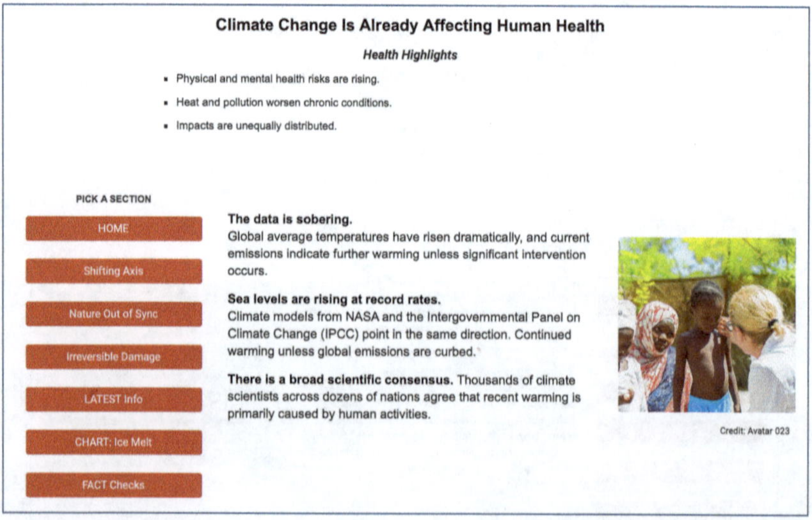


**Fig. 9.7** Button three: *Health Risks*

The fourth and final section button (Fig. 9.8) is *Irreversible Damage.*

**Button Four**
Recall that the structure of the original text story was divided into these four buttons. None of the words has been modified.

This page is a "call to action" page with some alarming information. One bullet that reads "Delayed action increases the risk of reaching climate tipping points" is accompanied by an explanatory photo of citizens taking action (protesting). Approximately 125 words of details appear.

The final three bottom buttons (Fig. 9.9) are not sections from the story. The button titled "Latest Info" serves two goals. 1. Motivate those who are already familiar with the study to check back for the latest update to the story. 2. Allow the current user to skip to the latest news if the other sections are not of interest.

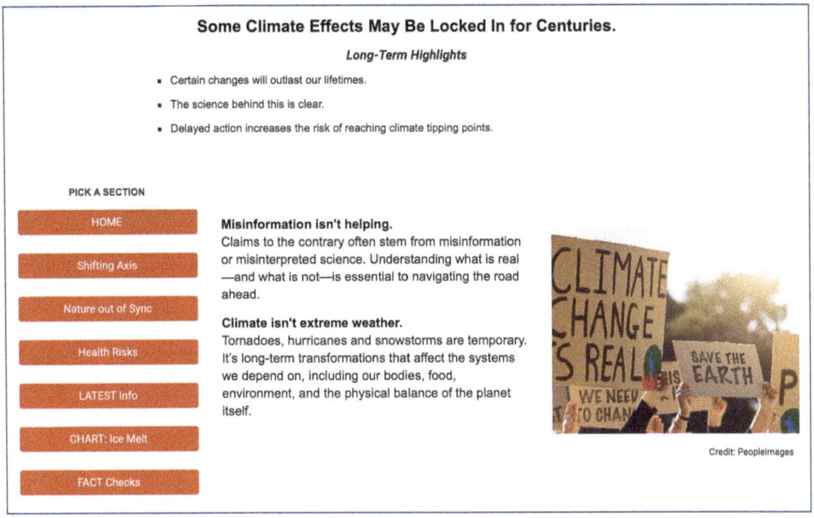


**Fig. 9.8** Button four: *Irreversible Damage*

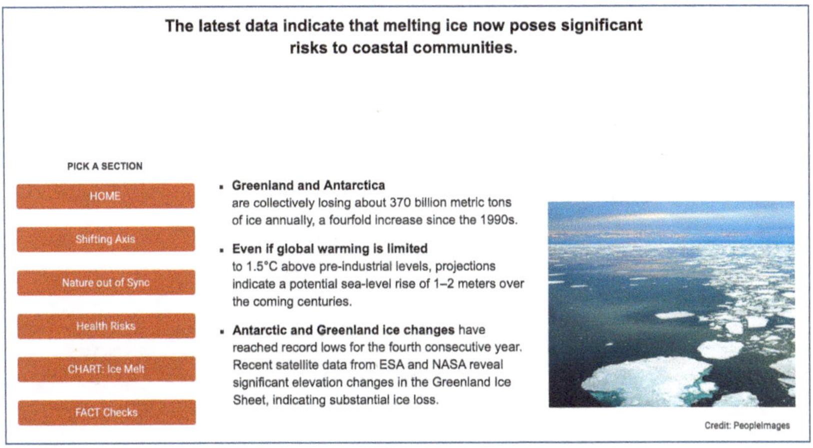


**Fig. 9.9** Button five: *Latest Info*

**Button Five**

One of the primary goals for organizations is to attract repeat visitors. The *Latest Info* option was added after the original story was posted to not only appeal to potential repeat visitors but also to "reserve" a page where the organization can continue to update this story, especially for users seeking this information and finding it with the most recent data.

Figure 9.10 represents the page dedicated to a data graphic, chart, or visualization. Other than the explanatory subhead and three short bullet point highlights to direct users to specific info in the chart, there is no other text to clutter the page.

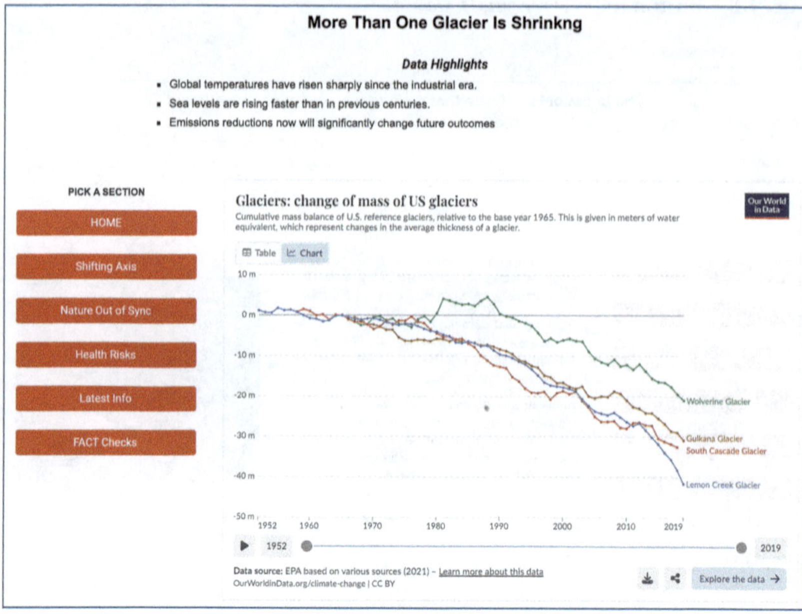


**Fig. 9.10** Button six: CHART: Ice Melt

**Button Six**

The data page always features a chart, video, or slide show to support the featured story. It is a clearly labeled choice for users who are not overwhelmed because interested users can devote as much time as they wish to view and inspect the explanatory visuals. In this story, an animated government-issued chart (from NOAA) illustrates the changes in the sizes of four US glaciers. This data can add credibility to the content. So does the final button, labeled *FACT checks.*

As noted earlier, despite the pleas for all users to verify the sources of information they receive, the unanswered question is to what extent is an *instant* fact-check page effective? Here, users can click to instantly confirm the sources of the information with links to each source and a short description of how the source contributed to the story.

**Button Seven**

The Smart Story Suite promotes source transparency to foster trust and enhance the likelihood that individuals will engage with, believe in, and share content. In the ongoing fight against misinformation, this design principle is critical.

When users know who produced a piece of content and understand why listed sources are relevant, they are empowered to evaluate the information on its merits. In this case, fact-checks are just a click away (Fig. 9.11).

In sum, the components of the Smart Story interface are illustrated in Fig. 9.12.

The lab is also experimenting with how artificial intelligence can instantly organize any digital content into a Smart Story and provide constructive feedback to authors and producers (Fig. 9.13). Using a SPICE scoring scale of up to 25 possible points, the tool evaluates how well the original content reflects SPICE engagement variables introduced in this book. For transparency, the display also includes the percentage of the original content represented in the AI-generated Smart Story. This experimentation is ongoing. For instance, while the AI version captured 98% of the original story, the question is what defines the missing 2%? Although

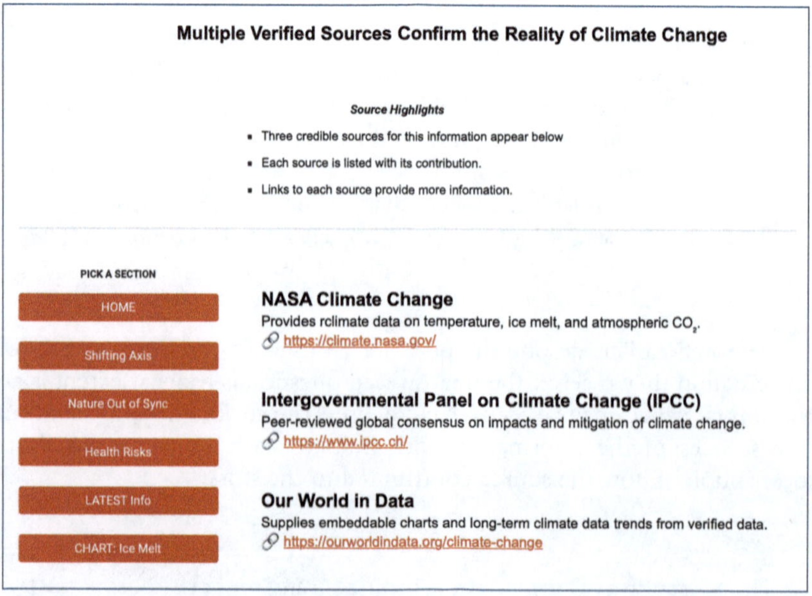


**Fig. 9.11** Button seven: *Fact Checks*

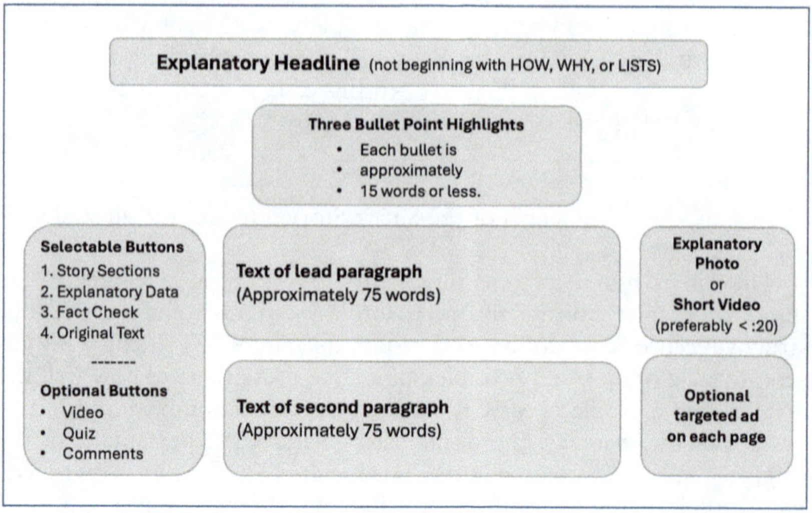


**Fig. 9.12** Smart Story components

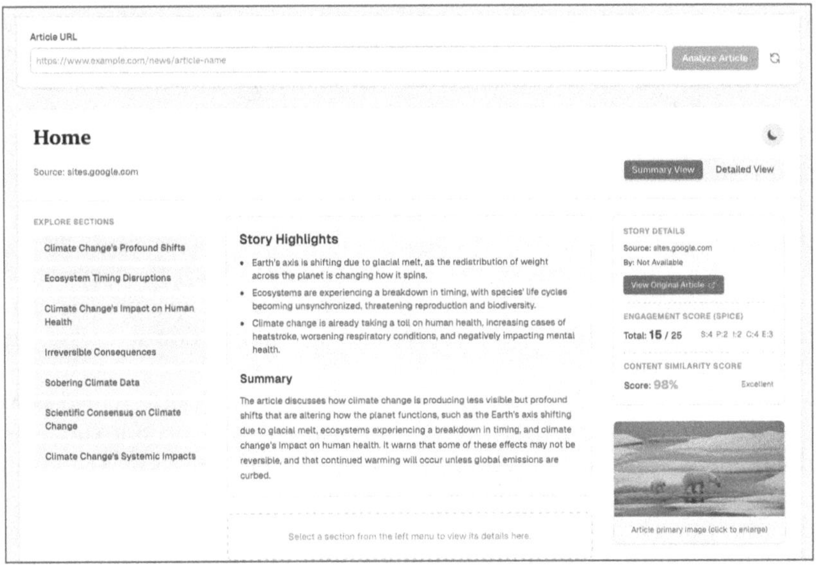


**Fig. 9.13** An AI-produced *Smart Story* of the original story. Programming by Viraaj Singh (Lab Team Manager), Matthew Chin, Sweta Dantu, Benjamin Wong, and Accessibility Manager Saumya Verna

the goal is 100% fidelity, further experimentation will improve the interface by determining whether the missing 2% of similarity reflects substantive content loss or merely minor editorial adjustments of the text to enhance its readability.

## 9.5 New *Latest Info* and *Fact-Checking* Options Promote Credibility

The *Latest Info* button is a reminder to users that they can return to this story for any later developments or corrections. Repeat visits are a primary goal for digital sites but are not always easy to generate. This space also facilitates corrections, which increase both transparency and credibility. Studies have consistently found that the credibility of the source delivering corrective information significantly affects its effectiveness [28, 29]. When corrections come from sources perceived as trustworthy, individuals are more likely to accept and share the corrected information. This effect is particularly pronounced in contexts involving contested or politically charged topics. Other studies showed that when users receive corrective information from sources they perceive as credible, they are more likely to accept and share that correction.

A study investigating the effectiveness of health misinformation on social media exposed participants to health misinformation, followed by corrective content. Results suggest the corrections were significantly more persuasive when they came from trusted expert sources, such as the Centers for Disease Control and Prevention [30]. When that correction was attributed to the CDC rather than a generic or anonymous user, participants were more likely to accept the accurate information and reject the false claim.

On the other hand, a meta-analysis of 32 studies with a combined sample size of 6,527 participants revealed that corrections do not eliminate the influence of misinformation [31]. Corrections were more successful when they were coherent and logically structured, aligned with the audience's existing beliefs or worldview, and delivered by the original source of the misinformation. Corrections were less effective when the misinformation originated from a credible source, when the misinformation had been repeated multiple times before the correction, or when there was a delay between the dissemination of misinformation and its correction.

The "Fact Check" button on every Smart story also deserves discussion. That dedicated page is reserved for all sources that contributed to the content, plus brief descriptions of how each source contributed. This allows users to actively assess the credibility of sources, including the author, publisher, or virtual agent [32]. The results suggest that users consider this as their primary criterion for trusting or dismissing information.

Across platforms, users are often expected to verify sources themselves, which takes additional time and typically involves clicking through links, searching for relevant information, or conducting independent searches. This effort can lead to reliance on intuitive judgments or emotional cues. Pennycook and Rand [33] found that individuals less inclined toward analytical thinking are more susceptible to believing fake news, suggesting that a lack of cognitive engagement, rather than deliberate bias, contributes to the spread of misinformation.

A meta-analysis of 91 studies representing data from more than 64,000 participants concluded that the trustworthiness and expertise of sources are crucial in shaping user responses to information, especially in the context of misinformation [34]. These findings reinforce the core design logic behind a Smart Story that the messenger matters.

However, not all attempts to expose sources enhance trust. When users were presented with metadata regarding authorship and editing in visual media, many misinterpreted the information [35]. Some started to distrust even legitimate content. This outcome may suggest that users can be confused about the distinction between media credibility and provenance credibility, indicating that how transparency is provided in content can be just as important as whether it is provided at all.

Bhuiyan et al. [36] conducted qualitative interviews, showing that both journalists and audiences value transparency. Results supported the notion that visible and well-designed source information can help to build trust in the information. Key takeaways from the study were that: 1. Both journalists and news consumers emphasized the importance of transparency indicators, including authorship, sourcing, correction history, and evidence of verification, and 2. Participants suggested that transparency cues be designed for easy comprehension.

Despite these shared views, the study also identified contrasting suggestions. News consumers focused on individual articles and transparency cues that related to the story's objectivity and evidence. Journalists advocated for broader transparency, including insights into the reporting process, organizational practices, and potential conflicts of interest. While consumers preferred simplicity that would not overwhelm them, journalists were concerned that overly simplistic cues might lack the necessary context. Finally, consumers proposed that third-party reviewers might offer more credible assessments. Journalists acknowledged the potential value of external evaluations but emphasized the importance of internal transparency.

These findings underscore the need for a balanced approach in designing transparency features. Allowing users to review and explore specific sources on a dedicated Smart Story page promotes simplicity. Incorporating assessments from independent organizations could enhance credibility among skeptical consumers. Providing context or explanations for transparency cues could help bridge the gap between simplicity and nuance.

On *Google* Search, the "About this result" panel provides context about the site, ownership, index date, and general description, but only if users click it. YouTube links to official sources below some videos about controversial topics. However, these features rely on content categorization and do not appear consistently.

X's *Community Notes* enabled users to add contextual information to posts, aiming to combat misinformation through community contributions. Notes become publicly visible once a diverse group of contributors agrees on their usefulness. The program has expanded globally and now supports various content types, including text, images, and videos. As of November 2023, it had approximately 133,000 contributors and reported receiving tens of millions of views per day.

Meta has phased out its Facebook Journalism Project and third-party fact-checking partnerships in the United States. In their place, Meta introduced a similar *Community Notes* system inspired by X's approach. Meta allows contributors to write and rate notes on content across Facebook, Instagram, and Threads. Notes are published only when contributors with diverse viewpoints agree on their helpfulness. Meta began testing this system in March 2025 and started displaying notes publicly in April of that year. While the *Journalism Project* website remained accessible at the time of this writing, its active programs and training courses have been discontinued, signaling a shift in Meta's strategy toward community-driven content moderation.

The deeper issue across all platforms remains the same: users are often expected to verify credibility on their own, typically by conducting searches. Time constraints, cognitive overload, and limited media literacy can make this challenging. That's why proactive source transparency integrated into the design is essential. The Smart Story Suite's Fact Check button is clearly labeled and always visible, ensuring users can access source information easily without needing to search for it. Clarity improves because, instead of merely linking to an external page, each source includes a brief explanation of how it contributed to the content. This credibility framing can emphasize why the source is important, not just who it is. Rather than providing source information deep within the text or in footnotes, the Smart Story's prominently displayed button allows users to verify supporting details about any source instantly. Providing guided context helps users avoid misinterpreting or overlooking information, a problem identified by Feng et al. [35]. The feature aligns the design of an interface with media literacy, explaining why a source should be trusted.

Deviating from traditional practices, the Smart Story Suite provides:

- A visible, easily accessible *Fact Check* button linking to core sources
- Plain-language summaries of each source explaining the source's contribution to the content

– Verification scaffolding: a consistent, repeatable pattern that teaches users to expect, find, and interpret credibility cues effortlessly

A Smart Story minimizes friction, supports critical thinking, and aligns with best practices from research in information science, psychology, and communication by integrating fact-checking directly into the interface.

## 9.6 Tests Confirm Short-Form and Long-Form Structures Can Co-exist

Testing the Smart Story interface and content that aligns with the variables of the Digital Engagement Model provided several significant results. An online experiment with a large, diverse sample of users tested the effects of the model's user DIET (demographics, individual interests, environment, and time) and the SPICE variables predicted to make content more scannable, personalized, and interactive, while increasing curiosity and emotional effects. The experiment collected data from 1,642 participants (42 percent male, 55 percent female, and 2.7% non-binary or preferred not to say. The age range was from 18 to 83, with a mean of 40.4 years.

Each participant was exposed to one of the two climate change story versions described above: either the traditional text-based news story or the Smart Story Suite version. They then answered a series of questions related to the variables specified by the model's user, DIET, and SPICE content. To begin, the study challenged the earlier point made. In contrast to the often-used yet abstract label "individual differences" to describe variances among individuals, the Digital Engagement Model (DEM) introduced the concept of individual similarities—a defined set of shared, predictable attributes that all users bring to any digital content.

The argument is that demographics, such as age, education, and the device used, often correlate with stable media behaviors that span broad user populations. More importantly, however, variations in two key situational variables—namely, a user's physical environment with distractions and multitasking, as well as the technological environment of a smartphone, laptop, or desktop—are predicted to play a role in engagement. The fourth user DIET variable is a user's available time for engagement. The model suggests that factors beyond demographics or long-term individual interests have a significant influence on engagement. This is especially true in the context of frequent, incidental exposure to content on mobile devices and social media platforms. Rather than tailoring content to individual differences, the DEM posits that the probability of engagement increases when attention is paid to these two DIET variables and SPICE content.

All participants were informed that a following screen would display a news article to read, as they would typically read any news online. They were told that there was no obligation to view or read any of the news story but to view it for as long as they remained interested.

Following the participants' preferred time of exposure to the story, they were asked to respond to the questions detailed in Table 9.1, along with their mean values. All questions asked participants to respond using a 1–5 scale of agreement or disagreement.

To measure the effects of demographics on interest and engagement, responses to three items were combined into an average score. Questions included: *The article was intended for someone like me, the presentation matched how I prefer to obtain news*, and *the news targeted my demographics.* There was no significant difference in the response scores to these questions.

The I in DIET for individual interest (in climate change news) was measured with three questions. *This story reflected a long-term interest of*

**Table 9.1** Comparison of mean engagement scores (1–5 agreement scale)

| | *Original* | *Smart* |
|---|---|---|
| ***User DIET measures*** | | |
| DEMOGRAPHIC appeal | 3.42 | 3.38 |
| INDIVIDUAL INTEREST (climate) | 3.38 | 3.37 |
| **No ENVIRONMENTAL effects** | 3.39 | **3.78** |
| **Supports TIME to engage** | 4.21 | **4.42** |
| ***SPICE content measures*** | | |
| **SCANNABLE content** | 3.81 | **4.21** |
| **PERSONALIZED content** | 3.49 | **4.22** |
| **INTERACTIVE content** | 3.66 | **4.27** |
| **CURATED CURIOSITY** | 3.54 | **3.81** |
| EMOTIONAL content | 3.24 | 3.12 |
| **FACT-CHECKING support** | 3.37 | 3.70 |
| **TIME on content** (in seconds) | **109.32** | 94.50 |
| **RECALL score of information** | 3.32 | **3.52** |

Shaded measures indicate statistically significant differences.

*mine. I have followed this news topic previously*, and *I care about the broader issues related to this topic (climate change)*. Again, there was no significant difference across both story versions. No significant differences in perceptions of how much the content addressed users' demographic and topic interest questions suggest no differences across participants randomly exposed to one of the story versions.

The confirmed reliability measure for effects of a user's physical and technical environments included the two statements: *I wasn't distracted by other tasks while viewing the content*, and *The content could be viewed without scrolling*. Results indicated a statistically significant difference in versions, with the Smart Story scoring higher. The final DIET variable, "time to engage," used the following three statements: *If I were interested in the topic, I had enough time to consume it; if I had more time, I would have explored the article further*, and *the article respected my time with options to view the content. There was a significant difference between versions, with the Smart Story receiving a high mean score.*

Turning to the effects of the SPICE content on engagement, two items measuring whether participants found the content scannable stated that *the presentation helped me find what I wanted to know* and *provided quick access to the core message*. The Smart Story produced a significantly higher mean score. The personalization measure employed three statements: *I could choose information in the story based on my interest, I could quickly view different parts of the story*, and *if I was in a rush, the format adapted to my needs for information*. Mean scores significantly favored the Smart Story. Perceived interactivity statements were, "*I had control over the content I wanted to consume*," and "*I could quickly skip content that I already knew*." Again, the Smart Story produced significantly higher scores. Two statements that tapped the curiosity generated by each story were, *I wanted to explore content beyond the first sentences*, and *compared to other stories, this one made me want to learn more about the subject*. The Smart Story produced a significantly higher mean score. The final SPICE variable of emotion employed three statements: *The article generated emotion, The content made the issue more personal or real*, and *I will remember this article because of how it made me feel*. There was no significant effect of emotion. One possible explanation is that although the Smart Story included more photos, the first photo of a polar bear coping with melting ice generated a similar emotion.

Given that the Fact Check button appeared only on the Smart Story, participants were asked to respond to the statement: *It was easy to fact-check the credibility of the information*. The higher mean score from participants viewing the Smart Story, along with the fact-check button, surpassed that of the original story. Two direct measures included the recording of time (in seconds) that the participant spent viewing the story version and the amount of short-term recall of the information, as assessed by five multiple-choice questions. We predicted that both measures would favor the Smart Story Suite, but an interesting result occurred. Although more time was spent on average viewing the original story, participants' recall scores were significantly higher for the Smart Story compared to the recall of details in the original story. One explanation is that not only was the Smart Story easier to consume in a short period of time, it transferred more memorable information than the traditional linear text story.

This study provided compelling evidence that, compared to the traditional story structure, the Smart Story Suite significantly enhanced users' perceptions of credibility, control, interest, engagement, and information recall for a diverse population of users that ranked the topic low in interest. While only one story was tested, the findings from more than 1600 participants support the core claims of the *Digital Engagement Model*. Designing for the shared individual similarities of environment and available time to engage can enhance digital content experiences.

## 9.7 The *Smart Story Suite* Offers a Guide, Not a Template

The Smart Story Suite's adaptive structure demonstrated that users who typically avoid certain topics or content can still experience increased interest in and recall of information when it is presented in a cognitively accessible and strategically designed format. Figure 9.14 compares the traditional concepts with Smart Story concepts.

These results challenge the persistent myth in digital communication that more likes and shares, or more time spent on content, represent more meaningful engagement [1]. Time is not always a proxy for depth. The Smart Story Suite is just one example that demonstrates the opposite. It was designed and tested in response to research supporting key user DIET variables, especially a user's natural environment and available time, which shape interactions with digital content. Our lab's research revealed that individuals raised on digital devices engage with information differently than those raised on traditional print media, such as newspapers [5].

Most of the content on social media is exposed to users incidentally rather than being intentionally searched for on Google. In this

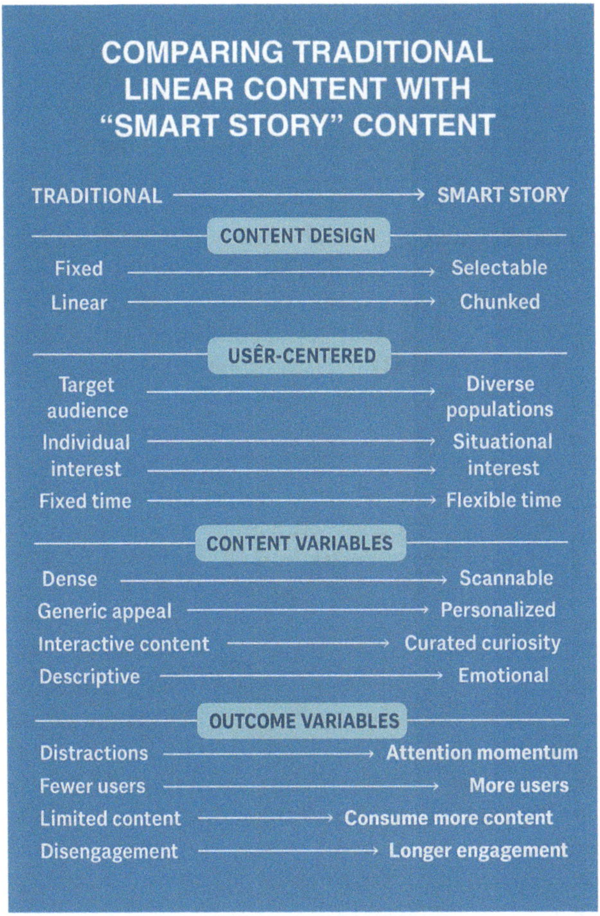


**Fig. 9.14** Comparisons of traditional content with smart content

environment, content must be structured not only to inform but also to generate attention momentum or the ability for the presentation of content to sustain attention. That's where the model's SPICE variables become essential. Content that is scannable, personalized, interactive, and evokes curiosity and emotion is more likely to engage more users and convert passive exposure into active interest. When modular content supports fast scanning and rewards curiosity with emotional resonance and personal relevance, comprehension improves, especially in an age defined by distraction and multitasking.

For some content producers, this could mark a turning point. Reaching beyond traditional audiences now requires more than algorithmic targeting, clickable headlines and video, or platform optimization. It demands a shift away from the illusion that any single design toolkit or plug-and-play template can guarantee engagement. What some might call a "template trap" reflects a misplaced faith in a least one solution [37]. The multidisciplinary research presented in the nine chapters of this book, which synthesizes cognitive psychology and neuroscience with journalism and human-computer interaction, points to a new reality. There is no "one-size-fits-all" content structure, not even the long-relied-on inverted pyramid [38, 39]. Instead, content can and should be adaptive, and the strategic application of the Digital Engagement Model offers a flexible, user-centered foundation for that adaptability.

The goal of engaging users challenges us to rethink not just where we place content but also how we shape it to invite interaction. The growing expectation for digital media to serve diverse user needs, especially in the context of news, justifies more experimentation. The Smart Story Suite is not the only answer; it is a model for how content can appeal to both users with stable personal interests and those who engage only when the content generates situational interest. Even topics that some might consider boring or irrelevant can become interesting and essential if the priority to produce well-written narratives also includes well-structured media.

Ultimately, the success of these strategies depends on a willingness to break from legacy formats and take creative risks. As discussed in the first chapter, the behaviors and expectations of digital users have evolved more rapidly than the content structures designed to serve them. We may now be at a moment where we recognize that to compete for attention in digital spaces, content must be designed for attention. And that design must not just capture users but keep them.

## References

1. Yaros, R., and A. Cook. 2013. Attention versus learning of online content: Preliminary findings from an eye-tracking study. In *Evolving Psychological and Educational Perspectives on Cyber Behavior*, ed. R. Z. Zheng, 132–154. Hershey, PA: IGI Global.
2. Yaros, Ronald A., and Anne E. Cook. 2011. Attention versus learning of online content. *International Journal of Cyber Behavior, Psychology and Learning* **1**(4): 49–69. https://doi.org/10.4018/ijcbpl.2011100104.

3. Yaros, R. 2009. Producing citizen journalism or producing journalism for citizens: A new multimedia model to enhance understanding of complex news. In *Journalism and Citizenship: New Agendas*, ed. Z. Papacharissi, 71–90. Routledge: New York, NY.
4. Yaros, Ronald A. 2012. Effects of mobile devices and text messages. *International Journal of Cyber Behavior, Psychology and Learning* **2**(3): 59–72. https://doi.org/10.4018/ijcbpl.2012070105.
5. Yaros, R., and J. Misak. 2020. Completing college writing assignments on mobile phones: Comparing students' attitudes and engagement across disciplines and age. *Journalism & Mass Communication Educator* **76** (2): 216–227.
6. Aldoory, L., et al. 2016. Piloting health text messages for rural low-income mothers: Effects of source similarity and simple action steps. *Health Promotion Practice* **15**(5): 702–710.
7. Mulupi, D., F. H. C. Wong, and R. A. Yaros. 2025. Investigating the effect of a physician's race and gender on user engagement with and perceived credibility of COVID-19 vaccine news. *Newspaper Research Journal* **46**(1): 96–117.
8. Yaros, R. A., J. Roberts, E. Powers, and L. Steiner. 2015. Serving the needs of the Latina community for health information. *Health, Culture and Society* **8**(1): 20–33. https://doi.org/10.5195/hcs.2015.158.
9. Sutcliffe, A. 2016. Designing for user experience and engagement. In *Why engagement matters: Cross-disciplinary perspectives of user engagement in digital media*, ed. H. Obrien and P. Cairns, 105–126. Springer International.
10. Said, N. S. 2004. An engaging multimedia design model. In *2004 Conference on interaction design and children: Building a community*. College Park, MD: Association for Computing Machinery.
11. Grinberg, N. 2018. Identifying modes of user engagement with online news and their relationship to information gain in text. In *Proceedings of the 2018 world wide web conference*.
12. Issam, K. A. R., and S. Patel. 2021. *Topic modeling based extractive text summarization*. arXiv preprint arXiv:2106.15313.
13. Li, Z., et al. 2016. Multimedia news summarization in search. *ACM Transactions on Intelligent Systems and Technology (TIST)* 7 (3): 1–20.
14. McKeown, K., and D. R. Radev. 1995. Generating summaries of multiple news articles. In *Proceedings of the 18th annual international ACM SIGIR conference on Research and development in information retrieval*.
15. McKeown, K. R., et al. 2002. Tracking and summarizing news on a daily basis with Columbia's newsblaster. In *Proceedings of the human language technology conference*. San Francisco: Morgan Kaufmann.
16. O'Brien, H. L., and E. G. Toms. 2008. What is user engagement? A conceptual framework for defining user engagement with technology. *Journal of the American Society for Information Science and Technology* **59** (6): 938–955.

17. Pernice, K. 2017. *F-shaped pattern of reading on the web: Misunderstood, but still relevant (even on mobile)* [cited 2025 March 3, 2023]. https://www.nngroup.com/articles/f-shaped-pattern-reading-web-content/.
18. Anderson, C. W. 2013. *Rebuilding the news: Metropolitan journalism in the digital age*, 218. Temple University.
19. Krug, S. 2014. *Don't make me think!: A common sense approach to web usability*. 3rd ed. Pearson Education India. 201 pages.
20. Norman, D. 2013. *The design of everyday things*, 368. MIT Press.
21. Deci, E., and R. Ryan. 1980. The empirical exploration of intrinsic motivation processes. In *Advances in experimental social psychology*, ed. L. Berkowitz, 39–80. New York: Academic Press.
22. Spencer, D. 2009. *Card sorting: Designing usable categories*. Rosenfeld Media. 162 pages.
23. Shneiderman, B., and C. Plaisant. 2010. *Designing the user interface: Strategies for effective human-computer interaction*. 5th ed, 624. Pearson Education India.
24. Shneiderman, B. 2003. The eyes have it: A task by data type taxonomy for information visualizations. In *The craft of information visualization*, 364–371. Elsevier.
25. Abou-Zahra, S., and J. Brewer. 2019. Standards, guidelines, and trends. In *Web accessibility: A foundation for research*, ed. Y. Yesilda and S. Harper, 225–246. London: Springer.
26. Chartbeat. n.d. *Scroll behavior across the web*. https://chartbeat.com/resources/research/scroll-behavior-across-the-web/.
27. Jackson, M. 2023. *Scroll depth* [cited 2024 March 15, 2024]. https://matt-jackson.com/seo-glossary/scroll-depth/#:~:text=A%20study%20by%20Chartbeat%20revealed,Essential%20Points.
28. Lee, S., et al. 2025. *Partisan fact-checkers' warnings can effectively correct individuals' misbeliefs about political misinformation*. arXiv preprint arXiv: 2505.08048.
29. Ecker, U. K., et al. 2022. The psychological drivers of misinformation belief and its resistance to correction. *Nature Reviews Psychology* **1** (1): 13–29.
30. Vraga, E. K., and L. Bode. 2017. Using expert sources to correct health misinformation in social media. *Science Communication* **39** (5): 621–645.
31. Walter, N., and R. Tukachinsky. 2020. A meta-analytic examination of the continued influence of misinformation in the face of correction: How powerful is it, why does it happen, and how to stop it? *Communication Research* **47** (2): 155–177.
32. Rieh, S. Y., and N. Belkin. 2000. Interaction on the web: Scholars' judgement of information quality and cognitive authority. In *Proceedings of the 63rd annual meeting of the american society for information science*. Citeseer.

33. Pennycook, G., and D. G. Rand. 2019. Lazy, not biased: Susceptibility to partisan fake news is better explained by lack of reasoning than by motivated reasoning. *Cognition* **188**:39–50.
34. Mang, V., B. M. Fennis, and K. Epstude. 2024. *Source credibility effects in misinformation research: A review and primer.* Advances in Psychology. https://doi.org/10.56296/aip00028.
35. Feng, K. K., et al. 2023. Examining the impact of provenance-enabled media on trust and accuracy perceptions. *Proceedings of the ACM on Human-Computer Interaction* 7 (CSCW2): 1–42.
36. Bhuiyan, M. M., et al. 2021. Designing transparency cues in online news platforms to promote trust: Journalists'& consumers' perspectives. *Proceedings of the ACM on Human-Computer Interaction* **5** (CSCW2): 1–31.
37. Gibbons, S., and J. Claire. 2025. *The template trap: How template culture is dumbing down UX.* NN/g Newsletter.
38. Yaros, Ronald A. 2011. Effects of text and hypertext structures on user interest and understanding of science and technology. *Science Communication* **33** (3): 275–308. https://doi.org/10.1177/1075547010386803.
39. Yaros, Ronald A. 2006. Is it the medium or the message? Structuring complex news to enhance engagement and situational understanding by non-experts. *Communication Research* **33** (4): 285–309. https://doi.org/10.1177/0093650206289154.

# Index




R. Yaros, *The Digital Engagement Model*, Palgrave Practical Guides in Communication, https://doi.org/10.1007/978-3-032-03822-7

FSC
www.fsc.org
MIX
Papier | Fördert gute Waldnutzung
FSC® C083411

Kolibri 360 GmbH
Ferdinand-Jühlke-Straße 7
99095 Erfurt, Deutschland
produktsicherheit@kolibri360.de